Reviews of *Parad...*

"... an incredibly detailed and passionate journey ... Kriete writes with drive, spinning a narrative that is both brutally honest and difficult to put down."

— *The Edmonton Journal*
July 27, 2021

"Avoiding the often-encountered trap of memoirs becoming self-indulgent, Marilyn Kriete releases her extraordinary life with mirth, a fine tuned sense of humor, and radiantly poetic prose ... Very highly recommended."

— **Grady Harp**
Amazon Top Reviewer

"*Paradise Road* is a fearless account of Marilyn Kriete's life of adventure. She unspools the tale of plunging into each chapter of her life with great candor and momentum. She has an uncanny knack for putting the reader by her side through each exhilaration, each heartbreak, each danger, each triumph."

— **Kimberley Cetron**
author of Fractals: The Invisible World of
Fractals Made Visible Through Theatre and Dance

"Watching Marilyn Kriete crack wide open and feel utterly wounded, only to watch her attempt to piece herself back together one mile at a time. From her happiness feeling truly ebullient to her crestfallen soul, we meet a woman furiously bicycling towards her future. Paradise Road is such a beautifully painted story, I felt as if I was with her and cheering her on the entire time."

— **Annie McDonnell**
The Write Review

From Readers—excerpts from Goodreads reviews:

"… A pilgrimage among the most extraordinary characters through events that compete with Hollywood in their drama."

"… Kriete is vulnerable, honest and engaging …"

"… A memorable, heartfelt, and thought-provoking memoir … a must-read …"

"… Men and women of all ages will find this book compelling."

"… A raw but utterly compelling and sometimes dazzling memoir by a writer who had gone through far more trauma and adventure in her first 25 years than most of us go through in our lifetimes."

National Indie Excellence Awards
Winner: Young Adult-Non-Fiction
Finalist: New Adult Non-Fiction
Finalist: Cover Non-Fiction

Book Excellence Awards
Winner: Adventure Non-Fiction

Paradise Road

A Memoir

MARILYN KRIETE

LU☾ID
HOUSE
PUBLISHING

LU☾ID
HOUSE
PUBLISHING

Published in Atlanta, Georgia, United States of America by Lucid House Publishing, LLC
www.LucidHousePublishing.com

© 2021 by Marilyn Kriete

Cover design: Troy King
Interior design: Amit Dey
Author photo: Taj Kriete

Library of Congress Cataloging-in-Publication Data:
Kriete, Marilyn, 1956-
Paradise road: a memoir/ by Marilyn Kriete–1st ed.
LCCN: 2021933095
ISBN: 978-1-950495-11-5
1. Biography 2. Family dysfunction 3. Teenage runaway
4. Group home 5. Solo travel 6. Sexual revolution 7. Hippie culture
8. Romance 9. Grief and loss 10. New Age beliefs 11. Adventure

BIO023000
BIO022000
BIO026000

Lucid House Publishing books are available for special promotions and bulk purchase discounts.
For details, contact info@LucidHousePublishing.com

For Laura, my huckleberry friend.
Who knows what duller path my life would
have taken, if not for you?

Contents

Prologue. 9

One: The Wall 11

Two: My Huckleberry Friend 19

Three: Broken Girl. 30

Four: Coal-Black and Fiery Red 34

Five: Jailbait. 40

Six: The Kindness of Strangers 48

Seven: Four Faint Horizontal Lines 59

Eight: Snails into Beer 69

Nine: Kenny Baron Specials 77

Ten: Unwrapped 84

Eleven: Sand Mandala 99

Twelve: Perfect Little World 108

Thirteen: Careening through the Wilderness 114

Fourteen: Silky Green Parachute. 118

Fifteen: Without You. 129

Sixteen: Sleepwalking. 132

Seventeen: Subterranean Lake 139

Eighteen: The Map. 148

Nineteen: Concentrated Storm Track 148

Twenty: DIY for the Newly-Bereaved 164

Twenty-One: Entangled 174

Twenty-Two: Stem, Seeds and All 187

Twenty-Three: Even Goddesses Get the Blues 206

Twenty-Four: Stranger in Paradise 222

Twenty-Five: Sea Change. 253

Twenty-Six: Outer Circle. 245

Twenty-Seven: Inner Light. 254

Epilogue. 272

Acknowledgements 275

About the Author. 278

I will complain, yet praise;
I will bewail, approve;
And all my sour-sweet days
I will lament and love.

—*George Herbert*

Prologue

Here's my theory: there's a moment in every childhood that shows exactly who we are. Pay attention to your child, and you'll see it. Scroll back in your own life, and there it is.

My son's snapshot involved moving from Africa to America, seeing his first pair of light-up shoes on Day One, and waking us at three a.m. to insist we go shopping at daybreak. He was six.

My daughter's moment involved pilfered wieners, the family dog, building a tent in her brother's room while everyone slept, and leaving a peace offering (the last wiener) on the hallway table in case she got caught. She was three.

The qualities at play in these snapshots— intensity, creativity, determination, manipulation, and an unshakeable love of shoes or campfires—continue to shape the course of both their lives.

I believe my theory. Like variety-pack boxes of make-your-own pizza, we're all born with our own set of raw ingredients. Life does the baking.

With that in mind, here's my moment. It's summer in Edmonton, Canada, 1962.

My dad catches me as I'm sneaking past the garage.

Hey! Where you going with that bike?

Yikes. I decide to go with a half-truth.

Um…just across the street. For a little ride.

It's your brother's bike — you know you're not 'sposed to touch it. Besides, you don't even know how to ride!

Yes, I do! I learned how! (Wishful thinking—I've been falling in the dirt for days.)

Really? You know how to ride a bike? Prove it!

He follows me across the street to a dusty vacant lot where bigger kids pound their one-speeds along a bumpy track embedded with purple thistles and gopher holes. Heart hammering, I hold my breath, perch my little bum on the hard seat, and push off. There's the familiar wobbling before the fall and then, to my utter amazement, I'm riding jubilant circles around my equally astonished father. It's a one-minute performance, but I can almost hear the angels sing.

The next day, there's a blue, second-hand bike propped against the garage wall: a *girl's* bicycle, with plastic tasselled handlebar grips and a dropped crossbar. I've surprised my father into positive action – perhaps for the very first time. And life has suddenly expanded.

And that, in essence, is me. I'm six years old, pushing at boundaries and grasping for early emancipation. I'd rather risk trouble than play it safe. If anything's worth learning, I'll secretly teach myself. Bikes will be pivotal. And someone from my gene pool must've bequeathed me their wanderer's heart, or rather, their *wandering* heart.

To wit: I can't wait to get away on my own steam.

1

The Wall

My mother and I are not friends. Her thumbnail synopsis is blunt; in her version, I pushed myself off her lap at twelve months and never came back. This puts the onus on one-year-old me – rather unfairly, I think — though I believe the bare outline. Still, there must have been a psychic push from her side. Something was always *off* between us, and the fault lines only widened with time. She simply didn't like me, and I sensed this early. Finally, when I was nine years old, she admitted it, loud and clear. *Marilyn,* she hissed at the end of another endless harangue about my character flaws, *I know I'm supposed to love you as my daughter. But I simply don't like you as a person.*

What do you do with revelations like that? I wasn't as tough as I pretended, so I simply built a wall to keep her out. Something about me infuriated her, though to be fair she often seemed angry at life in general. She'd wanted to be a singer but ended up married and teaching first grade straight out of university. Her teaching career lasted two years.

Nine months after her honeymoon, my oldest brother was born, the first of five consecutive birth control failures. I was the "can't-get-pregnant-when-you're-breastfeeding" baby, arriving eleven months after Philip, the slipped condom baby. My father's sperm continued to bypass a series of fruitful barriers, producing three younger brothers—all of us meant to be, accidental or not. My mother wound up with a brood of five, and although she was exemplary in the housekeeping sphere – the floors were waxed and the table ready — she fell woefully short in the emotional one.

And I bore the brunt. She needed a target for her anger and that was me, returning from school in knots, wondering what I'd be blasted for when I came through the door. I could never anticipate the day's transgressions, knowing only that whatever they were, she'd been stewing them all day, along with the eternal pot of leftover soup on the stove.

The attacks were soul-scathing ambushes, usually delivered between the back door and the living room before I had a chance to remove my coat. They reduced me to tears of frustration and wordless rage. The onslaughts left no room for self defense. And her grievances were endless; I'd never score a blameless day. I was a decent kid, a gifted student, who'd skipped a grade and brought home enthusiastic reports from my teachers. No one else saw a monster when they looked at me. But with her, I was always in the wrong.

While I served as scapegoat, my brothers learned to fly under the radar. Phil took cover in his art. Doug slipped in and out of the house like a mystical fox. Howard was quiet, learning from my mistakes and biding his time in the background. And Brian, who came years after the rest of us, inherited the classical music gene, giving my mother her golden child and a vicarious second chance at professional musicianship.

My father, a popular teacher and school principal, avoided unoccupied time at home and met his remaining emotional needs through golf and curling, leaving most of the parenting to her. As a couple, they bickered often and openly, and her fearsome stubbornness always won. She was barely five feet tall, yet no one could stand up to her.

Occasionally we breached the wall to suffer awkward moments of mother-daughter intimacy. At nine, I stumbled across a cardboard box in the woods one afternoon and asked her what "Tampax" was. She must've been waiting to get this talk over with, because she whisked me off the family picnic blanket and into a nearby thicket, dumping way more information on my blushing head than my idle question warranted. This was shortly after a mortifying sex education slide show at school, where Phil and I, sitting between our stony-faced parents and confronted with a series of shocking, flaccid and erect diagrams, were traumatized to learn what they had obviously done four times (!) to produce our current family.

Two years later, my mother summoned me into a public toilet stall to show me what actual tampons looked like – new and used. I was aghast. By the time my own periods started, we were so estranged I wouldn't speak to her about anything, let alone my menses. Six months into my budding womanhood, she discovered a box of tampons hidden in my room and chose another excruciating moment to confront my secrecy. It wasn't that I was ashamed of menstruating; as a relative late bloomer, I'd been pining for physical evidence that I'd actually grow up and be able get away from her. In fact, I longed to grow a body with breasts and curves, just not with her eyes watching.

Life with mother bled from one disappointment to the next. We clashed over everything—especially my wardrobe. Every inch of my exterior was under her rule, and not because I was her little princess. She and my grandmother selected all my clothes, frugally chosen and sadly received as Christmas or birthday gifts. They were boxy catalogue items, purchased at least two sizes too big so they'd fit for perhaps one of the three years I'd be wearing them. Both shoppers favored voluminous, scratchy plaid kilts and shapeless jumpers, preferably corduroy, paired with Peter Pan blouses and homely sweaters in muted shades of yellow, mauve, or brown, colors I hated. Photos from that time feature a small-faced, badly coifed child in huge cat's eyeglasses, miserably drowning in clothes befitting a frumpy Midwestern matron.

When the catalogues finally caught up with the Mod Sixties, my personal shoppers switched things up with lurid psychedelic prints, including a hideous pair of turquoise, yellow, and pink flower-power bell-bottoms, earning me the nickname *Fancy Pants* for my entire seventh grade year (and this bestowed by a classmate with the laughable surname of *Bumstead*. His dubbing automatically elevated him and put me in last place). Perhaps if I'd been able to burn the pants after their humiliating debut, my classmates would've eventually forgotten them and my new nickname. But no, at my mother's insistence, I wore the laughingstocks again and again, to fresh and riotous ridicule from Bumstead and his despicable minions.

But it wasn't just the pants ruining my miserable life. All my clothes, and the itchy, unaesthetic ways they never fit depressed me, and I yearned to break away and dress myself.

My mother also insisted I wear my straight brown hair in the same blocky, short cut every year, executed by her style-challenged German hairdresser. *Could you please not cut my bangs too short?* I'd whisper at each appointment, and he'd pretend not to hear as he hacked them short, halfway up my forehead. Or worse: for several cuts in a row, he sent me home with *Bat Bangs,* a bewildering take on the 1960s Batman craze, featuring two curves that culminated in a sharp point above my nose.

I'd rush home, mortified yet again, and stare in horror at the defilement in the bathroom mirror. Many of these haircuts were inflicted the day before school pictures. In desperation, I'd grab the nearest scissors and chop off the point, making my bangs both crooked and even shorter, and then wail at the prospect of being immortalized with my botched haircut in yet another bad school photo. Bat Bangs! Surely my mother knew how much I despised them! I was convinced she and her German mutilator were in cahoots, determined to keep me as ugly and demoralised as possible.

I didn't know if I was pretty or not, or even if I had the *potential* to be pretty. Apart from the hair and clothing battles, no one ever commented on my looks, except my brothers, who teased my round bum as captured in family photos taken from bad angles. Sometimes, after taking a bath, I'd cover my short, unlovely hair in a turbaned towel and sit on the bathroom sink where I could examine my face up close in the mirror. My skin was light and soft, my brown-green eyes thickly lashed under dark brows. My nose and mouth were neither large nor small. I'd stare into my eyes like a lover, wondering if they could entice and beguile, if one day someone would gaze into my hazel orbs and find me irresistible. I hoped so, badly.

There was one chance every year to get something I really wanted: at Christmas, Santa's single gift was clothing exempt. But sometimes even Santa didn't get it right. When I was eleven and had begun exploring downtown alone and on foot, I walked into Edmonton's only Indian import store and fell in love with everything: the beads, bangles, brocades, bronze ware, carpets, incense, silks, saris, and sandalwood adorning every shelf. Enraptured, I touched and smelled each item piece by piece, floating through the exotica like a stoned, deep sea diver.

Most captivating was a beautiful Indian dancing doll, dressed in a jewel-toned sari and shimmering with gold jewellery from the top of her braided hair to the tips of the bells on her toes. I *had* to possess her. And it was only October – plenty of time to petition Santa for the perfect gift.

I immediately launched my Christmas campaign, insisting she was the only, *only* gift I wanted. I drew a map of downtown Edmonton, clearly marking where she lived. I described her face, her hair, her clothes, and the shelf where she awaited me. I even included the price tag: eight dollars. Even on a schoolteacher's salary, she seemed affordable. I noted that the shop was only a few blocks from the department stores where my parents shopped. I talked about her every day. And then I waited for Christmas, anticipating how she'd light up my room and my life with her exotic charm.

You already know where this is going. It's not till I've opened the last package and shaken the bottom branches of the Christmas tree that reality hits. *They didn't buy her. They actually didn't get the only thing I been asking for, week after week, since October.*

I run to my room and cry. It's a double blow: not only is the doll absent, but there's only way I can interpret this denial. They simply don't care.

I end up saving my babysitting money, thirty-five cents an hour, and buying my Indian beauty in the spring. Luckily, no one else has spirited her away. And I love her intensely; something about the smell of India, captured in her hair and her slender limbs, excites me. But the emotional damage can't be fixed. I'm already resigned to years of wearing ugly catalogue skirts and blouses, paired with bad haircuts and baggy tights. But now I acknowledge another, darker truth: if there's something I really want, I know not to ask.

A year or two later, on another birthday, my mother gives me a pair of electric scissors and seems surprised when I don't light up. Electric scissors. She *knows* I hate sewing, at least as much as she does, so she must know that every time I use them, I'll be angry from the get-go. But maybe that's the point.

I share these little vignettes, not to throw stones, but to illustrate our dynamic. The cracks were always there, hot and icy, raw and deep. As I grew up, they deepened into canyons. The after-school attacks intensified and our respective rages mounted, though only one rage was allowed to vent. I took to hiding, sneaking, bypassing, and lying—anything to escape the teasing at school and the humiliation of dressing like a freak. Anything to cast off my mother's imprint and forge my own identity.

I yearned for affirmation, to be told that I was pretty, wanted, special. My intelligence was not in question, but my worthiness was. Yes, my parents acknowledged, I was smarter than average, but being clever was no credit to me.

I was a fledgling writer, a poet, a painter, and a sculptor. My mother dismissed my achievements and hung her own labels: in her eyes I was *sarcastic* and *conceited;* I was *selfish*, I was *as mean as Lucy in the Peanuts comic strips*. (And maybe I was. It seems most nine-year-old girls pass through at least one year of being epically unlikeable.) But I knew there were better aspects to me, qualities my teachers recognized and commended. And I wanted to believe my heart was basically good. I dreamed of being a nun or a missionary to Africa, or maybe a psychiatrist, so I could help people. This, I believed, was the real me, the Marilyn my mother refused to see.

I fought to hold onto that version of myself, and to not let my mother's diatribes define me. Above all, I knew to keep my true self hidden from her, deep behind the wall, or she'd rip the best of me to shreds.

2

My Huckleberry Friend

———————

Laura was my first angel. We met when her parents came to view the newly-built house across from ours. At that point the neighborhood was a muddy tangle of new roads and lumpy lots; lawns yet to be planted, houses yet to be built. But it was an amazing location, perched above the sprawling valley of the North Saskatchewan River, on the eastern outskirts of Edmonton. The river valley—or The Ravine, as we called it—would be our year-round playground, shaping our sensibilities and proclivities.

But I didn't know this yet. I was only five, soon to be six. Laura was a whole year and a half ahead of me, and I was instantly dazzled by her wisdom and sophistication. Laura *knew* things; she had a crazy imagination, and she was clearly the best friend I'd been craving since moving across town to our new house. But her family wasn't moving just yet: their house was still under construction.

I had my own room in our new house, but it was hardly the pretty room I'd envisioned before the move. It was square and drab, with boyish blue walls and a cold, high window overlooking the back alley. A mile beyond the alley, a ghostly city of refineries spewed smoke into the empty northern sky. The half-built neighborhood was deadly quiet, and at night the refineries emitted a frightening, eerie light that fueled nightmares of being lost and alone in a dark, metallic wasteland.

I longed to block the light and pretend the refineries weren't there, haunting my dreams, but the old pair of kitchen curtains my mother had hung covered only half of the window. The curtains also distressed me; their multicolored pattern of creeping ivy and brass cooking pots clashed with everything else in the mismatched room, and their utter uselessness as window coverings seemed further proof of my mother's disregard for me. I spent hours pondering the drapes and what they represented: how ugly they were, and how oppressed they made me feel. (Even as a child, an amateur interior decorator was trying to get out.) A few years later, I fashioned a pink and blue fringe out of cheap tissue paper to beautify the window, but it rustled so loudly above the forced air vent that I had to take it down.

Meanwhile, I was making do at my new preschool. I'd insisted on walking the seven unfamiliar blocks to class by myself on the first day, positive I knew the way. My mother, in a rare moment of capitulation, had secretly walked a half block behind me till I safely reached the church building. Then she slipped away, leaving me introduce myself to my new preschool teacher. After all, I was a seasoned preschooler, with three months' prior experience under my belt and not a trace of shyness. After that, I did the walk entirely on my own.

That spring, Laura's family finally moved in. My new best friend was in second grade, but she looked and acted much older. She was a beautiful child, with a slender frame, sculpted cheeks, and luminous gray eyes, all of which gave the impression of an older soul in a child's body. I envied her soft blonde curls and her feminine, color-coordinated bedroom. Across the alley, her window faced mine, and when we got a bit older, we used flashlights at night to send each other messages, like Anne of Green Gables and her best friend, Diana. Not that there was anything new to communicate; from the day she moved in, we spent every possible minute together, alternating between her house and mine when we weren't exploring The Ravine. As best, best friends, we emotively debated life's mysteries and sometimes fell out for the day, but we never tired of each other's company. She was my universe, and my portal into older, wiser things.

I was also envious of Laura's two-child family and her status as a Chosen Child — an adoptee. Laura was drawn to dark fairy tales, and she spun fabulous stories of baby factories and lost kingdoms to explain her origins. Her flamboyant father, a music professor in love with musical theater, smoked a pipe, wore a cravat, and sang bouncy Broadway tunes around the house. Her mother, a pretty transplant from Winnipeg, reminded me of a weeping willow; she was pliant and accommodating, and wept gentle tears—in front of us—when Laura's regularly unorthodox behavior undid her. To me, her tears represented *real* maternal love, an appeal for connection and delicate sorrow over her daughter's otherness, instead of the rejection I felt, and I yearned for my mother to cry over me, even once. I never saw her cry.

Even as a seven-year-old, Laura was sophisticated and curious, in step with the times, and she was possibly the first girl in Edmonton to own a Barbie doll. The week the dolls debuted in Canada, her father brought one home from a business trip to Toronto, and without having seen such a wonder before—a sexy, grown-up doll! —Laura knew exactly how to play with her. We dressed her in glamourous ensembles I'd never get to wear—though I imagined someday Laura would.

Laura knew all the lyrics to the Broadway tunes her father sang, and at the soulful age of eight, she taught me my first grown-up song, *Moon River*. The thrilling, mysterious lyrics (I had no idea what a huckleberry friend might be) broke my heart each time we sang it. A few years later, she'd be my introduction to the Beatles, and through her I'd be sagely instructed on the superiority of John Lennon, the sensuality of the Stones, and the superficiality of lesser, copycat groups. She was my ticket to the Sixties.

Before going psychedelic, we kept busy with our own version of show business, inspired by her father's record collection and our beginner's dance classes. We organized neighborhood variety shows, headlining ourselves, and spent months of our lives dancing precariously atop the six-foot-high fence that encircled my back yard. The fence was topped with painted six-by-fours, and on this narrow platform we honed our balancing skills, choreographing routines to songs like *Surry with the Fringe on Top* and *Good Ship Lollipop*. Our backyard performances were audience-free but might have generated curious crowds if we'd thought to advertise. We were fearless. As our skills increased, we even attempted to roller-skate along the fence—a short-lived triumph that ended in a mucky pile of dog poo festering in the back lane.

We built rickety stages and entered talent shows, convinced that our talent and charisma would net first place. (They didn't.) When we tired of singing and dancing, we named and mythologized the trails and groves in The Ravine: the Blue Forest, Blind Man's Walk, Belly-Ache Log, Carolyn's Way, and Drowner's Creek. The Ravine was still a wilderness full of deep, unexplored pockets, mostly ignored by the busy adults in our lives, and as long as we stayed clear of the river and came home by nightfall, we were free to go anywhere.

When we weren't exploring or rehearsing, we invented clubs and secret societies—nearly always an exclusive club of two. The most thrilling of these, The Black Hand Society, worked like this: Laura would ring a neighbor's front doorbell and strike up an inane conversation with whoever answered, distracting the homeowner while I snuck into their basement via the back door. (This was Canada in the 1960s; everyone's house was unlocked.) Once inside, I'd whip out my Black Hand Society notebook and frantically list the basement contents— *washing machine, dryer, fishing poles, boxes, winter boots*—never anything exotic (in fact, all the basements I explored were depressingly similar) but there was always the possibility of uncovering a den of iniquity at the next stake-out. We hoped so. We wanted to be shocked.

When I finished my list or got spooked, I'd blow my whistle. Laura also carried a warning whistle and even used it a few times, which must have startled the puzzled housewives she was stalling at the front door. But the crowning touch was this: before bolting, I'd leave our signature portent in a visible spot downstairs: a black construction paper hand, graphically warning the violated residents that The Black Hand had struck.

Such were the exploits of two evolving counter-culturalists. By 1967, we were ready for even deeper intrigue: a black-and-red Ouija board with invisible tentacles, waiting to ensnare our hungry little souls.

The Ouija board was an unsolicited and puzzling gift from Santa, who had no idea what powers the felted planchette would unleash into our lives. We were on it like suction cups on a wet vacuum.

Our fascination with dark fairy tales had fostered an obsession with ghosts and spirits, and the Ouija board promised to bring them right into our bedrooms. Bypassing silly questions about future boyfriends' initials and how many children we were going to have, we chose instead to probe the past: Could we connect with actual beings from ancient Egypt or medieval Europe? Apparently, we could. *Someone*—or maybe several entities—began spooking us with weird vibes and messages. For several weeks, we rushed home from school to set up our gypsy table and consult the oracles, captivated by this heart-stopping plunge into the supernatural. Over time, our sessions began to feel increasingly dangerous, and one day we agreed to renounce our spirit guides and pack the board away. By then it was too late: we'd already let them in. From then on, a residual darkness seemed to linger.

Laura's family and mine attended the United Church of Canada, a bland denomination for slant girls like us. Instead, we were drawn to the enigmatic Catholic Church, with its convents, priests, and confessionals, its mysticism and rituals. Of course, neither of us could actually *visit* a Catholic church; in those days, such forays across the divide would be considered heresy. Instead, we fed our imagination on tropes gleaned from *The Sound of Music* and old black and white movies. We didn't want Captain von Trapp; we wanted the secretive, cloistered life of wimpled nuns. I had a series of dreams in which I swung through the night sky in an enormous swing, robed in mystery and flanked by heavy, red velvet curtains. To me these were symbolic, potent dreams, full of an otherworldliness which I interpreted as my divine calling.

But soon another path beckoned, and we discarded our Catholic notions for the Beatles' eastern spirituality. As the Fab Four chased enlightenment, they became our religion, our lodestar. We already owned every Beatles record and had memorized and dissected every song. Now we studied pictures of our beaded heroes at the ashram and marveled at the robes and garlands, and at the beautiful long-haired women in their midst.

I bought a poster of the Maharishi and hung it next to my psychedelic poster of Pierre Elliot Trudeau, Canada's groovy new prime minister. Laura and I hadn't done any LSD (yet), but by sixth grade, I was yearning for India and my own magical mystery tour. The Ouija board had shaken us out of materialism, and now our mutual crush on John Lennon made the quest for cosmic consciousness as inevitable as our fast-approaching puberty.

A year later, Laura and her family left for ten months while her father completed a doctoral degree in the States. Ten months seemed a lifetime, and we clung to our cruelly separated friendship by writing daily missives and spending most of our allowance on stamps. To my unspoken envy, she was hanging out with an impossibly cool boy named Ira, who wrote opaque poetry and used impressive words like *non sequitur*. But despite our constant correspondence, I craved a local friend to fill the void till she returned. A quiet girl named Norma, newly arrived from Saskatchewan and assigned to the same homeroom, fit the bill. Ruminative and melancholic, Norma was less imaginative than Laura, yet surprisingly receptive to whatever dark subjects I chose to explore.

This time, I was definitely the leader. We walked two miles to school each day, and our relationship was epitomized by our walking dynamic: I attacked the course like an Olympian speed-walker, while Norma *almost* kept pace by alternating three walking steps with three running ones—the entire distance. Once we noticed the pattern, we found it hilarious, but it never occurred to me to slow down. I did everything fast: walking, talking, risk-taking, and jumping to conclusions. Impatient with the plodding pace of childhood, I was trying to grow up in record time.

Norma and I spent most of our time in her family's basement rumpus room, eating unmonitored Sara Lee chocolate cake straight from the freezer, fretting over our figures as we scrounged more sugar, and analyzing our dissimilar parents. Her father was a high-strung social worker who popped in and out the house with anxious queries about our activities. Compared to my father, he seemed highly attuned to his family's emotional frequencies and worried about his preoccupied children. Her mother was a plump, low-energy housewife prone to crying.

This disturbed me. Unlike Laura's mother's tears, these waterworks weren't about her children or even her marriage; they sprang from a deeper well. Maybe she was having an extended nervous breakdown, though in hindsight, it was probably a bad case of perimenopause. Whatever it was, this was the first time I'd witnessed unmasked adult depression, and the possibility of someday finding myself in a similar place terrified me. Although I was 25 years behind her, I had an inkling my own pockets of sadness could eventually morph into something similar if I wasn't rescued, or just plain lucky.

Norma had the dark hair, blue eyes, and pale skin of a classic Irish beauty, but instead of reassuring each other in the beauty department, we obsessed over our shortcomings: the too-long waists, too-short legs, and woefully underdeveloped chests that rendered us invisible to boys. Not that we were interested in any boys our age. I was still enamoured with John, she with George, and in our fantasies, we skipped junior high altogether and were utterly irresistible to men. Still, we longed for the imagined perks of present popularity, even as we disparaged the popular girls at school.

It was 1969. Woodstock was coalescing, Dylan and Donovan were on my turntable, and I was hankering for the alternate universe I'd discovered in a racy novel about Haight-Ashbury, a ripe read extolling the joys of free love and psychedelics. At school, teachers attempted to drug-proof our young minds by screening shockumentaries with titles like *LSD: Insight or Insanity?* Unlike most National Film Board yawn-inducers, these movies crackled with urgency and intrigue. As for this particular film, it couldn't have come at a better time, though on me it had the opposite effect from the one intended. Instead of being horrified by images of stoners' hands reaching into seductive blue flames, or of drug-crazed psychos leaping off skyscrapers, I was enthralled. I left the classroom determined to find some LSD.

This wasn't easy. Because I was an undersized, baby-faced 13-year-old, I had yet to be solicited by a drug dealer in our junior high school, so finding one was all on me. I studied the ninth graders and settled on a man-boy with the widest bell-bottoms and longest hair. Jackpot! But first I had to talk him into taking me seriously. This was a hard sell. I was obviously a complete neophyte, plus I was skipping the requisite steps: You were supposed to start with cigarettes, graduate to pot, and slowly work your way up (or down) to acid. But I wanted my mind blown, posthaste. My skeptical dealer finally relented, but not without overcharging me for the purple barrel blotter he carried in his requisite overcoat.

Norma was game to drop acid with me. But we talked ourselves out of taking a full dose the first night, taking only enough to trigger squiggly mind zaps and a mild anxiety attack. The next evening, we took a full hit and tripped the whole night. It was a claustrophobic, expansive rollercoaster of shape-shifting hallucinations, fleeting insights, and jolting fear. I hated it. I loved it. I wanted more.

We took more, as often as we dared, always fearful of blowing our young minds forever. I wasn't even sure what *blowing your mind* meant, but each trip was blighted by our fear of getting caught. I kept hoping for the ecstatic, free-flowing trips I'd read about in my Haight-Ashbury novel, but optimal LSD conditions don't include being underage, living with suspicious parents, and meeting an early curfew. Still, we kept tripping.

That summer I went to my last session of Christian camp and convinced Norma to come with me. Camp, I reasoned, would be the perfect place to drop acid without parents around. I didn't advertise our plans, but one of the girls in our cabin, an acid-head named Jinx, was clearly one of us, and she asked to share the trip so she could *show us something*. After a surreal night of tripping through camp while the counselors slept, it was time to be shown.

The sun was rising over the boggy lake as the LSD began to wear off, and nauseating blobs of seaweed and scum writhed on the beach in spongey hallucinations. Coming down is the unwelcome aftermath of an acid trip, a twilight zone of mental and physical discomfort saturated with a cavernous sense of depletion. I always forgot this depressing interval was part of the trip until it was upon me. *This* is what Jinx wanted to show us. She walked us to the end of the pier and made us look at her.

I know people, she said, gazing at us without blinking, *who took acid and got stuck in this place forever. Their brains are fried for life. They'll never get better, and they'll never leave this place. They're vegetables, but living ones; they know what they've done, but they can't escape. Their lives are ruined forever! It can happen to anyone: it could happen to you!*

She paused for effect and delivered the obvious punchline: *Stop taking acid!* She herself, she claimed, had stopped acid months ago and had only taken it now to enlighten us.

Her words, timed to coincide with the nadir of our trip, stunned me. Living here, trapped in a desolate limbo between two states of consciousness, would be hellish, if not the actual definition of hell. The prospect terrified me more than any trip so far. Listening to Jinx, it wasn't hard to imagine an eternity of in-between, a lifetime of brain-fry. But the lesson didn't stick. Like a speeding driver who slows down to rubber-neck a car wreck and ponders his own mortality for five minutes before speeding again, I wasn't done with psychedelics.

But things would soon be done with Norma. When we returned from camp, her father announced he was moving his family up north, and there were intimations he was trying to get his daughter away from me, the corrupter. He didn't say so directly, and maybe we were just being paranoid. But if keeping Norma safe was his actual motive, he chose the wrong city of refuge: he moved her smack into the middle of Alberta's most drug-infested community.

I cried to see her go. But Laura was coming back, and I couldn't wait to drop acid with her.

3

Broken Girl

Grade eight was a hazy year, and that year's archives retain no teachers, classmates, or classes, but only the countless hours I spent crying in the guidance counsellor's office on the second floor. Miss Russell, the spare, spinsterish counsellor at Hardisty Junior High, was my unlikely second angel. I was thirteen and in great pain. My father had fallen in love with his school secretary, a widow with four young children, and was contemplating leaving our family of seven.

This was a secret, but every night I heard my mother wailing in their bedroom next to mine, pleading with a wretchedness that made me burn with shame. My father's occasional murmurs, intermittent and faint, brought no comfort. The midnight sessions lasted hours and persisted for months. By morning the veil was drawn, and life crept on, but the simmering dread never lifted. My brothers, I assumed, were oblivious, though decades later we'd learn that each of us, apart from the youngest, knew at least some of the story, yet thought ourselves alone in what we feared.

I knew my father was drowning in desire. He wrestled for months, he was deeply in love, and he wanted to start over, to move to the sunny oasis of San Diego with this person who loved him back, along with her fatherless children. But I couldn't separate his longing to be with another woman from my certainty that he wanted to get away from *us*. He wanted different children, a better set; he wanted kids who didn't wear him out, like we did, driving him to rub his eyes and moan, *Oh my shattered nerves!* on school nights after work, as we got noisy and restless waiting for another late supper fraught with tension and argument, sure to be capped with at least one child's frustrated tears —usually mine.

I also knew that living with my mother meant misery, especially for him, now that he'd sampled sweeter fruit. Yet my heart simultaneously broke and hardened for her. *I'd* want to leave, too, if I were him. I could understand my father's impulse to escape and would soon be making my own exit. But my hard-edged mother was alone, almost friendless, with nothing and no one to prop her up. Perhaps that's why she blew so hard. I despised her for making him miserable enough to look elsewhere, and I hated his reducing her to such naked despair.

That year I had two confidantes: Laura and Miss Russell. But for once my precocious friend was out of her depth, and it was she who pointed me to Miss Russell and her open door. There were no other students clamoring for her time. My new angel was an odd duck, not someone I would ever imagine spending time with, but she was available, and her tiny office became my second home.

Miss Russell was knobby and angular, with short, yellowish-gray hair and a wardrobe of mannish dress suits that accentuated her jutting hip and pelvis bones. I sensed her personal life was equally embarrassing. But she became my rock, and I sought her company daily, sometimes even in the middle of a class, whenever I felt flooded. Our sessions— in which I alternately talked and fell apart—were endless looping tapes, dripping with despair. I was raw, aching, and deeply ashamed of my insatiable craving for love. Yet I returned to her office again and again, weeping in broad daylight like my mother howled at night, crushed by my father's abandonment and the bleakness of my parents' marriage. At this point, it didn't matter whether he'd decide to go or stay. What he *wanted* was plain to me, and he'd already chosen a better, more loveable family over us.

This belief, that he might forfeit but would never forget what he truly wanted, was cemented by a letter I found while searching my parents' bedroom drawers for clues. In it, my devout grandfather appealed to my father to *do the right thing* before God, to stay with his wife and family no matter how he felt. When my father ultimately decided to stay, I was certain this letter explained it: He stayed because it was his *Christian duty*. But to me, he'd already abandoned us in his heart of hearts—the place where these things mattered. He stayed, but he was merely doing the right thing, not the thing he really wanted. He was stuck with the family he'd spawned with his fertile and unhappy wife, but it was clear his heart lay elsewhere.

I don't remember a word Miss Russell said in all those months. She must have said *something* when I was crying too hard to speak. What I do remember is the chair by her desk and the shame, *my* shame, waiting daily in her office to undo me. I remember the broken girl with nowhere else to go. I remember the agony of misplaced attachment, of *needing* her, this odd misfit, so very much, though all she could offer was a listening ear. But her presence is what got me through. She was my port in a storm, an anchor when the hot and icy waters swamped my heart, even when they threatened to sink me several times a day.

At some point the midnight crying stopped. Outside my parents' bedroom, nothing was spoken of the crisis. I never learned the secretary's name, or met her fatherless children, or heard what became of them, or spoke to either parent about the affair. Life went on, and the storm clouds reconfigured. My father lived his happier life at school, with or without the secretary, and my mother made soup out of leftovers and stepped up her attacks against me.

The absolute deluge never came. But the sky was never really clear again.

4

Coal Black and Fiery Red

―――――― ～ ――――――

The next September I was set to follow Laura into high school. It wasn't a thrilling destination: McNally High resembled a prison, its grim concrete walls and narrow windows devoid of any architectural flair or warmth. The fortress hunkered on another edge of the river valley, across from the seedy side of Edmonton's core, and over that edge, beyond the sports fields, grew thickets of wild rose bushes where I'd nuzzled boys and guzzled my father's homemade wine at illicit summer river parties. The school's only redeeming attraction was the nearby 24-hour Night Owl Cafe, where three subsets — the ultra-cool, the truants, and the stoners – loitered at different tables over chips and gravy.

The year before, Laura had found our people among the garage band crowd, headquartered in the cafe. Our kind—the nonconformists and misfits who didn't join clubs or play sports—also glommed together in the school's smoking foyer, disconnected from whatever was unfolding in the mainstream. Our kind would never return for school reunions or be featured in the high school yearbook. We languished outside the social and academic scene, part of a shadowy species that slumbered through high school but came alive at night.

But this would come later. As summer ended, Laura and I were waist-deep in plans to run away, making high school irrelevant. Both of us were desperate to disappear and start over. My life felt precarious; I was spinning plates of secrecy at home, and it was only a matter of time until I slipped, and everything came crashing down. If that happened, even my limited freedom would be gone. I was weary of sneaking around to wear make-up or my own choice of clothes, or to go out in the evenings, or to possibly have a social life and find a boyfriend, and four oppressive, insufferable years stretched ahead until I turned eighteen. Anything, *anything* was better than living another week under my mother's regime.

Laura's struggles were less obvious. From my perspective, her parents seemed tolerant, reasonable, and even gracious, but Laura felt like a distant planet, light-years away from her parents' insular sun. Her show-casing father was a classic narcissist; her mother was his devoted handmaid. Their world was cozy, cultured, and adult; perhaps they should never have added children to the mix. Laura had outgrown her *special princess from the baby factory* narrative and was wrestling with a bottomless primal wound. Not that she could've articulated any of this at the time. That September, on the cusp of turning 16, Laura was simply in pain.

We'd fixed our sights on Vancouver, 850 miles to the west, and were waiting for an opportune time to escape before anyone noticed our absence. It was crucial to go fast and go far; we couldn't risk being caught. Once there, we'd melt into Vancouver's hippie subculture and reinvent ourselves. The only hitch was getting past my mother, who never left home. She was always watching, always suspicious, and always aware of my coming and going.

And then the impossible happened. My mother made plans, for the first time in our lives, to spend time away from the family, over a long weekend in Banff with several girlhood friends. My father jumped at this rare opportunity to take three of my brothers on a remote fishing trip. My little brother and I were to stay at my grandmother's house. It was a gift from the gods, a perfect trifecta. The coast would be clear.

I had some cash, around $40 from babysitting, and along with Laura's savings, we figured we were set. The biggest hurdle was figuring out how to leave town— literally. Neither of us knew which highway led west, and we didn't want to accidentally wind up in Saskatoon. Taking the Greyhound bus to Banff, 280 miles west, would solve that problem, and from there we'd hitchhike to the coast, as there was only one highway going west from that point. Of course, my mother would also be in Banff when we got there, but we'd have to take that risk. We were planning to dye our hair, jet black for me, deep red for Laura, and if we crossed my mother's path, she'd never recognize us. Simple!

Now all we needed was a ruse to get past my grandmother. Deceiving her would be unpleasant business, but my innocent granny was the final hurdle, a tricycle blocking our getaway car.

We decided to use my standard babysitting ruse and Laura's voice skills. Putting a handkerchief over the phone, Laura posed as Mrs. Client, smoothly persuading my reluctant grandmother to allow me to babysit, spend the night, and return by bus the next day. I held my breath, knowing my grandmother's *yes* contradicted the instinctive *no* in her gut. She was nobody's fool, as stubborn as her hardy Ukrainian roots were long, but for some reason she gave in. She'd meet me tomorrow at two, at a movie theatre across town. *Fiddler on the Roof* was playing, and she'd been waiting for months to see it.

Everything was set. It was a perfect, ruthless plan.

Sometimes there are scenes so pivotal, potent, and devastating that, even if we weren't physically there, we recall them as if we were.

Especially if we struck the match that sparked the devastation.

I wasn't there, but I see my grandmother on the corner of Whyte Avenue, dressed in her sensible catalogue slacks and a hand knit sweater, pacing in front of the cinema as two becomes three o'clock, four o'clock, five... I see her there, as the late August sun dims and bus after bus comes and goes, calming my little brother, trying to hide her fear, scanning each pedestrian and parsing the fake phone call, over and over, searching for clues and cursing herself for giving in.

Who could she call? Mrs. Client and her phone number didn't exist. Both parents were unreachable; did they even mention which hotel, which campsite they'd be at? No one expected to be found that weekend, back in those days when travelers said goodbye and broke contact till their return. How long did she pace before calling the police? Did they come right away? Or did they leave her waiting on the corner as the theatre emptied, once, twice, how many times, before until she finally gave up and went home? Did she sleep that night, or the next? Did she blame herself before rightfully blaming me?

I picture my little brother, the only blond, blue-eyed child in our dark-haired family, crying for me, his second mom, his muffin-maker, his fellow explorer; the one who took him for such long woodland treks, she'd have to carry him home, soft and sleepy in her arms; the big sister who always adored him, no matter how much she hated life under the same roof. I see a black cloud swallow the house as the family returns, minus one, in the wake of my disappearance. And I can hear my mother's endless rants filling the house and spilling into the neighborhood, making sure everyone knows that all of this, completely and unforgivably, is her wicked daughter's fault. The one she'd always known was rotten.

But most piercing is this: picturing my grandmother and my little brother on the same street corner at quarter to two, before the movie tickets are wasted, before this holiday weekend turns to tragedy, and before my hapless granny realizes her only granddaughter is *gone,* actually vanished, and she might never watch a movie with her again. (She won't.)

Before the punch in the gut.

And always, the realization: I can never rewrite this wretched script.

So, if anyone ever asks me, *What's the worst thing you've ever done?* I won't have to stop and think. The answer is on the tip of my dastardly tongue.

The Greyhound delivered us to Banff on Friday evening, soon after the mountains circling town had swallowed the sun. The alpine air was piney and cold, dense with fog, and I was on high alert, knowing my mother might be around the next corner, eating Salisbury steak with her friends and still unaware of my escape. Laura and I slipped through the tourist core and walked the fringes of Banff before locking ourselves in a grungy gas station bathroom. Here, under the greenish light of a low-watt bulb, we bent over a rusty bathroom sink and took turns dyeing our hair.

It was a night of firsts: our first Greyhound trip, our first night alone in a strange city, and the first time we'd colored our hair. When we finished, my face looked wan and lost under a wet swath of startling coal-black hair, and Laura, with her new, fiery-red curls, resembled a Klondike barmaid – hardly the subtle disguises we needed.

With absurd naivety, we figured a radical color switch would be enough to throw the police off our trail. After all, they'd be looking for two runaways with nut brown and dirty blonde hair, not these newly-tressed vixens who were still clearly underage and carrying their life's belongings in disposable bags.

But we weren't foolish enough to spend our first night in a gas station. Instead, we wandered the town again, toting our bags and shivering with cold and apprehension. Eventually we met a minister who invited us to sleep in his church. After a fatherly admonition that blew past our ears like fairy dust, he left us among the pews for the night and wished us well. We switched back and forth from pew to floor – the pews were curved, the floor was cold — before falling into choppy dreams permeated with the acrid smell of hair dye. At daybreak, we woke to more fog and slipped out of Banff in a blur—hours before my grandmother realized she'd been bamboozled, hours before she called the police, and hours before all hell broke loose— thumbing our way to the coast like two plucky bandits.

5

Jailbait

―――――≈―――――

September 1970 was a great time to be homeless in Vancouver. Thousands of hippies and runaways drifted west across Canada and north from the States to get high on the wide, sea-breezy streets and partake of the abundant free food and shelter provided by the city. There were also predators, grifters, addicts, and all the perennially homeless — the Natives and other unfortunates who slid south and west into their own tragic dead-ends. But if, in that brief epoch, distinctions were made between these sectors, I didn't notice. It seemed half the city lived free, gloriously free, and so Laura and I could, too. And for a few rapturous weeks, we did live free: free of parents, restrictions, and fear.

The safety net was easy to find. We slept in a quaint Victorian house sectioned into a no-questions-asked women's hostel. In the kitchen, antique cupboards and a roomy fridge were stocked with miscellaneous donated food, most of it stale, but one night there were stacks of ripe bananas, and I baked the residents a six-layer banana cake that threatened to slide off the platter like shifting tectonic plates. A few blocks from the hostel was a free clothing bank, which we shopped daily like a boutique, searching for vintage cloth sandals and gauzy blouses to perfect our hippie-girl make-over. With ample supplies of life's basics, we had enough money left to buy psychedelics and cigarettes (we still hadn't tried smoking pot). And since there was little to no scrambling for survival, we spent most of our days hanging out in an airy, light-filled armory that was now a men's hostel.

The armory was open all day, every day, serving as hub of the free-wheeling, hippie-twirling street scene. Despite its military origins, it was now a haven of peace and love, floating in a sunlit haze of hashish smoke and incense. Under its vaulted ceiling, minstrels, guitarists and bongo drummers jammed on dozens of cast-iron army beds heaped with backpacks and ponchos; on other beds, travellers slept or swapped stories, while scruffy guys with ponytails and old army jackets wandered in and out, selling, scoring, and smoking their goods. Their bra-less, beaded girlfriends drifted behind them like gypsies, whirling their beaded skirts. It was a delectable slice of Haight-Ashbury in a tidy Canadian bubble.

One afternoon, I was accosted by two pimps, though I didn't know the words *pimp* or *accost* yet. I'd never met anyone like them; so far, the extent of my exposure to dark-skinned people had been the occasional sighting of an African exchange student near the university in Edmonton. These were a different breed altogether: sinewy black men in fedoras and Motown suits, all teeth and honeyed speech. I must've been prime pickings—young, virginal, dewy-skinned, and obviously far from home. But they read me wrong. Zeroing in on my vintage sandals, they dangled the promise of new shoes, *sexy* shoes, *many, many pairs of shoes* if I'd just follow them out the armory door. Fortunately, trying to entice me with fancy shoes was as futile as trying to lure a vegan with a side of Kobe beef. I had no interest. My criss-crossed fabric sandals had taken weeks to find.

Except for observing the women's hostel curfew—in by nine, out by seven—our time in Vancouver was formless, and the days passed in a blur of spacey interactions. We wandered from the hostels to the streets, falling in and out of conversations and 60-minute friend-ships, and harboring secret attractions to pony-tailed draft-dodgers, who seemed leagues cooler than our home-grown hippies. Apart from the pimps, no one tried to seduce us — or if they did, we were oblivious. Maybe the word *JAILBAIT* was stamped all over us. I like to think we had a vigilant crew of angels watching our backs. They must've thrown up their arms in dismay the day we decided to go to California.

Apparently being in Vancouver wasn't enough. I can't remember what prompted our decision to head south, though it was probably linked to my obsession with Haight-Ashbury and our fantasies of serving as muses for whichever famous rock band needed us. We still adored John, but Yoko had taken up all of John's space, and we were tired of waiting for his situation to change. Or maybe we just wanted to put more distance between our parents and ourselves. Whatever the reasons, California beckoned like a fairy godmother, ready to grant our every desire.

There was also the oversize bulletin board in the armory. Plastered with handwritten notes about missing friends, ride shares, potential bandmates, and upcoming music festivals, it made everything seem pos-sible. All you had to do was thumbtack your wish to the board, and ping! Your wish would come true.

That morning we got to the armory early and posted this sign:

Two screwy chicks

need a ride to California.

Ready to leave today!

P.S. No Mafia need apply!

This last sentence was Laura's — her half-serious, half-madcap way of screening out any possible scoundrels. We'd thought of everything.

For the next hour we circled the board, waiting for takers. It didn't take long. Quicker than you can say, *Out of our minds and into the madness*, we had our drivers. Indeed, they *were* ready to leave today. To celebrate, or just to be even stupider, we both took a big hit of mescaline as soon as our new companions were out of sight. We'd be riding high to California!

Let's call them Sleazy and Smarmy; whatever names they gave us were probably fake, but they had a red convertible and two empty seats in the back. There was one minor glitch: they needed help with gas money. No problem! We jumped in the car and went to collect our stuff at the women's hostel – four small plastic bags of cast-off hippie garb and our last bit of cash. Not enough cash, according to Sleazy and Smarmy. We'd go downtown and panhandle for more. Laura and I would be the mendicants, while the men minded the car and made sure our stuff was safe. Being pretty young girls and all, this made sense. We'd collect more money, much faster, than two guys ever could.

By the time we got downtown, the mescaline was kicking in. Laura and I split up and worked opposite sides of the street; even stoned, we knew that a single, repentant runaway, eager to scrounge bus fare so she could get home to her parents, would stir the sympathies of tourists and grannies better than two of us together. Soon we were pulling in handfuls of change, as well as one, two, five, and even ten-dollar bills, and trotting it over to our ride pimps, who splayed in the convertible like bored sultans, working on their tans. With each deposit, they urged us to bring in just a little more. Of course! We had no idea how much we'd raised, or how much gas to California would cost, but we were hard little workers.

By now it was noon, or later. The mescaline had flooded our brains and it was hard to keep track of where we were or what we were supposed to be doing. The sun was too bright, and I was spinning like an upended paper boat in the stream of lunch hour pedestrians – sensory overload. Ducking into a sedate, upscale restaurant—there was the hush and tinkle of fine dining and a sudden blast of cool air—I began to move from table to table, soliciting diners. Within minutes, a very angry man—the Maître d, no doubt—grabbed my arm and pushed me back onto the street. The trip turned dark. I needed to find Laura and get my bearings.

Ten or fifteen minutes of terror seized me as I searched for my anchor, till we finally found each other and the world tipped straight again. We could do this. We just needed to find our way back to the red convertible, and we'd all be on our way to California. Laura was navigating better than I and knew where the car was parked. Holding on to each other so as not to float away, we inched our way back to the corner to rendezvous with our drivers, and there they…weren't.

Sleazy and Smarmy, their pockets fat with the cash we'd collected, had absconded, along with our wallets and the plastic bags containing everything we owned. It was as if they'd stolen our souls. Shipwrecked, we stood on the sidewalk as the world dissolved, trying and failing to read the time on a giant clock that told us nothing. Their betrayal, amplified a hundred-fold by the mescaline, was cosmic, unfathomable. Our dreams were dashed, our identities stolen. We had nothing; we were nothing; we'd been scammed to the bone. It was the scariest, loneliest feeling in the world.

It didn't occur to us to find a city park, to simply wait till the mescaline wore off, and then to panhandle enough change to get back to the hostel and start over. In hindsight, this would've been an excellent plan. But we were way beyond logic or reason. At least I was. Laura had a last card up her sleeve and knew someone to call: the teenaged son of her parents' friends, the only person either of us knew in Vancouver. Byron would help us. He'd know what to do. He was cool, she assured me; he wouldn't tell his parents. Laura was sure of it. I wasn't so sure – the world had suddenly flipped into a dangerous, treacherous place — but I was too wasted and scared to think of a better plan.

We were still capable of finding a phone booth and depositing a dime to make the call. Laura did the talking; the street signs kept morphing into starbursts and lurid paisleys, but somehow we managed to give Byron our location. He was cool. He'd be there in half an hour to meet us. We just needed to stay put so we wouldn't lose ourselves or each other again. We tethered ourselves to the booth and waited. The trip got mellower. Eventually a sleek Volvo pulled up and Byron bounced out to greet us — from the passenger side.

Did Byron even drive yet? It was too late to find out. His father smiled benignly at us from behind the steering wheel as if he were picking us up from the airport. His voice was like maple syrup.

Laura! How nice to see you again! And this must be Marilyn! Hop in, both of you – there's plenty of room in the back. We'd love to take you back to our place for a visit, Laura, and Carol's looking forward to seeing you, too! It's not far from here...

And so, for the second time that day, we ignored the alarms that must've been screaming in some corner of our mescaline-drenched brains, and heedlessly climbed into the back of another shady car.

Byron's West Vancouver house was almost as beautiful as the ocean view it overlooked. It was the kind of house owned by patrons of tony restaurants like the one from which I'd just been ejected. We sank into a plush sofa in the shag-carpeted, sunken living room while Byron's mother fussed in the kitchen, preparing sandwiches and muffins for her sudden guests. Byron and his father sat with us, pretending this was simply an unexpected but delightful social call. Laura and I tried to act normal, but we lost it when lunch came, dissolving into giggles and babbling about having *met our muffins and faced the cake.* We were clearly out of our minds.

In spite of our drug-fueled inanity, our hosts kept up the charade. Unsurprisingly, we were too stoned to eat, but we could giggle and even relax a little, sinking deeper into the sofa as Byron's father put a record on the turntable. It was Bob Dylan, bleating the lyrics of *Like a Rolling Stone,* a song I'd heard but never *heard* like I was getting it now. Suddenly the song was the only thing in the room: Dylan's sarcastic jeer, mocking the girl who used to dress so fine, now living on the streets and having to get used to it, this lost and diminished girl who'd squandered all respect and had no direction home. The words hammered me, flattened me, and once again the trip turned dark. Was this a warning, a message, a rebuke? It sure seemed like it, especially when someone—Byron? his father?—kept playing the song over and over and louder and louder as the conversation petered out, and now there was a chill in the room, and I looked up to see two uniformed, unsmiling men step onto the shag carpet with shiny, black, thick-soled shoes.

Canadians don't wear shoes in the house.

But apparently Canadian policemen do.

6

The Kindness of Strangers

So many firsts! I'd never been in a cop car or a police station, never been shuffled from one hard plastic chair to the next, never been interrogated by one heartless cop after another, never been fingerprinted or strip-searched or given a bottle of lice shampoo and ordered to shower under the contemptuous gaze of a warden. And I'd never had such a long, hellish drug trip, a trip that lasted almost 20 hours, absorbing and amplifying every ounce of bad energy coming at me. There wasn't a single smile or a glimmer of compassion from any of the uniforms that night. Laura and I were criminals, and they split us up the moment we reached the station to make sure we suffered alone through our arrest and incarceration.

I also hadn't known that a juvenile detention centre is essentially a jail, and a harsh one at that. The strip search and the supervised, cold shower set the welcoming tone. Then another hostile warden, furious that I'd interrupted her night rest, confiscated my clothing, threw me a pair of scratchy, over-bleached pajamas, and locked me, alone and still tripping, into a pitch-black room.

It was probably two or three a.m. by now, and I'd been in full-blown panic since the cops had materialized. Now, alone in the dark, fear ate me alive. No one had told me that mescaline trips could last almost a full day. There was nothing to tether me, no sane or reassuring thought I could think of to stop the fear, and no chance of sleeping even a few hours before my first day in juvie began. I was doomed, reduced to reliving all the foolish decisions that had landed us here – if I could even think straight.

By six in the morning, the mescaline had worn off, replaced with a new layer of dread as another grim-faced warden delivered my prison garb: a boxy, short-sleeved, faded cotton blouse; a pair of cheap, ill-fitting canvas shoes; and the ugliest pair of jeans I'd ever worn. Everything reeked of bleach and ammonia. Apparently, part of the punishment was to make us feel as hideous and discomfited as our supposed crimes deserved.

In the dining hall I found Laura, as sleep deprived and miserable as I felt, where a pasty breakfast of lumpy creamed wheat and stale slices of white bread awaited us. Our fellow inmates looked as pale and listless as the food. After breakfast, it was time for chores – the sole morning activity. I was assigned to scour the long basement hallway with ammonia and steel wool, while Laura was banished to fold clothes in the overheated laundry room.

We met at noon for a joyless lunch of white bread and bologna sandwiches. Everything about the center was oppressive, even the so-called 'free time' in the afternoon. After lunch, all the inmates were herded into a stark common room with nothing but hard furniture and each other's sad histories to occupy us. If our captors couldn't break us with bad food, scratchy clothing, and mind-numbing chores, they'd do it with boredom.

The detention centre was designed to make every aspect of juvie life as unpleasant as its architects could get away with. Beds were planks, blankets were stiff, wardens were merciless, and chores were pointless and punitive. I guess this was a good thing, if the point was to turn junior delinquents from a life of crime at their first offense. But the architects' failure to make distinctions based on the level of crimes committed — or *not* committed, no formal charges had been laid for most of us — dismayed me. There were kids in juvie who'd stolen cars and wielded knives!

What had we done? Run away from our unhappiness and searched for meaning with psychedelics? Panhandled for spare change along with most of the street people in Vancouver? It was hardly the same. But another aspect of the punishment was denying us any opportunity to speak with someone in authority. If any of the planners had suggested compassion as a useful adjunct to our treatment, his colleagues must have laughed him out the door. Our human rights were confiscated, along with our watches and underwear.

If there were social workers in the background, determining the length of our stay or our next destination, they were invisible. Laura and I had no idea if we'd be there for months, if our parents were involved in the decision, if we were expected to go to court, or if they'd ship us somewhere else. This made our 12-day stint feel like eternity – no doubt all part of the architects' plan.

One morning we were summoned to the juvie office, ordered to change back into our old clothes (still ripe with the smell of hostels and fear), and then delivered to the airport in the company of two cops who would escort us back to Edmonton. Another first: my first plane ride. Once again, the police split us up, Laura in one row with her officer, I in another with mine. The cops had nothing to say to us; their job was to keep us from running again. And they were right to think we might: I'd have done almost anything to never face my mother again.

It was a quick and awful flight. At the airport, Laura's parents greeted her with bear hugs and tears before sweeping her out the gate without a glance in our direction. My parents stood stone-faced at the far side of the terminal, waiting for me to approach them. My mother looked ten years older. There were no hugs, no smiles, not even a sense of relief. *We're glad you're back safely,* my father said woodenly, as if he'd been told what to say but hadn't practiced saying it with feeling. Nobody was glad to see me. I felt my stomach contract as it always did around my mother, and the age-old dread she stirred in me flooded every pore. *The worst is yet to come,* my body was telling me. *Something worse is going to happen.*

And it was. As we walked to the exit, my mother finally spoke. *I found your diary,* she said, *and I read every page. I know everything about you.*

I kept my diary stashed at the bottom of my pink wicker laundry basket, along with other secrets of my barely-lived life: my forbidden bras and make-up, my beloved Haight-Ashbury novel (which my father had originally confiscated from a student and hidden in the basement). Some of these things I'd taken with me. Others I'd re-stashed. But how could I have forgotten to take my diary?

This diary, like the journals of most teens, was a portal into my darkest thoughts. It simmered with the rage I harbored against my mother. It burned with resentment towards my father for never defending me against her. It clung to every past grievance and injustice like welded pearls in an iron oyster. It forgot nothing, and it forgave nothing.

And of course, it contained other secrets. The first boy I'd French-kissed – a complete stranger, encountered in a forested playground while my mother was just yards away. The sexual fumblings I mistook for love at boozy river parties. My persistent attraction to psychedelics and long-haired stoners. And every crush and heart hunger I'd experienced since the age of eleven.

My diary was also a portal into my overactive imagination. Besides my confessions and transgressions, I'd written pages of things I might *like* to do, or at least fantasized doing, even though I knew I never would. But my mother couldn't make those distinctions. For her, my fat leather confessional only confirmed what she already believed: I was rotten to the core.

Her words hung in the air as we walked to the car and drove into the city. No one spoke, which was another first — both parents typically filled space with words, words, words. I scanned my brain for something to cut the tension, something that would humanize me. *I baked a six-layer banana cake at the hostel where we stayed,* I ventured. Baking was a nice, normal thing, wasn't it? And a six-layer cake was special. I wasn't spending *all* my time in Vancouver being deviant! This got no response. My father turned off the highway, heading west instead of north, and eventually pulled into an office building parking lot.

You need to see a psychiatrist, one of them said. *This is his office.*

Another first. I'd fantasized about *being* a psychiatrist but had never actually met one. This appointment was sudden – I had no idea what we'd talk about — but being at his office was a relief. At least I'd be able to explain myself to someone who'd listen. But I quickly realized it wasn't to be a private session. As soon as we sat down, my mother erupted into a tirade that blasted any chance of me, or even the psychiatrist, saying anything. She ranted for an hour without pausing for breath, periods, commas, or questions marks. When the hour was up, the doctor pulled me into another room and asked me to sit. Finally, an adult other than my father had seen my life up close and witnessed what I could no longer bear.

The psychiatrist spoke slowly, enunciating every word as if my life depended on it. *Your mother is a very, very angry person,* he said, *and I can see that you're alienated from both your parents. Very alienated,* he said, looking to see if I grasped what he was saying. *A very extreme case of alienation.*

He paused to let his words sink in. I wasn't familiar with the word *alienation,* but I could guess what it meant. It sounded like I either deserved a medal or had contracted a fatal disease.

In fact, he continued, *your mother is so angry, I'm afraid she'll harm you if I send you home. So I'm sending you to a Children's Home for a few days, until she calms down. After that…*

His words trailed off. He got on the phone and arranged my stay at the Home. A social worker would drive me over. Then he wished me luck and stepped cleanly out of my life.

My mother's rage was as likely to abate in a few days as coconuts were likely to grow in Edmonton. Nevertheless, I spent a few desolate days at the safe house before being dropped back into the family maelstrom. No one, not even the other lost children of trauma, spoke to me while I was there. Who was in charge? Did anyone suggest getting a social worker involved in my transition? Apparently not. My talk with the shrink had been a meaningless blip.

It was a cold reprieve, completely overshadowed by fears of what faced me at home, and the heartless regime I dreaded went into effect the minute I walked in the door. The New Rules, my mother informed me, would remain in effect until the day I turned 18. From now on, there would be no friends in my life. No phone calls. No extra minutes to get home from school. No going out, ever, besides going to school. No babysitting, no extra-curricular activities, and no chance of earning any brownie points through good behaviour. No nothing. I would essentially be under house arrest for the next three and a half years.

My father would be the nighttime enforcer. To prevent me from running away, he planned to sleep outside my bedroom door for the first few weeks. McNally High was put on daytime alert. If I missed even a single class, the principal would call my parents and initiate a search. In an instant, whatever freedom being in high school might have bestowed was snatched away. I did the math; if I left home the day I turned eighteen, 1,236 miserable days stretched before me.

It was incomprehensible. The centre could not hold.

Within a week, my father went back to sleeping in his bed. I imagine the cold linoleum hallway had something to do with it, though nothing was said. But his concession would make my next escape much easier. Laura was ready to join me again, even though her parents had taken the compassionate route and were trying to woo her back. I still couldn't see why she found her situation insufferable, but did nothing to talk her out of accompanying me. We were best friends, and best friends stuck together, no matter what.

In hasty consults between classes, we weighed our options. Unless we started dealing drugs or robbing banks, the only thing we could be arrested for was truancy. So we figured if we stayed in Edmonton and kept attending school, we'd be untouchable. Would our parents try to physically apprehend us and drag us home? Even in my mother's case, this seemed unlikely. She'd be raving and gnashing her teeth at home, but I couldn't see her showing up at school to wrestle me into the car.

At this point I had nothing to lose. Still, I wanted my getaway to be foolproof – and final. My last home art project – and there'd been many since the day I first clutched a crayon – was making a Marilyn-sized dummy, replicated with my own pink hair curlers under a patterned scarf I'd once worn as a Halloween gypsy. I arranged her neatly under my bedclothes; she'd be waiting for my parents to check on me during the night. I packed a few clothes. Then, crossing the linoleum floor where my father should have been sleeping, I crept to the sundeck above the garage and threw my bag over the railing.

And then, in a move I'd been perfecting since the age of ten — possibly for this very moment — I straddled the railing, inched my way to a spot above the gate post and swung myself over, pausing to catch my balance before jumping onto the lawn. The gate barely shook as I leapt into the night.

No one talked about 'couch-surfing' in 1970, and there was nothing remotely cool about sneaking into the basements of friends and acquaintances at night, then creeping out before dawn to avoid parental detection. Laura and I were lucky if we got a two-night stay. Most hosts risked taking us only once, and after we ran out of friends with basements, we took our chances sleeping in beds with strangers – young men who lived on their own and promised to let us sleep in peace. These promises often wavered as the nights inched toward morning, in which case we'd spend the hours before dawn fighting off advances. It was exhausting. But we were still virgins, and still getting ourselves to school each morning, where the administration had apparently taken a "wait and see" approach to our homelessness. As we'd expected, our parents had not swooped in to arrest us.

After a fortnight of basement hopping and advance fending, it was a relief to discover that Edmonton also had a free hostel. The Soft Machine was a creaky, four-storey manor near the university. It was seedier than the Vancouver hostels, and housed a raunchy clientele known for hosting "balling contests" in the malodorous main floor bunk room. We instinctively avoided the bunk room at all hours. Instead, as the hostel's youngest, most vulnerable residents, Laura and I were chastely bedded on the fourth floor, where Keith and Danny, the 22-year-old hostel managers, paternally watched over us.

Danny was a scrawny, pointy-bearded draft dodger who read underground newspapers and resembled a scruffy leprechaun. Keith, pale and cerebral, had an afro of dark, glossy curls and wore John Lennon glasses. As avowed pacifists, they also avoided the main bunkroom, unwilling to take on the downstairs biker crowd. As long as no one was getting knifed, it was safer to ignore the fornicators than to call them out.

I was immediately drawn to Keith, and he to me. He was the first adult in my life to really lean in and ask the right questions, and we spent hours talking about parents and life and books and dreams. He was a gifted listener and a wise friend. Of course, I fell deeply, desperately in love with him and his sweet attention.

Once he understood my situation, Keith had a plan. He had a degree in social work (the Soft Machine gig was his first job) and he'd apply to be my guardian, guiding and encouraging me in the safe haven of the hostel – on the fourth floor, of course, where he and Danny could continue as mentors and make sure I did my homework. All we needed was my parents' consent.

Keith phoned my parents and the three of us went to meet them, confident my liberation was at hand. It seemed like a win-win for everyone. I'd be out of my parents' hair and secure enough to finish school. With Danny's assistance, Keith would help me navigate the years till my independence, protecting me from predators. My mother was curious enough to listen to our longwinded proposal – for about 15 minutes. Keith and Danny looked straight out of Woodstock, but they were wildly articulate, and this briefly impressed and silenced my parents. But when they got to the punchline—that *Keith* was proposing to *parent* me—my mother exploded, and for the next two hours she ranted without stopping. As usual, the venom was directed at me and my utter incorrigibility. I was mortified. I'd lied to Keith about my age, adding two years to my actual fourteen, and the pathetic truth embarrassed me.

The guardianship was dead in the water, but at least Keith and Danny knew I hadn't been exaggerating. We returned to the hostel, chortling over the *But Meeting* we'd just endured – thus dubbed because of the dozens of "buts" they'd tried to interject as my mother raged. It was the only word they could get in edgewise: my mother's verbal prowess was as formidable as ever.

Despite the failed rescue attempt, my life at Soft Machine might have continued indefinitely if Laura and I hadn't made more stupid mistakes. One chilly autumn evening as we hitchhiked around Edmonton looking for something to do, we got into a car with two men in their early twenties who suggested driving to Calgary and back, a six-hour round trip.

There was no reason for the trip; they simply had a full tank of gas and nothing going on. And they weren't our type. They were *greasers*, not hippies, and they weren't offering drugs or alcohol. It was just a bad case of four-way boredom. And the car was warm.

The drive was as dull as our companions. At two a.m., we parked along a deserted street in downtown Calgary and got out of the car. Seconds later, the sickening yowl of a police cruiser closed in. We were sunk: two underage girls in the middle of a weeknight with no ID, no reason to be downtown after midnight, and no idea of who our companions were. They let the men go and hauled us in. This time, the cops at the station were convinced we'd been smoking weed and wanted us to admit it. We hadn't. Our clothes reeked of patchouli oil, the classic hippie perfume, and not pot, but the police couldn't make the distinction. It was their word over ours.

All the things I'd sworn would never happen to me again—the strip search, the lice shampoo, the humbling prison garb—happened again. This time the juvie stay lasted a week before we boarded our second flight back to Edmonton. But not everything was the same. This time, our escort was a lone social worker, and when we landed, she handed us over to an Edmonton colleague. This time, there were no parents waiting at the airport to embrace us or push us away. And this time, they weren't sending us home.

7

Four Faint Horizontal Lines

ister Mary Magdalene greets us at Cottage Four, cradling a black chihuahua atop her ample bosom. The dog resembles a squirmy rodent, wriggling and nibbling at her face as she coos at him. This is my first peek into the actual world of Catholics, but Sister is nothing like the nuns in *The Sound of Music.* She wears a burgundy polyester dress hemmed precisely at mid-knee—the shortest she can get away with, post-Vatican II—and her token veil barely covers the long, silvery hair she's pulled into a ponytail. A narrow face and hawkish nose peg her age at around 40, but she carries herself like a young girl: self-consciously. The moment she introduces herself, I wonder what sordid personal history moved her to become a nun and name herself after the notorious Mary of Magdala.

And this is Chico, she warbles, *my lovely, perfect, splendid little man!* She leans forward to give us a closer view of the rodent, but Chico only snarls at us. I instantly hate him.

Chico, Chico, be nice now! Sister seems to forget us for a moment as their love fest continues, replete with tongues and lips and canine belly gyrations. We wait for her to come back. *Chico, lovely Chico, my little man, let's show these girls their new home!*

Laura and I have just come from the main building at The Maple Ridge Home for Girls, where we briefly met the Mother Superior and Mr. Ramsay, the unctuous social worker in charge of fifty or so wayward souls. Unbeknownst to us, we've been fast-tracked past the Assessment Unit, the locked basement quarters beneath Mr. Ramsay's office, where girls are held for observation till deemed fit to live in one of the four cottages, or be held in long-term incarceration.

We're amazed they haven't split us up yet, that they've taken us to the same cottage, and now Sister is walking us upstairs in the roomy house to the *same bedroom*. It's a huge room, with enormous closets and matching twin beds and dressers at both ends of the room. Not only do Laura and I get to share a room, we get privacy, too. I wonder if someone's made a terrible mistake, and if this wondrous gift will be snatched away before we get to enjoy it.

And there's more. As we examine the empty double closets, Sister explains how we'll fill them.

I'll be taking you shopping soon, she says, *to get some new clothes. You'll each get to spend $150 at Zeller's for a new wardrobe. But we'll be going separately, so you can take your time and I can help you find everything you need. I hope $150 is enough; you don't seem to have anything with you. Oh, and you'll get more money to spend on school supplies and toiletries—you know, make-up and jewellery, whatever you need.*

I almost pinch myself. $150 for new clothing is a fortune, probably close to what my parents have spent in my *entire life* on all the clothes I hated wearing. The only time I've gone shopping carte blanche was a few summers back, when my suitcase went missing after camp and my mother grudgingly took me to replace my entire summer wardrobe. We fought the whole time, but eventually she let me spend $35 on a lime-green mix-and-match ensemble: shorts, pants, jacket, and two stripy T-shirts. The $150 being offered is stupendous! And no one's ever given me money to spend on make-up or earrings.

Sister nuzzles Chico while I stare back at her, gobsmacked. *Now we'll show you the other girls' rooms, and where Chico and I stay in our own little suite. It's private, but we're all on the same floor. Right, Chico, my little man? Let's go show the girls our house!* Nuzzle, nuzzle, nuzzle.

We follow her down the hall and peek into four other large bedrooms, each furnished like ours and spotlessly clean. Sister's suite occupies half the upper floor, but she gives us only a quick peek into the plushly-carpeted foyer of her hideaway.

The girls will all be home from school soon. There are six of them, besides you two. Come on, Chico, let's show them the rest.

I admire Sister's perfect posture as she leads us downstairs. She has shapely legs, and I'll learn later how proud she is of her gams and the slim figure she diets to maintain. She reminds me of the original Mary Poppins, as vain as she is plain. As the days progress, we'll get to admire the dozens of nearly-identical, tunic-style polyester dresses she's sewn to showcase her best angles.

The main floor has a tiny television room without a TV—*We might put one back later, but we don't want you girls watching too much TV*—and a primly decorated living room, which *does* have a TV, but the whole room is out of bounds unless it's your turn to vacuum (*We vacuum the house every day, don't we, Chico?*) or unless Sister invites you to watch her favorite programs on Friday nights. She tells us what they are, and we get a window into the romantic fantasies of a middle-aged nun.

The FBI Show, Friday nights, with Efram Zimbalist Junior — I love, love, love *him! He's so incredibly handsome, and so smart, I never miss a show. Oooh, we love Efram Zimbalist Junior, don't we, Chico? And I love, love, love Johnny Cash, his voice is so deep and he's so handsome, too, isn't he, Chico? We never miss watching Johnny Cash. And there's Tiny Tim, with his ukulele. Tiny Tim is so, so cute, so handsome* — *we love when he plays* Tiptoe through the Tulips, *don't we, Chico? Don't we think Tiny Tim is just so handsome, too?* Nuzzle, nuzzle, nuzzle.

She lifts her chin and gives us a stern look. *If you're very good, I might let you watch a show with me sometime.*

I'm gobsmacked again, hearing someone say *Tiny Tim* and *handsome* in the same sentence, because he's absolutely creepy and no one in their right mind would call him *cute*. But Sister thinks so, and she'll be faithful to her four heartthrobs – Chico, Efram, Johnny, and Tiny — for all the years I'll know her. I'll never hear her mention Jesus, though there's a huge crucifix in her foyer, and she dutifully attends Mass every morning with the other nuns.

The kitchen is as spacious and spotless as the rest of the house, and Sister explains the cooking rotation: The girls take turns making dinner, and we can plan any menu we want. She takes us to the basement level, also immaculate and enormous, and into the largest pantry I've ever seen. It's practically a grocery store, its shelves stacked to the ceiling with boxes and cans, its freezers stuffed with meat and ice cream, its fridges crammed with condiments and cellophane-wrapped vegetables. Everything looks fresh and modern.

Just let me know the day before your cooking night if there's anything else you need, Sister continues, *and I'll make sure we get it for you.*

I've died and gone to heaven. Since our second escape, Laura and I have been subsisting on cast-off food – on too many smooshed, stale jelly donuts, in particular, which seem to find their second pasty life in hostel pantries. Fresh food! And I love to cook.

We pass through a toasty laundry room, where we'll be washing our skin-tight bellbottom jeans every night and only partially drying them, letting them dry on our bodies for a perfect fit. We'll start most days with damp jeans and wet hair, heading out in sub-zero temperatures with our jackets unbuttoned, as cool girls do. All of this is tolerated, even condoned, at Cottage Four. There'll be no more sneaking out to apply eye shadow and change into forbidden clothes. Even smoking is fine, as long as we smoke only in the last room Sister shows us, the rec room. It's big and shiny, like the rest of the house.

This is where you girls will spend most of your time, unless you're cleaning or cooking, Sister tells us. *Make sure you empty the ashtrays every night. Those shelves are full of cards and there's the stereo, and lots of albums the girls have collected.* She points to a shelf and I check out the titles: Ten Years After, Deep Purple, Chicago, The Who, and dozens more.

Sister finally releases her hold on Chico, and he scuttles past her feet and starts humping a footstool. She regards him like a mother watching her son play the violin. *Oh, and at three o'clock you'll meet Pat, the social worker. She comes here every weekday to spend time with all of you, playing cards and making sure you get your homework done.* At the mention of homework, she pauses, as if she's forgotten something.

And indeed, she has. *Oh yes, and by the way, we've decided that both of you should keep going to McNally High instead of going to the school here. We think that would be much better, so you can catch up on what you've missed and get your grades up again. Is that okay with you?*

She looks at us quizzically, as if we might think otherwise. It's more than okay. It's like getting a heavenly upgrade.

At 3 o'clock we meet Pat, who welcomes us with a genuine smile and promises to be available for whatever we might need. I immediately like her. She wears cool jeans and a fisherman's knit sweater and looks like a teen with her tiny figure and pixie cut. She also promises to teach us Canasta and Whist, which turns out to be how we spend most of our free time at Cottage Four: playing cards and rolling tins of Drum tobacco into stacks of cigarettes.

I'm not sure if Pat's role is mostly to keep her eye on us and make sure we empty the ashtrays and finish our chores, or if she's supposed to be initiating deeper talks, but she keeps it light, preferring to mentor us through the lyrics of Gordon Lightfoot, Carole King, and James Taylor. Months later, we'll find out she's been going through a devastating divorce, and the heart-rending lyrics make sense, but not the sickening realization that someone as lovely as Pat could lose her dream marriage so soon. The disillusionment I experience over this news is profound; I'm shattered to learn that a head-over-heels young marriage can fail. I've been deceived by fairy tales. Divorce is for stale, old couples who never really loved each other, not for beautiful dreamers like Pat.

And then we meet our housemates. Gradually, we'll learn bits and pieces of each other's back stories. There's Jenny, who looks part Native but will neither confirm nor deny it, pregnant with a baby rumoured to be her father's. Patrice, from up north, whose sad features and years of abuse at the hands of her brothers and cousins make her look much older than 16. Faith is tremulous, pretty and blonde and rumoured to have a genius IQ, yet completely incapacitated by familial abuse she won't discuss. Susan is an angry, shockingly obese 15-year-old, whose scowling face, stringy hair, and putrid body odor will render her an outcast even among our band of misfits.

You'd think there'd be compassion to spare amongst such similarly damaged girls, but no, we compare and assess and rank each other, drawing up alliances and boycotts. There's plenty of gossip but no show of vulnerability among us. Only later will my heart break for all of us.

And there are other girls who'll come and go during my time there, broken girls who'll either sink or swim once they're tossed back into the big pond after their stint at Maple Ridge. Most of them, I believe, will sink.

For a program supported by Social Services, the counselling resources at Maple Ridge are woefully thin. There's a nun presiding over each of the four cottages—rivalling, quarreling nuns who barely speak to each other—but the house nuns are mother figures, not confidantes. The cottage social workers, like Pat, are more like babysitters. Mr. Ramsey, ensconced in his wood-panelled office, is the only social worker available for one-on-one sessions, and he makes most of us squirm. There's something oily about him, something off about his family-man persona. I instinctively feel shame in his presence, even though I've confided nothing.

My early sessions with him are attempts to bridge the chasm between my parents and me, but it's a lost cause. Each meeting is the same: my mother hijacks any semblance of a dialogue with rants against me, leaving Mr. Ramsey speechless. I can't even look at her. I turn my chair and face the wall, waiting for the hour to end. After several repeat performances, Mr. Ramsey admits defeat by cancelling the meetings; there'll be no reconciliation. I could've told him that from the outset, if he'd asked.

However, I'm still expected to meet alone with Mr. Ramsey. I quickly put an end to these sessions with the same chair-turning strategy.

The only other man on the premises is Dr. Higgins, who shows up once or twice a week to deal with our acne and prescribe birth control pills for every resident, whether we want it or not. I'm not sure how the nuns morally justify the enforced birth control, but perhaps they simply leave it to the discretion of Dr. H, who, being English, is probably an Anglican. He's concerned about my weight; I'm hovering around 85 pounds, low for my current height of 5 feet, in spite of the abundance of food at the Cottage. I'm living on coffee, apples, and the occasional bag of chips, and I'm fainting, frequently, but I don't see myself as anorexic or particularly thin. I just like feeling empty and wispy and light, light, light. The fainting is a minor inconvenience as I'm too featherweight to cause much damage. When I faint, I collapse neatly, like a deflated dancing man balloon at the local car lot.

Within a few weeks, Laura and I have our first serious falling out, and at night we simmer in our distant twin beds, hissing slurs across the frosty room. A new girl, Cora, joins Cottage Four, sent by her parents in an attempt to sever her romance with a drummer who's ten years older and black. Cora has the tall, thin build of a supermodel and the temperament of a shrew. But she can also be exceptionally charming, as sociopaths usually are. Feigning a passion for Chico and for Sister's television heartthrobs – Efram, Johnny, and Tiny — she speedily wins Sister over, knocking Laura off the pedestal of favorite girl status, a position Laura's netted through her artistic talent: She's temporarily captured Sister's heart by sketching portraits of the nun and her dog inside their inner sanctum. It's a hard fall for Laura, losing my affections first, then Sister's. Then, as if to twist the knife and keep me from returning to my original friend, Cora woos me into her net. And Sister, swayed by Cora and tiring of the tension between Laura and me, moves me into Cora's room.

I'm not among Sister's favorites, not having hit upon some arbitrary key to her fickle heart. This matters, not because I necessarily want to spend more time with her, but because Sister holds the key to weekend passes, and I've yet to score one. All the other girls spend weekends away with relatives, but for me going home isn't an option. Instead, I spend my lonely weekends at the Cottage with Sister, helping her scour the floors of the main building for pocket money (three dollars and a bottle of Tab for three hours of ammonia-and-steel-wool drudgery on the stairs) every Saturday afternoon, and then kicking around the house by myself until the other girls return. I manage to persuade a boy at school to pose as a Responsible Boyfriend and sign me out for Friday night dates, whereupon we go our separate ways. But I want more; specifically, I want to spend weekends at Cora's house and enjoy the unlimited freedom she's wrangled from her browbeaten parents.

Sister's not budging; I've got the stair-scrubbing covered, and perhaps she doesn't want to give up the pleasure of my company as we sip our bottles of Tab after the work is done. So Cora and I hatch a sympathy plan. One Friday afternoon, I close myself in the bathroom and slit my wrists: four horizontal lines (still, after all these years, faintly visible), not enough to send me the ER, but enough to elicit gushes of blood and a wellspring of compassion from Sister. Dr. Higgins patches me up. Cora and I are overly optimistic, hoping Sister's change of heart will spring me from the Cottage that very night. It doesn't; she wants to keep me on suicide watch at least until Sunday, but the following weekend, I get my weekend pass. And not without an unexpected bonus: I've jumped to second place in Sister's books, at least for now.

Now we're at Cora's every weekend, leaving the cottage on Friday nights to wander the city before landing at her parents' house to sleep. We launch ourselves into the night with an inviolable routine: two hours of primping, slathering our faces with shimmery blue eye shadow, navy-blue mascara, and viscid lip gloss, and then squeezing into damp jeans and sheer bubble tops before admiring our skinny bodies in the mirror. Finally, eschewing winter boots, hats or scarves for beauty's sake, we prance into the frigid nights, hitchhiking back and forth across town in search of companions or a party. Cora's in charge of saying yes or no. We're mostly looking for a boyfriend to replace Cora's forbidden lover—someone, preferably another drummer, with a friend on hand for me. This quest lasts for months, through two seasons of man-hunting and close calls, until the balmy summer night we finally find him.

8

Snails into Beer

Blair is—literally— fresh off the farm, a well-built 18-year-old from the country with crinkly blue eyes and a springy brown afro as boisterous as his raspy laugh. His roots are Scottish, not African, but with his drum kit and crazy hair, he sort of resembles Cora's ex, and before long, he's fallen into her sociopathic brew like a snail into beer. We met him the usual way, hitchhiking. Mike, his dreamy long-haired friend, was more my type, but he slipped through my fingers like a beautiful trout.

Now the three of us—Cora, Blair, and I—are getting wasted every weekend in Blair's basement suite. These nights, too, follow an inviolable routine. After the first communal hour of drinking, the lovebirds lock themselves into Blair's bedroom for the rest of the evening, leaving me to share the dregs with whoever drifts in and out of the suite. I spend most nights languishing like a forgotten patient in a waiting room, occasionally falling into short-lived relationships like the gin-soaked liaison that squanders my virginity. This event is such a disappointment that I break up with my Lothario immediately, whereupon he smashes his arm through a window to show how much he cares.

I never know who'll drop by while I wait in Blair's cramped, dingy living room. But the calibre of visitors vastly improves when some of the grad students who live next door start calling. Jim, a social worker from Ontario, is the first. His interest in me is different. Jim stops short of carrying a notepad with him, but my family history and current life at Maple Ridge fascinate him; perhaps I'm thesis material. Still, I can tell that beyond his professional curiosity he actually cares, and his questions go deep, where I want to go, and where I could never go with Mr. Ramsay. I welcome his visits, and start viewing my circumstances with more interest, too.

Soon after meeting Jim, I get a glimpse into my future. One of Jim's housemates, an American philosophy student named Jack, comes over one evening to introduce himself. He's vibrant and inquisitive, and that night we talk for hours—an effortless, expanding conversation about books, relationships, Woodstock, America, sexism, philosophy, and Vietnam. The connection is immediate, and the conversation we start that night will sparkle and grow for years. It's a foretaste of the most wonderful and devastating relationship I'll ever have.

But neither of us know that yet. For now, it's just the start of an increasingly addictive friendship.

Back at Maple Ridge, there's constant change and secrecy. Before her due date, Jenny is quietly moved elsewhere to have her baby. Patrice turns 18 and outgrows the system, leaving Cottage Four without a single goodbye. Susan and Faith disappear overnight, on different nights, and are rumoured to be in psych wards. Other girls move in. Laura falls into an undiagnosed dissociative state and moves back home. She's found and married by a gentle boy, a year or two older, who hopes to fix her. Pat's divorce is finalized, and she still won't talk about it, though she seems older, sadder, and less engaged with all of us.

I'm in grade 11, flailing at chemistry and floating through my other classes. Except for chemistry, which baffles me, my grades are good, but nothing I learn at school sticks. As I experienced in middle school, my classmates, subjects, and teachers leave barely a mark, because my real life is lived elsewhere, in the Cottage and with Cora on our weekends away.

The only memorable class is drama, which takes place in a large, circular room with a sunken stage, darkly illuminated by jewel-hued stage lights. Here we sprawl on the carpet, listening to the soundtrack from Woodstock and giving each other head and back massages. There are no plays or productions that I'm aware of, no reading of scripts or taking notes. Many of us, including the teacher, smoke dope before each class. Drama is the only class that resonates, and the only class I never skip. It's like being back in the armory, this time at night.

One day Sister tells me we're going to Family Court. The powers-that-be at Maple Ridge want to make me a ward of the Province of Alberta so I can be released early without parental interference. This is news to me, and I'm petrified: I haven't seen my parents in over a year, and the prospect of seeing them again, even in the presence of a judge, is heart-stopping. On court day, I'm shocked by my mother's hollow appearance, but we don't exchange looks or cross the room to say hello. Even if we wanted to—and we don't—greeting each other would be absurd. This is the decisive battle, the final showdown. My parents aren't fighting the Province because they want me back; they're fighting for their reputations. It rankles my mother that the authorities consider her unfit to parent me.

As soon as I see them, I shut down, afraid to listen to either side. My representatives must convince the judge that returning home and living with my mother would be detrimental to my mental and emotional health. They speak about what they've witnessed between my mother and me, and without hesitation the judge concurs. I'll be free as soon as the school year ends.

It isn't me who suggests leaving the system at age 16 and moving into a cheap apartment with Cora. It's probably Cora's idea, and Sister backs it. Or maybe Mr. Ramsay wants me out. Maybe it's a government budget issue, but nobody tells me. And I don't think to ask if there's an option to stay. Besides, haven't I been chasing this carrot of emancipation all my life? For Cora, moving out is the obvious next step. She's turning 18 and is about to graduate. Her parents will coddle her, but they won't take her back. Even they know their limits.

So the plan moves forward. I land two jobs that start as soon as school gets out, and I promise to put myself through grade 12 when classes resume. I have every intention of doing so, but there's no strategy in place, and no one ever follows up to see if I do.

Which would've been wise, because I don't.

If school has been stifling and dull, work is its stimulating opposite. It's thrilling to live in the adult world, to be treated like a grown-up and get a paycheck for the privilege. I like working hard, happily juggling a 60-hour workweek for the first few months before dropping a hospital kitchen job for a full-time position managing the record department at the Hudson's Bay Store.

I *love* my new job. I get to reconfigure the music department and bring it into the Seventies with hipper music. Record company reps treat me to extended lunches and flattering flirtations. I get to play my favorite records all day, saturating half the fifth floor of the department store, and to discover new artists. I befriend the regular customers and special order the music they haven't been able to find anywhere else. All of this is heady stuff for a 16-year-old, with a predictable outcome: though I complete one correspondence course that fall, I abandon further plans to finish school. Why bother when work is so much fun?

On the home front, Blair moves out of his basement suite to share a bedroom with Cora, and together we serve our imperious queen. Cora pushes him to earn more, to work overtime and midnight shifts, even to move north and work in the oil fields, and not for the common good, but for her shopping pleasure. She insists on being pampered like a world-class courtesan.

I'm the house servant in this saga, cooking, cleaning, and paying the bills at her command, and Blair is alternately her gigolo or her cash-strapped sugar daddy. She wields her steel-trap charm to pull us in and throws outrageous tantrums if we balk. None of us is happy in this fairy tale, nor do we know how to break the spell.

Blair is banished to the oil fields, and in the dead of winter, Cora and I take a weekend trip to see if he's working hard enough. He's wretched, bunking alone in a cheap hotel and working 12-hour shifts with steel pipes in 40-below-zero weather. Cora comes with an even longer shopping list, and she's in spectacular form: icy, domineering, caustic, and peevish. Nothing's good enough, and Blair and I are idiots. If one of us isn't failing her, the other surely is. She plays us off each other like a puppeteer. Every hour, sometimes several *times* an hour, we fall short of her impossible demands.

On one of those nights, when Cora has mercifully stormed off from both of us, a weeping Blair pulls me into his room, and we wail in unison. It's too much. Cora's like my mother; she elicits the same feelings of helplessness and rage, and no wonder. She's a classic abuser and I'm her perfect victim. Once, for no memorable reason, she pushed me down a full flight of stairs onto a concrete floor and never apologized. On another day, she sucker-jumped me from behind as I walked to school, all six feet of her, landing me face-first in a sand-crusted snowbank. Then she sat on my back and pummeled the rest of me into the snow. She's pinched and slapped me, too, but mostly she's meted out cruelty with her forked tongue. Blair and I are watching her rip the other apart, and this is finally bringing clarity to our own abuse. We hold each other as we cry, and exchange our first kiss.

Still, it takes a few more months to reach breaking point. Blair moves back to Edmonton (he's back on gigolo duty), and we commiserate when Cora is at work. One spring morning, we move from the sofa to the bed and exact some horizontal revenge. I'm not strongly attracted to Blair, but our minds have melded in shared misery, and it's inevitable that our bodies follow suit. We need a lot of comforting.

This happens only once. We don't touch each again till we've vanquished Cora, but our carnal transgression breaks the spell. We don't have to be victims. We can be happy, safe, and free—together. I move to a studio apartment to prepare for the split, leaving Blair to drop the bomb. Cora is blindsided and explosive. To her, Blair is the innocent victim, seduced by her duplicitous, former best friend, and I'm the snake.

For weeks she stalks us, wailing and pleading for Blair to come back and threatening to destroy me. Unhinged, she phones at all hours of the night until we're forced to leave the receiver off the hook. She calls my workplace, posing as a string of outraged customers denouncing my expletive-laced customer service, until my employers finally call her bluff. At closing time, she waits for me outside the store, ready to pounce, and I beg the door-closers to sneak me out of secret doors. I'm scared to go home, where she might be waiting outside with her rage, and maybe a knife.

When I go home and Blair's not around to protect me, I barricade myself in. One night there's a gentle knock on the door, followed by a timid voice.

Marilyn, it's me. It's Vickie. This is Cora's downtrodden mother, who's become my second, much nicer mom over scores of weekend visits. She sounds as friendly as ever, and harmless.

I'm not mad at you, Marilyn. I just want to talk to you, to see how you're doing, and if there's anything you need.

For a moment I actually believe she's on my side; that perhaps, as the most long-suffering victim of Cora's abuse, Vickie understands all my reasons for absconding with Blair and escaping her nightmare daughter. I open the door a crack...

...And the Philistines are upon me. Within seconds, Vickie, Cora, and Norman, her checked-out alcoholic father, are in my space, slapping me, pulling my hair, and screaming invectives. Once they've reduced me to a snivelling sack on the floor, they storm the kitchen and empty my cupboards of every second-hand cup, plate, and pot Vickie's ever given me, stuffing some into garbage bags and smashing the rest on the floor. I guess they're *all* mad, even Norm, who before tonight has had nothing but boozy winks for me. Like raging Gestapo, they ransack my closets, looking for contraband. When everything I own has been manhandled and trampled, they leave as they came – rabidly screaming, a three-headed Caligula. None of my neighbors investigates the commotion.

Crass materialists, all of them. They haven't taken anything that matters. I'm shaken, a bit beat up, but mostly relieved. What more can they do to me?

After the siege, Cora moves east and continues her harassment with high decibel phone calls in the middle of the night before finally going silent. This, of course, this only deepens my alliance with Blair. We fall in love, and what sprouted from desperation to escape our tormenter grows into a vigorous plant. With Cora excised, Blair and I can nurse each other's battered self-esteem. We can be best friends, laughing at each other's jokes and drinking coffee in bed. We can chase our own dreams instead of pandering to a borderline tyrant. And we can have a high old time doing it, smoking Blair's inexhaustible cannabis supply and amassing a rocking collection of all our favorite record albums.

9

Kenny Baron Specials

———————⟋⟍———————

I f "first love" means your first requited love, then Blair was mine. I'd just turned 17 when we moved in together; he was 20. We spent our first month in the luxury high-rise Cora had insisted Blair rent for her, furnished with nothing but a thick mattress on the floor and the cases from Blair's drum kit, artlessly arranged as makeshift tables and chairs. But the penthouse wasn't *us*, and we jumped at the chance to move into the communal house next to Blair's old suite, the grad house where Jack still lived.

By then a group of us were becoming The Gang, a devoted circle of friends that endured for decades, losing and adding new members over the years (mostly without me). That summer The Gang hung out constantly, congregating in parks and living rooms, going for midnight bike rides on warm summer nights, and leaving town as often as possible to backpack the Rockies or float by canoe down lazy rivers. In late July, a dozen of us rode our bikes from Jasper to Banff, recruiting my brother Doug to move our gear by car from one campsite to the next. That way, we could save money and put our amateurism on display by riding with cumbersome backpacks instead of proper bike touring equipment.

The Gang did pretty much everything in a cannabis cloud. There's a photo of me from that trip; I'm pulling the string of a tent bag with my teeth and glaring at the camera, determined to set up camp before the hash pipes are lit and everyone loses the plot. Most evenings, my appeals for law and order are ignored the minute our ever-generous Blair brings out his stash, but at least our own tent will be pitched before sunset. If my friends want to stumble around in the dark, looking for level ground and lost tent pegs before pitching their tents on rocky lumps and headache-inducing inclines, that's their choice.

From Banff, Blair and I leave The Gang and head to the Okanagan Valley, where we live in an orchard for the rest of the summer, picking apples, plums, and pears by day and stuffing ourselves with homemade pie by night. I grow a little tummy. When the warm days fold and the work ends, we hitchhike to Vancouver and rent a studio apartment on the top floor of a narrow Victorian house near Stanley Park for a mere $80 per month. We paint the walls and curved ceilings a warm, sapphire blue, transforming it into a cozy nest, and place two crimson-painted stools at the window of our closet-sized kitchen, overlooking the sordid back alley of Davie Street. Whenever we aren't at work or asleep, we perch on our red stools, baking bread, smoking pot, and discussing the fascinating stream of drug dealing, propositioning, and dumpster diving going down in the alley. It's like watching endless episodes of *Cops,* minus the cops. Life is happy and peaceful. We feel safe and alive, free from our tormentor, starting to create a world shaped by our own choices.

I walked the seedy side of Vancouver and found a job at the State, Hotel, a decaying flophouse improbably located above the city's finest French bakery. No application form or interview was required. I was hired on the spot by virtue of having climbed the pee-stained stairs to the grimy lobby and inquiring about the help-wanted sign. If I could do that, I could chambermaid the sorry rooms at the State Hotel.

The hotel was run by a merry gang of delusionals. Mr. McGillivray, a silver-haired retiree with no prior business experience, had just purchased the State and was confident that replacing the flickering fluorescent lights and shabby linoleum in the lobby would transform the hotel into a profitable tourist inn. To this end, he'd hired a lanky, pale young Mexican, Will Padilla, to man the front desk. Will had just arrived from his parents' Acapulco resort and seemed not to notice that his Canadian clientele were not well-heeled tourists, but rather dealers, pimps, prostitutes, alcoholics, drifters, and poverty-stricken pensioners. He was a sleepy-eyed amigo, and he sprawled all day across the front desk, dreaming about the Canadian house he imagined buying and the patterns he'd use to *paper-wall* it, and about the beautiful Canadian wife he was planning to find and marry. There was little action at the front desk during the day, and when he wasn't handing out keys, his mind swirled with quixotic visions of his imagined bourgeoisie.

Neither Mr. McGillivray nor Will ventured from the lobby floor into the guest rooms, nor did Lottie, the wizened head housekeeper, who'd earned the right, after 30-odd years, to spend her days chain-smoking in the laundry room or gossiping with Mr. M when she wasn't barking orders at Cindy and me. Cindy, a gorgeous 18-year-old best described as a *babe*, had been hired the same way as I had, around the same time, and we ran the upper three floors like flirty den mothers, tag-teaming the cleaning (though Pine-Sol only amplified the decomposing rooms) and befriending some of the long-term residents. Every day was an education.

At least half the tenants at the State were permanent guests, or at least as permanent as anchorless, shattered souls can be, and Cindy and I had our favorites. Our first new buddy was Kenny Baron, a rakish 57-year-old who dressed himself by nine each morning in a shirt, tie, and plaid vest and forthwith invited us into his room to share a "Kenny Baron Special": a tumblerful of cheap sherry and rotgut whiskey, mixed over his rusty sink.

To be polite, we'd take a sip or two and then watch Kenny drink his, transforming from a cheerful morning person into a sobbing wreck over his Life's Regret: the drinking that had capsized his first marriage, over 30 years ago. At each recounting, he'd pull out a fading wartime photo and show us his lost bride, weeping as if she'd walked out just yesterday. It was a wretched and bracing way to start the day, and Kenny's daily performance never failed to stun me. Even at 17, I could see how his self-crafted, entrenched narrative kept him mired in a rut he'd never escape, even if he wanted to. It was the perfect excuse to drink himself to death.

Later in the morning, we'd visit Earl, a beguiling pimp from Detroit, who enchanted us with his blinding white teeth, honeyed speech, and endless innuendo. He made us feel sexy and off-balance, in danger of melting on the spot. Earl stayed in bed till well past noon, and he'd play host from under the covers, languorous as a cat, his ebony eyes wandering our bodies like feathers. On Mondays, he'd mentally undress us and let us know if we'd gained a pound or two over the weekend. Once, after I'd spent a full weekend baking and feasting with Blair, he called me "Thunder Thighs." He liked fresh towels and white girls and making us blush and burn. But Cindy and I had boyfriends, and that was that. Still, there was something tantalizing about Earl, and for a while I harbored a heart-stopping crush, simultaneously imagining jumping into bed with him and being appalled by my wicked, unfaithful imagination. Cindy and I never talked about Earl; the thoughts he stirred were too intimate. Instead, we just kept going back.

By mid-afternoon, Alabama Dan would be waking up down the hall, ready to invite Cindy and me for a smoke from his professional drug stash. Dan was a drifter, a draft-dodger, and a mediocre con artist. He wore a wide leather hat over his long, greasy ponytail, even in bed, and, unlike Earl, never requested fresh towels because he never bathed. While we shared a joint, Dan compulsively strummed his guitar to accompany his anti-war ramblings. It was hard to keep his stories straight, even for him. We felt sorry for Dan, who'd lost most of his brain to drugs and bad ethics. Like Kenny, he served as a cautionary tale for Cindy and me: Do drugs, but don't overdo them. Never reach the point where you're wearing hats to bed. And mind your personal hygiene if you hope to have friends. Alabama Dan appeared to have none, and while we understood why, we bravely tried to fill the void while trying not to breathe through our noses.

Another favorite resident was a tiny, bright-eyed pensioner named Mr. O'Leary. Mr. O kept to himself; he'd lived in the hotel for years and did his own cleaning. But every Tuesday afternoon we had a standing appointment to exchange laundry. Mr. O wore a suit and was always chipper; still, his circumstances made me sad. Years ago, he'd been a fire-fighter with a wife and a home, but life had stripped him of all but his government pension, barely enough to pay rent at the State and subsist on a diet of noodles and hotplate soup. Still, he carried himself with dignity and self-discipline — rising early, keeping to himself, and maintaining a tidy schedule of walking, shopping, and visiting the library. He seemed to inhabit a cleaner, better world than his neighbors.

One Tuesday afternoon, Mr. O' Leary missed his laundry appointment, but we barely noticed. The next Monday, realizing no one had seen him come or go in days, Lottie sent me with a spare key to investigate. As soon as I cracked the door and was assailed by the stench of death, I knew what I would see. But I had no idea how thoroughly three pounds of brains could splatter a floor, four walls, and the faded bedspread of an army-tucked bed. Otherwise, his orderly room was immaculate. On a bedside table was a slim ledger book, itemizing every purchase he'd made in the past year. Crackers, tinned milk, bars of soap. No next-of-kin.

I looked and didn't look for twenty seconds before bolting, and someone called the police. Cindy and I spent the rest of the day avoiding the fourth floor. This time, Mr. O's room was professionally cleaned by discreet workers who locked the door behind them. For a long time, maybe till the State Hotel met its own death, the room stayed locked.

Poor Mr. O: his fastidious, miserable existence was over. But the violence of his death haunted me. Why a gun, why so gruesome an exit? I couldn't bear to imagine what he'd been thinking. And I couldn't fathom a death where there was no one left to mourn.

And thus, the State Hotel became my second, vicarious life for six unforgettable months. Cindy and I were free agents, as long as we dealt with the vomit, needles, empties, and mystery-stained linens from the unseen, overnight guests and didn't bother Lottie with complaints. We bounced from floor to floor on our springy young legs (no elevators in the State), chortling over Will and Mr. McGillivray's shared lunacy and Lottie's tenured uselessness, and marveling at the perks of a job where getting high all day was not only free, but expedient.

Indeed, we couldn't have coped with the despair and putrefaction of the State without cannabis and sips of Kenny Baron specials. On rough days, when the overnight guests were deplorable and Mr. McGillivray sensed we needed extra encouragement, he'd splurge on treats from the French bakery downstairs, bringing the exquisite aroma of golden butter and almonds to jostle with the rank air in the lobby.

And when melt-in-your-mouth pastry wasn't enough, Cindy and I would fortify ourselves with a beer-and-tomato-juice lunch at the local pub before wobbling back to work at the strangest little universe in town.

10

Unwrapped

———

Although we'd come to Vancouver in a roundabout way, Blair and I had a goal: we were saving to buy the ultimate hippie accoutrement, a Volkswagen van. This was part of an even greater plan. We'd heard you could drive straight north, stake out a piece of land, and claim it, simply by building a log cabin on site. It would take only a few months of savings to buy the van and equip it with a propane stove, a foam mattress, a retractable table, and funky fringed curtains; even sooner if we could resist going to weekly concerts and buying more and more record albums. Indeed, by now we should've have been musically set for life. That Christmas, Blair had surprised me with 50 brand new albums, each individually gift-wrapped and ready to be played sequentially over the course of the only Christmas I've ever spent entirely in bed – a once-in-a-lifetime indulgence that was perfect at the time.

Right after Christmas, we lost our beloved dog, Fritz, only to find him on New Year's Day behind a neighboring house, frozen in rigor mortis and still frothing at the mouth. This was also Blair's birthday. It seemed he'd been poisoned, maybe deliberately, or with rat poison used by the local restaurants. We were devastated. Fritz was family; he'd run alongside our bikes as we cycled from Jasper to Banff until his feet gave out and Blair had to carry him, riding single-handedly and balancing the terrier's shifting weight on his elbow and thigh.

Losing him unleashed a flood of mourning and homesickness. We needed our friends, so we splurged on plane tickets for a quick trip to Edmonton. Being able to reconnect with The Gang was a stopgap tonic, but the hours I spent talking with Jack that weekend only stirred my desire to be near him, and as Blair and I flew back to our two-person life in Vancouver, I wept the entire way for my secret soulmate, who suddenly seemed as vital to me as air.

In spite of our musical splurges, we had our funky van purchased, refurbished, and ready to go by late spring. We'd survived a winter of Vancouver rain and darkness, and now, just as the clouds were lifting and the city was spectacularly born again, we were leaving. After stocking the van with sleeping bags, cooking pots, dried beans, and our entire record collection, we headed 850 miles east, north, and then west again through B.C.'s nearly unbroken wilderness.

Blair drove, singing in his raspy voice and drumming on the steering wheel, while I rolled joints, my feet on the dashboard, mesmerized by the endless tracts of forest and the dearth of human imprint. On the third day we reached our destination, the coastal town of Terrace: Cedar Pole Capital of the World and annual recipient of more than 50 inches of rain. That's over four feet of water, enough to grow trees as tall as Westminster Abbey and ferns the size of mountain goats. It certainly wasn't the scrubby Alberta forest where we'd been hatched.

At midday we pulled into town and set off to find work. Within an hour, Blair was hired at a local pulp mill and I got a job at the town's only drive-in, a brown and pink burger joint improbably called the Dog N' Suds. Our new jobs started the next day. *That* part was easy. Now for the epic part: scoping out land for our future homestead. To find it, we got in the van and bumped along an old logging road until the tracks petered out and we were forced to park. Trembling with excitement, we disembarked and looked around. This was it, the magical, preordained site where we'd build our cabin, plant our garden, raise our chickens, grow our marijuana, and milk our goats—for the rest of our long, idyllic, and purely organic lives. This was the land that would birth our legacy, the earth that would feed our dreams.

It just wasn't ... how we'd imagined it.

As we stood beneath towering cedars, swallowed by smothering green, I could practically *feel* the rain forest growing around me, huffing the humid air and swelling into prehistoric specimens of outsized botany. Like massive seaweeds, tentacled ferns grabbed at our waists, and in spite of the sunny day we stood in semi-darkness, the overhanging canopy as thick as a nun's wimple. We weren't even thinking about the overgrown creatures that could be lurking in such a jungle; the flora alone would swallow us alive. Suddenly, we felt very alone, very small, and utterly inadequate to the task of taming even a garden-sized finger of this enormous beast.

Blair looked at me and said exactly what I was thinking. *Let's get the hell out of here.*

We'd been in Terrace for two, maybe three hours. In fact, we hadn't even driven to the town center yet. And we never would. The forest had spoken: this was not our Shangri-La.

I nodded at Blair. Without another word, we jumped back into the van and gunned it east: Alberta bound.

It was nearly solstice in Edmonton, when nights claim only a sliver of the long, intoxicating days. We were back with The Gang, back in our city, and back to ourselves. Jack returned from a trip to Guatemala, and, as he did on each return, he found us first. We were his base camp, his Canadian headquarters, always ready with fresh food, cannabis, and conversation. And love, so much love. Blair and Jack were nearly opposites, but they cracked each other up and shared a deep, affectionate bond. Blair and I verged on hero worship; we were in love with Jack's energy and his joyful, adventurous spirit. For me, Jack was a magnet, awakening a hidden, more beautiful version of myself I hadn't known before.

But Blair and I were engaged, and I wore his diamond ring. I was half of *Blairilyn*, as our friends dubbed us, and Blairilyn was a certified, peer-reviewed package: as comfortable and pragmatic as a warm bath. Besides, Jack was eight light years older and courted ultra-cool, university women, women beyond my ken in life and love. If I ever dreamed of being Jack's partner, my conscious mind suppressed it. I'd always be too young for him, too far behind, too late. It was enough to delight in our perpetual conversation, and to know that he delighted in it, too.

Blairilyn was always busy, always planning and doing. We planted an enormous garden around our rented bungalow and painted the walls of our bedroom black, plastering the furniture with psychedelic white, orange and blue contact paper so we could find our way in the dark. Our house was always full of friends. I cooked huge feasts for everyone. We moved easily from one job opportunity to the next. At one point, we started our own janitorial service, cleaning restaurants by contract seven mornings and nights a week. Blair was the floor mopper, I was the vacuumer, and we swapped out the bathrooms and windows.

One of the restaurants occupied a huge, converted church building, featuring a lit-up 70s disco floor, several tiers of dimly-lit tables, and an indigenous mice colony that took turns leaping over my feet as I vacuumed in the dark. I hated mice, and even if ten critters in a row vaulted my sneakers or zipped past the light of the vacuum, I startled each time. The owner's wife shared my name, Marilyn; she spent her mornings slumped beside the disco floor in the dishevelled restaurant, nursing her hangovers with rum-spiked coffee while Blair and I cleaned around her.

This other Marilyn was well past her prime, 40 years old and prematurely haggard. One morning she simply dropped dead. Her death freaked me out more than all the manic mice, and because we shared the same name, I couldn't help wondering if her early death portended anything for me. I'd sensed her sadness from the first day, which seemed to intersect mine, as other people's sadness usually did.

That year I became an obsessive walker, taking long, ruminative hikes through the river valley that transects the city. In winter, I walked through the dazzling, untracked snow atop the river, delighting in the solitude and the soft crunch of snow beneath my feet. No one else in the city walked on the river, or if they did, they left no tracks. Most days I hiked at least six miles, and many days up to twelve – to the disco-floor restaurant and back. The daily treks were therapy; they calmed my restlessness and soothed my spirit, at least for a few hours during and after.

I was anorexic again, and we were smoking too much cannabis. Blair thrived on round-the-clock smoking, but for me the THC turned my thoughts inward and provoked a depression I'd been trying to out-run for years. Marijuana made Blair happy, a carefree, jolly sort of happy. It also made him oblivious to my sadder moods. Since physical activity was the only way I could keep myself from despair and Blair saw me in almost constant motion, his failure to notice my depression was understandable.

I was a high-functioning depressive, with limited insight into my own psyche. That winter, Jack left Edmonton again to travel throughout Mexico, and I missed him more than I let myself feel. I began to hang out with Gwen, one of The Gang and my newest best friend, and over long, conversational games of Scrabble and creamy cups of instant cof-fee, we listened to Joni Mitchell and analyzed our world. I was longing for something I couldn't admit, even to myself.

The next year I switched careers and became a cook. I'd learned my way around the kitchen from an early age; at eleven, when my youngest brother was born, my mother had gone into hospital for a week, leav-ing me to cook 21 family meals without menus, instruction, or the con-venience of prepared foods. It was immersive, thrown-in-the-deep-end learning, with *Better Homes and Gardens Cookbook* as my guide. Since then, I'd studied other cookbooks and honed my skills, landing my first cook-ing job at a 24-hour truck stop diner where I worked fast-paced, 12-hour shifts, long shifts that channelled my restless energy and showcased my strengths: stamina, instinct, and speed.

And now it was summer, and Jack was back in town. He started crossing the city to surprise me at the diner, waiting at a corner table for my next coffee break. We'd cram as much as we could into twenty min-utes of talk – or thirty, if the customers were fed and he'd timed it right. Our endless conversation spooled on. He was my bright light, the radiant face that lit up every corner of my heart, no matter how I'd been feeling the moment before his smile met mine.

Meanwhile, Blair was growing closets and garages full of marijuana plants, long before home-growing evolved into the sophisticated world of hydroponics. None of this horticulture was for personal profit. This was the farmer in him, coupled with his generous spirit. He loved sharing and never tired of toking up with friends. We talked of marriage and kids, without a timeline since there was no rush; we were in this for life. The ring I wore had been Cora's, recouped by Blair after their breakup, but I didn't mind. I was used to leftovers. The extent of my shadowy, subterranean depression was a secret, even from me. If anyone had asked, I'd have said I was happy—enough.

And then someone did ask.

My long walks often ended at the city library, and one afternoon I was curled in a leather chair with a stack of books, speed-reading a book from cover to cover, when a middle-aged man approached me.

He got straight to the point. *Excuse me,* he said. *I've been watching you read for the past two hours.*

This was alarming; I'd been lost to time and space. I pulled myself out of the book and stared at him.

He went on. *I've never seen anyone devour books like you! And I'm curious to learn more about you — you intrigue me. Would you mind if I take you for a cup of coffee and ask you some questions?*

He looked to be in his mid-40s, respectably dressed, vaguely academic, and definitely not on the make. I'd almost finished my book, and his curiosity piqued mine. Plus, a free coffee would be excellent, so I agreed. We exchanged first names as we seated ourselves at a nearby café, and he ordered two cups. Would I like something to eat, too? *No, thank you.* I was too curious to think about food.

And then the questions began. *How old are you? Why are you wearing those scruffy work clothes? Why are you so thin? What kind of work do you do? Is that why your hands look so ragged and old for your age? Did you finish high school? Why not? What do you plan to do with your life? Since you're such a voracious reader, so hungry to learn, why aren't you at university?*

I was right about his appearance: he *was* an academic; in fact, he was a psychology professor. He appeared to be from India or Pakistan and spoke with a cultured accent, vaguely British. He obviously valued education and had no trouble asking personal questions. I was secretly flattered that he'd been studying me so avidly, even though he'd managed to suss out nearly all my weaknesses. But the one question he *didn't* ask is what book I was devouring as he watched me from across the library. It was a book about anorexia: if I couldn't eat food, I could stuff myself with words about *not* eating food.

And the reason I was speed-reading? Simple. There were two kinds of books I unshelved at the library: books I skimmed on the spot, which I'd never admit to reading, and books I'd check out and take home. This was a skimmer, and taking it home would be tantamount to admitting I was anorexic—which I wasn't, of course. I was just fascinated with the subject of girls who really *were* anorexic.

My stranger had noted the obvious: my ravenous reading, my thinness, my faded corduroy jeans and plaid work shirt, my work-wizened fingers, and the insecurities I hid behind my long curtain of hair. After his initial questions, he probed deeper.

Who do you live with? Why are you with this Blair person, this farmer, *planning a life* on a farm (these words spoken derisively) *when you're obviously meant for something different? Why aren't you doing what you're* meant *to be* *doing?*

I met his questions with plain answers until the last one, which stumped me. Now I felt exposed, as if he'd been slowly unwrapping a deluxe chocolate bar, only to find a stale saltine inside. In retrospect, the opposite was probably his intention, and closer to the truth. He stared at me as I fiddled my raw, tell-tale hands, and I felt my face turn a similar red.

What could I say?

The interview was over. My interloper paid the bill and stood to leave. He offered no advice, no business card and no follow-up, but simply squeezed my hand and thanked me for my time. Then he wished me luck and disappeared as suddenly as he'd appeared.

His questions and my feeble answers lingered. They confirmed what I already knew inside, that life with Blair would never be intellectually stimulating, nor would I ever begin to explore other aspects of my potential if I stayed in his world. I was too accommodating, too willing to go with the flow of his easily satisfied lifestyle. But I couldn't see a way out without breaking his heart, and that was something I couldn't imagine choosing.

Soon after my strange library encounter, Blair and I moved again, this time to a cozy bungalow in Riverdale, a character neighborhood nestled between the river and downtown. The Gang followed us to our new home, and that season our shared passion was playing softball in the park across the road. Baseball was the only sport I'd ever played without being forced to participate in a gym class, but that summer I lost whatever zeal I had for the game after a fast ball missed my glove and broke my nose.

Jack was back in our lives, having returned from his latest travels with a girl in tow, someone he'd met in Idaho. As soon as he introduced her, I could see this was no great passion, but simply a case of two travelers slaking their loneliness in a mismatched fling. In fact, he confided, he'd wanted to leave her at the border, but she'd always dreamed of going to Canada and, well... But she wasn't his type and whatever had sparked them was long gone. Within a few weeks, she drifted off with someone else and disappeared.

Our stint in Riverdale was also short-lived. To save money—and prepare for our future life as farmers—we decided to move to Blair's parents' farm, thirty miles east of Edmonton. We planned to live rent-free by camping in the shady poplar grove at the middle of their quarter section. I also wanted to plant our biggest garden yet, a market garden, next to the old pig barn. Blair had always rhapsodized about the farm, and particularly about this spot, where decomposing layers of pig manure had surely turned the potent black Alberta soil into even richer gold. *The best soil on earth*, Blair assured me. It was time to find out.

Our new home was a huge tent, fitted with a fake Persian carpet, a lamp, a dresser, a double bed, and Blair's state-of-the-art stereo system. Several yards away, we dug a pit for bonfires and circled two barbecues and three wooden picnic tables under the trees. There was still plenty of room in the grove for more tents, and we invited The Gang to join us over the weekends. At some point during the summer, everyone came.

Blair was right about the soil: the seedlings exploded like Grow Monsters in the perfect loam. Every morning I rose at dawn and walked six brisk miles around the farm's perimeters before working all day in the garden. The sun shone up to 18 hours a day and I hauled endless buckets of water from a hand-pumped well to keep the plants from drying out. Rooting in the soil under the prairie sky, I was as happy as I imagined the pigs had been—before they met their Maker. Now their transmuted poop was growing sunflowers as big as banjos. And my days of rooting in the mud were numbered, too.

Jack came for weekend visits with the rest of The Gang, but in mid-August he showed up with a tent, a tool kit, and a plan. He wanted to build Blairilyn a geodesic dome. As Volkswagen vans were to vehicles in the 70s, so were geodesic domes to domiciles: the ultimate hippie-home project. He'd supply the wood, the labor, and the vision, camping in the grove with us till it was done. It would be a labor of love. But building a dome required at least two people, and Blair, unbeknownst to Jack, had just found some steady carpentry work off the farm.

I was busy with the garden, but couldn't I help? As a child I'd hammered a few tree houses and makeshift stages, to say nothing of designing some impressive toothpick sculptures. How hard could it be to build a dome? According to Jack, it was as simple as screwing two-by-fours into stars, then joining them all together to form a cupola. Working together, the two of us could probably get the shell up in no time.

And so, we began. Jack had never looked as beautiful as he did in the filtered light of the poplar grove, his denim sleeves rolled above tanned wrists and perfectly shaped hands, his hair as burnished as the turning aspen, his blue eyes lit with years of affection. Our five-year conversation spooled on. Jack had grown up in Arizona and studied in Tennessee, and as we worked, we talked about the things he loved—baseball, deserts, mountains, cycling, and Central America; bluegrass music, philosophy, and

Being Here Now. We talked about American politics and his lucky exemption from the draft by virtue of being—like me—allergic to wool. We talked about the songs and books and tragedies that had shaped his world, and those that had shaped mine. We talked about the straight line that ran from Phoenix to Edmonton and our opposite origins: the long, crystalline Alberta winters that dwarfed our brief summers, and the sweltering months of Arizona heat that cheated his people out of winter. Jack was fascinated by life, and his fascination ignited mine.

Like the Walrus and the Carpenter, we spoke of many things. But we'd never spoken about what lived between us. Never had I verbalized how much he meant to me, even to myself, or how at home I felt when he was near. Nor had he verbalized such thoughts to me. In any crowd, in any room, we gravitated to each other like long-lost twins, like mother and child, like the only person in the world who spoke the same language. Our connection felt intrinsic, as if bred in the bone before birth.

But there were no words for these feelings or places to put them, because we also loved Blair and couldn't conceive of a future that would devastate him.

But building the dome – bantering over procedure, steadying boards while the other sawed, watching each other bend and lift the fresh beams skyward—brings everything to bursting point. The air is thick with the unspoken.

One evening Jack finds me at the well, pumping water for our weekend guests. He lifts a filled bucket to carry back and sets it down again. His eyes meet mine and five words rush out, a mixture of anguish and joy.

You have completely captivated me.

These simple words upend my world forever, but our hearts are in our throats. How can we contemplate smashing the obvious hurdle? A living soul, a *friend*, stands in the way. Blair is devoted to both of us, and I know his love is true. He's been ever kind and trusting. And as crushing as my leaving him would be, Jack's betrayal, betrayal at the hands of his hero, could be even worse for Blair. As unthinkable, it seems, as a murder.

Still, the one I love is waiting for an answer.

And you have completely captured me.

The words are out, and now we know exactly how the other feels: the same. Drowning, flying, saturated, locked. I set my too-full bucket next to Jack's, sloshing the water over our feet, and fall into history's saddest, most exquisite hug as the world spins out and away.

This is Jack's last night on the farm, though not because of his admission. The dome is unfinished, but as a teaching assistant, Jack needs to be back for the start of university. He also has one day left to claim a room in the communal house where he hopes to live. It's the last weekend of the summer, and that night we party in the poplar grove with the rest of The Gang, trying to act normal while our hearts do cartwheels and swan dives in the dark.

The unfinished dome floats under the harvest moon, a witness to our hidden courtship. Only a top section of the shell waits to be joined to the other beams, but for that we'll need a third person's long arms, and now that might never happen. At least we've been honorable; there's been no kiss and no touching, apart from brushed hands as we worked

and the hug at the well. After our confession, our eleven-word incanta-
tion, we've spoken no further, made no plans or promises, but our union
feels as certain as the moon, as insistent as the sea.

We're spinning, compelled to do *something* to express the overflow.
As the outdoor party progresses, we take turns slipping into the tent
and playing love songs on the turntable, searching for lyrics to say what
we dare not speak. We avoid being close to each other, afraid our eyes
and skin will betray us. No one seems to notice the electricity dancing
between us, or how often the albums are being changed.

Once the party ends, I fret and burn through a sleepless night, longing to see Jack in the morning yet dreading his departure. I've fallen into
a bottomless, churning waterfall. When he emerges from his tent, I see
he's spinning in the same whirlpools. We pretend it's just another morning, and after eating breakfast with Blair at the picnic table, Jack packs up
his tools and his tent and drives away.

Blair seems oblivious to my restlessness after Jack leaves. Perhaps
I'm a good actress, concealing my racing heart as best I can. There are
bushels of vegetables waiting to be harvested and sold or blanched and
frozen for winter. I try returning to the work, but it's impossible to concentrate, even on mindless tasks. I want to run crazy circles around the
farm or roll on the ground, screaming. And with everybody gone, the
farm is suddenly too quiet for both of us.

Maybe Blair senses my agitation. There's a summer's worth of laundry waiting to be washed. Why not go to Edmonton, he suggests, and
do our laundry there? We can hang around a few days, regroup with The
Gang, and bring some fresh vegetables to share. The garden can wait.

We bag our laundry and drive to the city. That afternoon I meet Jack
at a spot overlooking the river—a particular patch of grass where we'll

end up having the most significant talks of our lives. It seems we've been in constant communion, an extrasensory link bypassing space and time. But we need to make a plan, to find a way to be together, as much as we dread taking the next step. There is no other course. Blair must be told, today.

There is no painless way to break your first love's heart. The best I could do was to find a quiet spot to plunge the knife. I stood with Blair on a friend's leafy back porch and watched his face dissolve as I spoke the crushing words that had nothing and everything to do with him. It was over. As expected, he was gutted and stunned, but surprisingly not angry—at least not yet. He didn't try to convince me to stay. He knew what he was up against, the strength of Jack's charisma and the bond I shared with him. There was no contest to consider. The Jack of Hearts had won, hands down, after drawing the first card six years earlier.

For a long time, Blair and I held each other and wept like lost orphans. And then, like the noble man he is, he pulled himself together and drove me over to Jack's for the first night of my new life.

11

Sand Mandala

I cannot boast, as some do, of a photographic memory. Nor is my memory a ledger, recording every detail with pinpoint precision. My memory is a slippery fish, darting through frothy, hazy rapids and sudden clear pools, often a flip and a turn out of sight, and only occasionally lingering where I can count its spots.

But there are moments where the spots are crystal clear. I remember the peaceful room, the soft light, the fragrant bed. I remember Jack's lips and fingers on his recorder, the song he played for us before we finally embraced, and the first kiss of our slow-brewed love, filling the room like a drug. I remember it all in slow motion. I was *home*. I remember waking in his arms throughout the night and falling deeper into a secret joy that had been waiting, all these years, to surprise and overwhelm me.

We spent our first days and nights sequestered in Jack's basement room, sporadically coming up for food and conversation with our new housemates. Our love overflowed the house; we were like honeymooners, gently teased and indulged by our new friends. It was another house of grad students, everyone renting rooms from Saul, also known as the Silver Fox, a silver-haired psychology professor with a fondness for pretty undergrads. He had recently cast off his wife and kids in the suburbs to pursue a second act as a serial seducer and New Age purveyor.

Now he organized esoteric workshops on campus and hosted Karma-Cleansing sessions in his living room, in which housemates and guests sat lotus-style on the room-sized carpet and bared their souls while meticulously picking lint off the rug. Saul was playful and outrageous, and amenable to whatever degree of involvement his housemates desired. For Jack and me, the degree was measured and occasional; we were busy downstairs, exploring our own brand of consciousness.

Our first two months together were untouchable. Everything about being with Jack was wonderful, but most wonderful was realizing that he *knew* me, so very, very well, and that he'd *chosen* me, above all other eager contenders. He wasn't in love with a fantasy girl, soon to be exposed as a fraud by the harsh light of reality, but with *me* — the restless, insecure, hungry, prone-to-the-blues girl he'd known since I was fifteen. And I was in fathomless love with my favorite person in the world, someone whose passion for life—and for *me*—was unmatched.

We seized every opportunity to be alone, at home and away, driving to the Rockies for total seclusion on weekend hiking trips. Two of these trips revealed facets of Jack I'd only glimpsed before. On the first, stormy weather trapped us in our tent after the first day of hiking. This was fine; we had no trouble filling time while the wind howled outside. But food and drink was another matter. Jack's idea of meal planning consisted of packing three boxes of Harvest Crunch granola. He figured eating dry cereal all weekend was simpler than planning a menu and toting a camp stove, and it made perfect sense—until the afternoon of our second day when, well into our next-to-last box of sugary oats and craving a hot drink, I had to admit that my perfect Adonis had shortcomings, too.

On the next hiking trip, we slept in Jack's van the first night: inclement weather again. Soon after falling asleep, I woke in the dark to tell him I was feeling sick, very sick, and as I leaned over his sleeping form, my roiling stomach heaved hot chunks of vomit all over his lovely face. His immediate reaction—once he realized what had woken him up—was pure compassion, not disgust. He sat up and slid open the van door so I could crawl over him and get some air. And then, as I leaned over the side, I puked again, right into his only pair of shoes, parked outside the van in readiness for morning. I was doubly mortified, but Jack found it hilarious. He waited till daybreak to rinse his Adidas in a mountain stream before cheerfully wearing the ice-cold shoes (which stayed wet all weekend) without a word of complaint. This, of course, completely absolved him of the granola gaffe.

Every Thursday night Jack and I went dancing with friends at the Hovel, a coffee house/dance hall with low lights and ceilings and the best bluesy folk bands in town. One night between sets, I suddenly felt claustrophobic, and I staggered down the long hallway and upstairs to the street, holding onto the walls as Jack followed. Outside, the cool air failed to rally me, and now I was swooshing through a kaleidoscopic tunnel, faces and flashes from my 20 years on earth rushing past in a torrent. It felt like dying, the ultimate letting go, and I almost surrendered. But something powerful was pulling back, a strong energy—Jack's energy— like the pull of a tide or an anchoring moon. The rushing stopped. When I opened my eyes, I was lying on my back and looking into Jack's face.

I felt as if I'd been gone a lifetime, though only ten minutes had elapsed. From the outside, it looked like a seizure, followed by unconsciousness. From the inside, it felt like a death call. And it wasn't drug or alcohol induced; I'd had only a single beer. By now, our friends had gathered around us on the street, speculating. Maybe I'd taken some kind of cosmic leap in consciousness. Was that possible? It was a radical theory and a reassuring alternative to the possibility that I'd almost died. Still, twice in a lifetime seemed far-fetched: I'd already taken a cosmic leap when I fell in love with Jack.

We lived just a few blocks from the university, where Jack taught and graded papers, and I found work as a cook again, this time at the university daycare centre. It was a delightful job, preparing meals and snacks for sixty children and twelve staff members. The kitchen, now stocked with home-baked goodies and a happy new cook, quickly became the social center. The daycare was situated in an enormous glass building called The Hub, which also housed students, coffee shops, bookstores, and bulletin boards. There was a big picture window in the kitchen, dividing the center from the inside mall, and at least once or twice a day I'd look up to see Jack's love-lit face beaming back at me. He came by as often as he could, walking the extra blocks across campus just to share a smile. Like skaters in a pas de deux, we were always circling back to each other.

Jack's love for me restored a confidence that had been plummeting since late childhood. With him, it was safe to be nine years old again, or five, or fourteen, and to let those different Marilyns emerge and seek their healing. It was safe to share my secret wounds, my exiled dreams and my buried talents. I began to draw and write again, outlets that had defined me in childhood but which I'd repressed since becoming a teen.

For the first time since leaving Maple Ridge, four years prior, I felt ready to visit Sister Mary Magdalene and maybe even look Mr. Ramsay in the eye. I harbored no reproach (some of that came later), but despite having made my own way in the world, I'd always felt too insecure to go back. With Jack, I was a new person: being loved by someone as brilliant and beautiful as Jack made *me* feel brilliant and beautiful. I no longer needed external achievements to validate my life; I was in love with the most wonderful and enchanting person on earth, and he was in love with me.

We went on a weekday. With Jack at my side, I climbed the red linoleum stairs to the main office, no longer smelling the ammonia and steel wool from all the lonely Saturdays I'd spent stripping the wax from their well-worn tiles. (I wonder now why Sister felt compelled to strip the floors *every week*.) The dour green waiting room no longer induced the sickening anxiety caused by its proximity to Mr. Ramsay's office. I rang the buzzer, and ancient Sister Helen, still teetering on death's doorstep, shuffled in to greet us. She seemed not to recognize me, but she would let Sister and Mr. Ramsay know we were here. Sadly, she told us, it wouldn't be possible to visit the Cottage, alone or with Jack: I was no longer a resident.

This was a huge disappointment. I wanted to show Jack the icy blue room I'd shared with Laura, where we'd heartbreakingly murdered our friendship, and the long hallway I'd charged in the middle of the night, leaping over a battalion of cockroaches I hallucinated in a nightmare, and the downstairs alcove where I'd jumped onto a chair to escape them, screaming the house awake till I woke myself up, too. I wanted to show him the bathtub where I'd slit my wrists, and the TV-room-without-a-TV where I'd fainted more than once from self-induced hunger. I wanted to stand in the kitchen where I'd accidentally poured scalding water over my foot after another hollow, sleepless night, and to walk him through the magnificent pantry, describing the stuffed green peppers, the chicken cacciatore, and the instant mashed potatoes we took turns cooking for each other, our fellow lost girls — Susan, Cora, Patrice, Jenny, Laura, and Faith. I wanted to sit with him at the round table where we rolled cigarettes, played Canasta, and put off doing homework till we aged out or were otherwise deemed ready for release into the outside world, and were henceforth forgotten.

But not, I hoped, by each other.

Still, there were living ghosts. Mr. Ramsay, as unctuous as ever, invited us into his office to chat, but he looked smaller, less menacing, and didn't insist I sit in the wooden chair I used to turn away from him. He was charmed by Jack—everyone was—and seemed to look at me with new eyes. I introduced Jack to him as *my lover;* the term *boyfriend* couldn't encompass what he meant to me. As always, five minutes with Mr. Ramsay was more than enough. But this time I wasn't trying to escape the ineffable sense of shame he used to evoke in me; this time he'd lost his power. There was nothing to talk about, except the million things I'd never dream of telling him.

Sister, on the other hand, was delighted to see me. She carried an older Chico in her arms but still wore a figure-skimming polyester dress and her short veil. She'd aged over the past four years, and many things, she told us, had changed. The Home was now entirely run by Social Services and the residents were all Indigenous. Cottage Four was no longer the White Girls' enclave, and she no longer lived there. Her nemesis, Sister Margaret of Cottage Three, had gotten sick and died. She missed her.

Now all the remaining Sisters, bickering and ailing, were housed together in private quarters out back, and she found the situation insufferable. She stopped short of confessing regret over her decision to become a nun, but I could see it in her eyes, and she would admit it, several years later, on my second and final visit with her.

All of this made me sad. The closest thing I'd had to a loving home no longer existed. And there was nothing else to see. The past had dissolved, Maple Ridge had evolved, and so had I.

Next were my parents. I hadn't spoken to them for six years, nor had I wanted to. In fact, every day I didn't accidentally run into them was a relief. We lived in the same city, yet in different worlds. But now that Jack was working part-time at the bike and ski shop where my parents bought their cross-country ski gear, our worlds had intersected. Somehow they'd heard about Jack and were coming round the store, not to shop, but to ask about his schedule. It took a while for the store owners to figure out who they were and what they were after, but once they connected the dots, we deduced that my parents were hoping to inspect their daughter's new boyfriend, incognito. This shocked me. It hadn't occurred to me that they'd ever be curious about my life. I was dead to them—my mother had uttered those words—and dead was dead.

But now, with my newly-restored confidence, I decide to phone them and call their bluff. It's a snowy November day.

My father answers the phone. *Hello?*

Dad? It's Marilyn.

There's a long, nerve-wracking silence before he speaks. *Marilyn?*

Yes. It's me. I give him a second to digest this breaking news and get straight to the point.

It's about George's Cycle. The shop owners told me you've been coming round a lot, asking questions about my boyfriend. Jack. They say you've been there lately, asking about his schedule.

More silence. I've caught him off-guard, but I've got nothing to lose. I press in.

Does this mean you want to see me? Is that why you've been going there? Is it because you want to see me again?

My father finally speaks, but he sounds wary, and his voice is shaky.

Let me ask your mother and see what she thinks.

I picture him standing in the front hallway, receiver in hand, and I hear him calling her, repeating my name several times. I expect to wait a few minutes while they hold a whispered discussion, perhaps even suggest calling me back later with their decision, but within seconds, my mother is on the phone.

Marilyn?

She sounds eager, breathless, but I keep the tough girl stance, repeating what I know about their sleuthing at George's.

So, does this mean you want to see me?

There's no hesitation. *Yes,* she says, *I do. We do. When can you come over?*

This unfamiliar warmth is not what I expected, but I'm heartened by it. We make plans for the next Sunday afternoon.

And so, a chasm is crossed, or at least a makeshift rope is tossed my way. I decide to go alone the first time, without Jack, giving my parents privacy to address our complicated history. But nothing is addressed.

Our past is a sealed box and will remain that way forever. My parents ask no questions about the last six years of my life or of the troubled years that came before. My mother never will.

There will be no apologies, no intimations of remorse from her side of the wall. It seems the only way we'll go forward is by erasing the past, like monks sweeping away a sand mandala, leaving an inscrutable pile of muted, indistinguishable colors. We'll start with a fresh slate, like distant relatives who have only just met. We are no longer parent and child, and in many ways, it seems we never were. Instead, we talk about cross-country skiing and the weather, about my father's golf and curling, my mother's choir. We talk about my brothers, especially Brian, the youngest, the apple of their eye. They invite me to bring Jack over for Christmas dinner, five weeks away, and I say yes.

All these things happen quickly, sparked by the energy Jack's love has unleashed in me. My heart is full. I'm not only in love with Jack; I'm in love with the person I *am* with Jack. I've stopped going for long, mind-numbing walks and instead I'm living in the moment, eager for every minute I can spend with him, with and without other friends. It seems my life will be amazing after all.

But there's a thief afoot, an ambush at hand. It won't be what I dare to dream at all.

12

Perfect Little World

———————

One afternoon I finish counting pumpkin cookies into melamine trays and glance through the kitchen window into the Hub. Jack is looking back at me. He's wearing his dark denim shirt over a soft green t-shirt and faded jeans and clutching a folder to his chest. But he resembles a ghost. He stands motionless, not smiling, his face pale, his eyes haunted. This is a Jack I've never seen.

I pull off my apron and run outside to meet him. He pulls me in, as always, and we melt into a hug. There's fierceness in the way he holds me, and we're both spinning, but this time it's the spin of drowning, of being on the edge of an abyss. I look into his eyes.

What is it? What's wrong?

I saw the doctor today — I went for my six-month follow-up results. It's not good. The cancer... it's come back, it's metastasized...He says it's in my lymph glands now.

Did I forget to mention that Jack had gone through a bout with cancer? I'd completely forgotten about it, too. His cancer was a brief episode before we became a couple, after he'd discovered a lump in his testicle and waited too long to take action. He'd downplayed the whole affair, undergoing a quick surgery to have the tumor removed and rarely mentioning it again. I hadn't even known he was going for follow-ups. The doctors said they'd gotten all of it, and everyone wanted to believe the happy-ending version. The cancer was history.

But now it was back.

It was 1 pm on a Wednesday afternoon. We stood motionless by the window, clinging to each other on our crumbling island as fear climbed our legs and students rushed or ambled by on their way to classes, naps, or lunch, unaware of the sinkhole tearing through our perfect little world. The inconceivable was screaming in our ears, and we listened for several howling minutes before pulling back and jumping onto the flimsy raft of *everything's-going-to-be-fine*.

Treatment started right away. For six months, there'd be radiation, then chemotherapy. There'd be no short or long-term prognosis until the treatments ended. The only good news was that we lived within walking distance of Alberta's best cancer hospital, as well as the university hospital, making it easy to be at one or the other for treatments.

Back in the 1970s, when chemotherapy was relatively new, the dosages were much stronger, and no one received chemo as an outpatient. Each round required several days of hospitalization so patients could be monitored and rehydrated during the unremitting, body-wracking vomiting that ensued. My chief memory of those months are stacks of kidney-shaped, stainless steel vomit bowls overflowing with the vile, watery-green slurry that spewed from Jack's body. I'd hold the bowls for him as he puked and then run to the toilet to flush the contents, trying not to vomit myself or to spill the seething toxins before rushing back for the next eruption. The liquid was hot and seemed infinite and radioactive. Jack's hair fell out; he lost weight and turned greener and paler as the months progressed, never losing the metallic stench of chemicals and decay that oozed from his pores. The vomit bowls waited at the hospital for his next round.

But we stayed positive. We cracked jokes and held hands, playing choppy games of Mastermind and Boggle between projectile sessions, and sleeping as close to each other as Jack could tolerate with his constant nausea. We were still floating in our love, confident that once this hell was over, our lives would fly again.

Jack fought hard. In an effort to enhance the battle being waged in his cells, he spent hours visualizing thousands of vinblastine and bleomycin soldiers blasting his cancer cells into oblivion. Even on his greenest days, he was relentlessly optimistic and outgoing, making him a favorite among the doctors and nurses. These days were just a blip on his joyous life trajectory, a transitory combat zone. He was convinced that with the right mindset, the treatments would work.

The sessions were weekend affairs. Outside the hospital, he mustered enough energy to live as vibrantly as ever, working two jobs, romancing me, and even teaching a night class on quantum physics—a subject in which he was entirely self-taught—at the university. I went to all his lectures in an attempt to grasp elusive concepts like bosons, wave-particle theory and eigenstates, but mostly to sit in the mid-rows and feast my eyes on all five-foot-eight-inches of him as he explained the marvels of the universe. I was in love with every inch of him, but particularly his hands, his eyes, his lashes, his shoulders, his smile...

Fortunately, I wasn't compelled to take an exam at the end of the course, or I'd have failed abysmally and been outed as a stalker, not a student.

On Jack's treatment-free weekends, we attended various New Age workshops. We talked a lot about spirituality, and were surrounded, in Saul's house and among our friends, by dabblers and devotees of teachings sprung from an eclectic pool: Allen Watts, Ram Dass, Carl Jung, Gurdjieff, transactional analysis, Tarot, the I Ching, Sufism, the teachings of Lao Tzu, rebirthing, lucid dreaming, soul travel, spirit guides, and an assortment of eastern gurus. The smorgasbord appeal of these offerings—take as much or as little as you like, in any combination—and their promise of ongoing transformation made them highly palatable.

In high school, Jack had been converted to Christ and had even chosen a Christian college for his first degree. Since moving to Canada, he'd drifted away from the faith, starting with a Christian study group that devolved into an encounter group, its members, one by one, enticed by the prospect of achieving cosmic consciousness. But he remained a seeker and was still amenable towards his former faith; he read and reread Tolkien's books with religious fervor, and every book in his small but carefully chosen library had a spiritual theme.

While we waited for this dark chapter to close, we planned our future. Marriage was a given; we'd wait till Jack was healthy and the timing was right to host the perfect outdoor celebration with friends. We wanted two or three children, and although we hadn't gone as far as choosing names, one of our most heated arguments was about the kids: Would it ever be okay to bring donuts home as a treat? (I said no; Jack, the freer spirit, would be an indulgent father.)

But before the wedding and the babies, we planned to spend two years on a bicycle trip, starting in the middle of Canada and touring all of the Americas. Along the way, I'd get to visit Guatemala, where Jack wanted to return someday as a medical missionary. We'd spend extra time in South America, perhaps Columbia or Chile, working on our Spanish. And after the trip we'd come back to Alberta so Jack could get his degree in medicine. These were more than mere pipe dreams: Jack was already on track for medical school, and our bikes, maps, panniers, and hearts were ready to go. All we needed was the expected all-clear from the doctors.

That March I turned 21. From Jack I was learning to keep a positive mindset, especially to myself. But my body knew otherwise. Since Jack's diagnosis, I'd been battling crushing fatigue, returning from work exhausted at 3:00 pm every afternoon and crashing into leaden, insatiable sleep. I felt cold; my skin itched, and I struggled to concentrate. Eventually I saw a doctor and was diagnosed with hypothyroidism. The medication, which I would take for the rest of my life, lifted the symptoms, but I failed to read the signals my distressed body was sending me. I saw no connection between my own disease and the stress of living with a cancer patient. Everything was going to be fine, wasn't it?

My mother, like most people, was very fond of Jack, and instead of buying me yet another item of ill-chosen clothing for my birthday in early March, she registered us for a weekend Christian retreat. I missed this sign, too. She probably perceived what I couldn't: that Jack's life was very much hanging in the balance. I'd have vetoed the invitation, but the fees were paid, and Jack, strangely enough, was eager to go. Even stranger, my mother had persuaded the camp director to give the two of us—unmarried and thus immoral—our own private room. No doubt Jack's cancer was the bargaining chip in this concession.

The retreat was held in the Rocky Mountain foothills, at a camp my grandfather had proudly helped build two generations before. Once there, Jack threw himself into every session with unmitigated zeal and spent hours discussing theology with the keynote speaker, who happened to be a writer Jack admired. They bonded quickly. But I took an opposite tack: I retreated. Most of my time was spent hiding in our room, perplexed by Jack's enthusiasm for a religion that made me queasy, and terrified of being proselytized by an earnest evangelical on the prowl.

We emerged from different ends of the retreat tunnel, unscathed.

After the retreat, Jack resumed the last of his treatments. We didn't discuss the weekend or the speaker or Jesus, or my visceral rejection of all three, or his openness to revisiting Christianity. But Good Friday was approaching, and Jack wanted to attend an Easter service. Would I go? Not a chance. For me, the Christian message was inextricably linked with my parents, and the last thing I wanted was a faith that resembled theirs.

13

Careening through the Wilderness

It's May 1977, and Jack's treatments are over. According to the doctors, the cancer is in remission, and as far as we're concerned, he's been cured. Spring, always late and skittish in Edmonton, has finally melted the lingering snow, and along with the rest of the winter-sick population, we're ready for fresh adventures.

We join three other couples, all friends, for a white-water canoe trip in the Rockies; the *white water* aspect a first for me, if not the others. The canoes are rentals from George's Cycle; our team leader and amateur guide, Clive, is a hardy swashbuckler from England whose credentials include crossing the Sahara by Jeep and navigating life by the seat of his pants. He's chosen the roaring McLeod River for this escapade, which is fuller and louder than any of us had expected, churning with the debris of a heavy spring melt and positively deafening. This is white water to the nth degree. But cowards we're not; we've driven four hours to get here, and Clive's bravado is contagious. After loading the four canoes with camping gear and three days' worth of food, we push off, careening through the wilderness at breakneck speeds.

The morning is bright and cool. This is no leisurely paddle, but an exercise in hypervigilance and lung power, trying to avoid collisions with waterborne trees as we holler "RIGHT!!" or "LEFT!!" at our water-drenched partners seated two feet away. Clive and his plucky wife Paula take the lead; Jack and I are in fourth place. I can't see Clive up ahead, but I picture him like a sinewy voyageur, imagining he can subdue the river on our behalf, and I suspect he's ranked us by experience.

The first hour is pure adrenaline, and not the good kind. I can't take my eyes off the water for a second. But as the hours pass, I relax a little and dare to glance periodically at the fast-moving scenery. Lots of blue sky, gray rocks, blurry green forest. At two o'clock, Clive spots a sand bar, and we pull ashore for lunch. We agree to canoe for two more hours before making camp for the night. Once again, Jack and I assume fourth place on the river.

There's a limit to how long anyone can concentrate, especially under pressure. We're flying downstream for another hour when the river takes a wide turn, but my arms are weary, and my brain's been fried by the sun and the roaring current. I dully notice that Roy and Minna, in the canoe ahead, are waving their arms and shouting something I can't make out, but my mind moves too slowly to grasp the danger. Jack sees what's coming and starts yelling "LEFT! LEFT!" but even if I have any arm strength left to draw upon, it's too late. We're being sucked into a gigantic sweeper (I'll learn that useful word a little too late) of deracinated, water-logged trees, and before I can grasp what's happening, the canoe flips over and disappears, leaving me trapped beneath a mountain of smashed and twisted pines and sucked into the vortex of a maelstrom, experiencing, in a visceral way that transcends all prior life experience, the fearsome power of big water and centrifugal force. I'm a twig in a tornado, an egg in an industrial washing machine, about to be both drowned and disappeared. Time slows, as it does when one stares death in the face, and I dispassionately note where life has chosen to deposit me. The thrashing water bobs me up and down like a cork, and on the ups I grasp at sodden logs above my head, but they're unwieldy and so slippery I know I'll never get a grip. *So this is it*, I think. *This is how it ends.* I feel strangely calm in the midst of my imminent demise; there's nothing I can do, and some primal part of me accepts this without alarm.

Suddenly an arm reaches down and yanks me into daylight. It feels like the arm of God, but it's actually Roy, who pulled ashore several hundred meters ahead and ran back to save me. Roy is not only a quick thinker, but also a spry sweeper climber and a very fast marathoner. Working in tandem with God—who's placed him third in the flotilla where he kept an eye on us—Roy's caught me in the absolute nick of time, at the very moment I've surrendered to the river and let go. I'm back in the land of the living.

But where is Jack? Roy walks me off the sweeper and seats me safely on shore before bounding off to find him. This rescue's easier; Jack's been swept downstream and bashed around like a bumper car on speed, but the river delivers him to the left bank, where we all need to end up for the night, and he's managed to drag his battered body ashore. Running on pure adrenaline, Roy carries Jack's river-whipped body upstream and places him beside my convulsively shaking one.

Jack's eyes tell me we've both stared death in the face, but our chattering teeth preclude any talk. We're shell-shocked, river-shocked, and hypothermic—the river is barely melted ice—and Jack's legs are ravaged with rock-inflicted bumps the size of golf balls. Roy and Minna build a fire and we practically stand in it. Eventually Clive, Paula, and the second canoe mates portage their way back to us. Our canoe and everything in it are long gone. Minna collects dry clothing from the group to dress us, props us by the fire, and feeds us warm liquids before we split up and squeeze into two friends' tents for the night.

We're miles from civilization, and there's only one way out. In the morning, our friends will canoe for two more days to where the cars are parked. Jack and I, with only the clothing on our backs, will hike our way out from the river until we're lucky enough to find a road. We all hope to be reunited on the third day.

Morning comes fast. After filling our bellies with hot oatmeal, Jack and I turn our backs to the river and strike out, mapless and empty-handed. I should be scared, but I'm not; I'm with Jack. The sun shines high and hopeful through the trees. And God is with us. We walk into the afternoon until we find a gravel road, and one hour later there's a truck, and we're rescued again.

We spend the next eight weeks getting in shape for the epic bike trip. One afternoon we're riding a 40-mile loop in the country when a small plane lands on the empty highway ahead of us. A tall, very familiar-looking white-haired man with impeccable posture climbs out of the aircraft, and Jack gives a whoop. It's Pierre Berton! I'm amazed to see this prolific Canadian writer and TV personality in the middle of Nowhere, Alberta, and even more amazed that Jack, my Arizona-born, all-American fiancé, not only recognizes him but is thrilled by the sighting. We cycle past the plane and wave to Pierre, who's engaged in a deep conversation with his companion. Perhaps they're discussing Vimy Ridge or the War of 1812 or the Dionne Quintuplets. Or maybe they've just run out of fuel. Who knows?

It's a great Canadian moment.

14

Silky Green Parachute

~

July 31st marks our last night in Edmonton. It's also the last night of The Hovel, reluctantly closing its doors after five years of the best local music in the city. The whole Gang is here, boogying one last time inside these hallowed walls before sending us off with hugs and tears.

By noon the next day we're on a train to Thunder Bay, our bicycles boxed and ready in another car. It's a three-day trip, and once again Jack's taken care of provisions. This time it's an enormous bag of trail mix, one step up from last fall's Three Days of Harvest Crunch, for at least the mix comprises various food groups: cashews and dates and chocolate chips. Jack, at home in the world wherever he goes, makes a handful of new friends in every passenger car, while I finish a fat novel and wonder how many grueling miles of riding it will take until I'm *really* in shape.

The train deposits us in Thunder Bay at nightfall, and we cycle the town's outskirts, hoping to find a place to pitch our little yellow tent before it's completely dark. We're off to a lucky start; someone invites us to sleep on the floor at the Rowing Club, above the skiffs that sleep in narrow cubbies below. We're grateful, and despite the hard floor we crash into our first good sleep since leaving Edmonton, only to be awakened at 5 am by a dozen startled rowers preparing for their pre-dawn workout. So much for sleep; we might as well get an early start, too.

Jack has planned a route that takes us south into Minnesota, where we'll catch a ferry to a magical place called Isle Royale, and then continue cycling on the Michigan side of Lake Superior before heading back into Canada. Apparently, the hills and headwinds on the Canadian side are rough, and this route will ease us more gently into the trip.

Day One is brutal, especially after three days of railway inertia. My bum is sore, and my back is scorched after tackling the hilly miles that take us to Grand Portage, our first stop. But now there's a glitch. The ferry service to Isle Royale doesn't allow bicycles; in fact, the island forbids wheels of any kind, except wheelchairs. We'll have to ride the same fifty miles back to Thunder Bay and start over. And we'll end up having to ride the north shore of Lake Superior whether we want to or not, all 630 miles of it to Sudbury. Besides uncountable hills and strong winds, there are vast armies of mosquitoes, black flies and no-see-ums waiting to devour us. But there are compensations. We'll get super-fit, super-fast. And it'll be all-Canadian, all the way to Maine, and beautiful, because I'm riding with Jack.

Before leaving Edmonton, we made arrangements to send monthly articles back to the city newspaper, the Edmonton Journal. Fifty dollars per submission is a lot of money, enough to finance almost a week of biking. And we both love writing. Still, co-writing with any-one, even a soulmate, can be challenging. We bicker over syntax and adverbs, style and content, and how to fit as much as possible into the limited word-count. It's exasperating and fun. Our articles will flesh out the postcards we mail back to friends, but as we ride, I also write letters in my head to Gwen, my closest girlfriend. She'll be my lifeline in days to come.

The largest freshwater lake in the world is like an ocean, choppy, wild, and desolate. We ride into Wawa, the town that everyone in Canada loves to hate (after Toronto), battling great winds and wondering what prompted this woebegone town to exist. At night, bloodthirsty insects hone in, and we escape them by zipping ourselves into the tent. Thankfully, the netted windows are fine enough to keep out even the tiniest biters. I'm beginning to grasp the vastness of the Canadian Shield, formerly an abstraction I'd colored and labelled in years of Canadian social studies classes. We're cycling only a sliver of it. I'd always pictured a knight's shield, hugging the earth, but it's more like a half-buried continent, pushing through the earth in giant heaps of stone.

After ten days of wilderness camping, we ride into the blackened, nickel-mining town of Sudbury. For the first time on our trip, it's pouring rain, and everything we're wearing and carrying is soaked. We're on a tight budget, around eight dollars a day for both of us, enough for food and a weekly wash at a laundromat, but not enough for luxuries like camp sites or cabins. My mood turns sour. Even if there were a campsite along this urban-blighted stretch of highway, we'd be shivering in damp bedding, and rolling into wet clothes in the morning. We pull into a gas station and huddle under an awning.

I wish there was such a thing as a three-dollar motel, I lament. Jack concurs. *Wouldn't that be wonderful?* It's not remotely possible, so we banish the thought, shake out our ponchos, and keep riding. Ten minutes later, I'm blinkered by a red neon sign: ROOMS $3.00 PER NIGHT. If this isn't an answered prayer, I don't know what is. We rush in to pay before someone changes the sign.

The three-dollar room is just what you'd expect for three bucks: grubby and rank. Its cheap rate probably attracts a lot of hourly customers, too. But it's dry! We can hang our wet gear over the vinyl chairs till morning! There's a droopy double bed and a one-burner hotplate! Best of all, there's a ceiling over our heads and a soak-proof roof! We're ecstatic. I never see rooms for three dollars again. But that night we get exactly what we need.

Jack's route to get us from Thunder Bay to Mexico has a multilayered agenda. It isn't the most *direct* way, but rather the most historically rich, aesthetically pleasing, and socially engaging itinerary he could create. There are old friends he wants to visit along the way, scattered from Michigan to Montreal to Morristown, Tennessee. And he's a huge history buff: Our route will take us through chunks of Civil War territory, through the White Mountains, the Green Mountains, and the Great Smoky Mountains. The journey includes some back-tracking and side-tripping, with no fixed timetable. All we have to do is keep one step ahead of winter as we wind our way south.

The next leg of our trip takes us west again, to visit Jack's college friend, Carol, at her earth-mother cottage in Kalamazoo. Carol reminds me of Mama Cass. She's big and buoyant, with long flowing hair and a buttery personality. She's crammed her cottage with jars and bins of homegrown foods, and every room is pungent with the earthy smells of herbs, handmade soap, and goat's milk cheese. Carol is very fond of Jack, and she extends that fondness to me by attempting to fatten me up with hourly feedings from her garden and pantry.

One afternoon I'm standing in Carol's garden, munching on fresh peas, when something wet and disgusting hits the left side of my face. Hot and slimy, it slithers down my chest and gurgles down my legs. I touch it with my fingers; it's an enormous, sun-blasted, rotten tomato.

A few rows over, Jack and Carol are doubled over, laughing hysterically. It's obvious Jack's the instigator. And I'm enraged.

Jack stops laughing long enough to explain himself. *I've always wanted throw a rotten tomato at someone!* He's grinning at me, like this is a perfectly rational explanation. Doesn't everyone harbor that secret wish?

Really? I'm thinking. *You think this is funny? Splattering your fiancée with a rotten tomato? In front of a friend who thinks this abomination is hilarious, too?*

We're facing the unbridgeable chasm between those who think practical jokes are funny, and those who find such blindsiding antics both humiliating and humorless.

My rage is immense, intransigent: I feel violated. In all the years I've known Jack, he's never hurt me, never done *anything* that's made me feel ridiculed or disrespected. But this comedic failure has crossed the line.

It ends up being the worst argument of our relationship. Jack apologizes, over and over, but being the target of a hot tomato, however intended, fills me with shame and indignation, and I have a hard time letting go.

From Michigan we ride through southern Ontario, stopping in the little town of Chatham to visit Jack's former housemates, Jim and Carolyn. He's the social worker who'd taken such an interest in my life at fifteen. They're shocked to see us as a couple—our age difference, for starters, and it's a surprise visit—but thrilled to see both of us. They're no longer hippie-ish grad students. Now they have a squalling baby and a square little house drowning in infant paraphernalia. Jim seems restless. Bizarrely, he takes Jack and me to a nearby strip club to check out a stripper with 50" boobs, which confirms my suspicion that he hates his life. The stripper is a freak show. We nurse our beers and reminisce while she waves her grotesque appendages at the crowd. The following morning, we say goodbye to Jim and Carolyn. I hope, in spite of Jim's obvious life crisis, that he's still validating lost children in the system, as he once did for me.

We pedal on to Quebec to visit Zosia, an almost-girlfriend from Jack's past. Jack's friendships, male and female, are always deep. He's incapable of superficiality and falls a little in love with almost everyone he gets to know.

I'm certain I live in the sweetest chamber of his heart, so these relationships aren't threatening; I'm just amazed at his capacity for love. Still, there's the rare person in Jack's circle of friends who triggers my insecurities, and Zosia is one of them. She's Jack's age, a gorgeously exotic French-Canadian who dresses like a gypsy. She's witty and intense, in all the right ways, and cooks magnificent meals with ingredients I've never heard of. Her book-lined, picture-perfect apartment reflects her refined intellect and exquisite taste. And on top of all these incredible attributes, she's kind. She's a flawless jewel.

As for me, I'm wearing the same white gym shorts I've worn every day since we started riding, along with the same thrift store tank top. My lacklustre hair is suffering from lake water shampoos with Dr. Bronner's 18-in-1 All-Purpose Peppermint Soap, one of the few toiletry items we carry in our panniers. I wear no jewellery apart from a single pair of plain earrings I never remove, and I've given up on shaving my legs. My nose is perpetually burned, though I rarely glance in mirrors to assess the damage. None of this has bothered me until now, but next to Zosia...

Still, Jack introduces me like I'm Guinevere to his Lancelot, and when we slide into our zipped-together sleeping bags, fragrant with wood smoke and lined with our silky green parachute (an inspired purchase from Edmonton's Army & Navy Surplus Store), I know I'm The One.

From Montreal, we cross the border into a slice of Maine and then Vermont, which is like riding through a series of postcards, apple green and rustic, dotted with tiny white churches and red covered bridges. We fall into a pace as peaceful as the clear sky and the meandering roads linking one village to the next. The atmosphere is different in this corner of the world. We're no longer battling the winds and isolation of the northern lakes; now the space between towns is condensed, and pockets of history, far richer to me than my Canadian quota of fur traders and voyageurs, wait to be explored.

Jack is in his element, a history buff on an extended field trip. In every town, there are locals and eccentrics to meet, and like a seasoned journalist he seeks them out, engaging them in long, inquisitive interviews.

While he listens and probes, I wait on the sidelines, tuning in and out as my patience dwindles: I want to clock more miles, set up camp, sit by a fire and drink tea. The expansive talks conducted in grocery shops at the end of the day are the worst. *I'm hungry, dammit!* But I keep such traitorous thoughts to myself. These interludes invigorate him as much as my evening routine will invigorate me, and I can wait.

As we cycle through New England, where small-town grocery stores are plentiful and better stocked, our evening meals become predictable. Jack gets addicted to Kraft Dinner and a bag of Fritos every night, while I buy sardines, tomato juice, carrots and potatoes. Every night I resolve to never again eat another corn chip, before digging into Jack's bag and keeping pace with him as we talk into the night. For breakfast, we seek out diners that feature 75-cent specials, and ripe bananas—the ultimate cycling fuel—are regularly featured for lunch.

When the roads are quiet, we often ride side-by-side, resuming the conversation that started six years ago. Otherwise, Jack rides a bit ahead, turning back at me to grin and point out sights along the way: An eagle! A tunnel! A horse and buggy! A funny sign! Apart from the tomato episode, there's no conflict, no stress. We're getting stronger, browner, and leaner, and one day we stop at a thrift store to exchange our mini-wardrobe for replacements a size or two smaller. I savor every part of every day, but the nights – munching on Fritos, feeding a campfire, laughing and touching for hours inside the tent – are best of all.

Somewhere in Vermont we meet another cyclist who invites us to visit him in Cambridge, Massachusetts. Jack's made another friend and quickly accepts; besides, he's always wanted to see Boston. But his focus changes as we near the metropolis. He's been complaining of a sore knee, which surprises me since he rarely complains. Now he wants to reach Boston to get his knee checked out. We're sure the pain is from overuse—all that cycling—and probably isn't serious, but it's affecting his equilibrium and could stop us down the line.

After weeks of fresh country air, riding into Boston's heavy metro traffic is hell. The polluted air triggers one of my life's worst migraine headaches, and Jack's knee pain becomes excruciating. We arrive in Cambridge like two wounded soldiers. Our new friend is eager to show off his city, but most of our time is spent chasing doctors. The x-rays and tests reveal nothing. All Jack can do is try painkillers and hope for the best. We leave Boston and head for New York and Pennsylvania.

Our next goal is to beat the incipient snowfall in Virginia's Blue Ridge Mountains and make it to eastern Tennessee, where we'll stay with friends from Jack's college days and give his knee some time off. We pedal hard, barely missing the snow, and make it to Morristown as the last brown leaves are clinging to the trees.

Several of Jack's classmates still live in Tennessee, and it's been ten years since they met as freshmen. Jack's reappearance sparks a brainstorm: why not plan a reunion over Thanksgiving? Someone secures a gigantic farmhouse in the Unaka Mountains and the invitations go out: A Decade of Decadence. Dozens of friends arrive. Over the holiday weekend, I get glimpses of how decadent this decade actually was among these former Christian College students; there've been divorces, debacles, and breakdowns, and two of the married women are in the throes of a very public affair while their husbands do their best to ignore their spontaneous make-out sessions. Even after the loose morals I've witnessed among pagans, I'm surprised by how far these former evangelicals have fallen.

But they are energetic, funny people, thrilled to be together and to see Jack again. I organize the meals and serve as chief cook, capping the weekend with a succulent turkey dinner. Although I'm clearly the odd one out— eight years younger, Canadian, and lacking any shared history apart from my connection with Jack—the cohort embrace me as one of their own.

After the reunion, we briefly head south towards Georgia and Florida, but in spite of the rest break, Jack's knee is getting worse. So we return to Tennessee, visiting the Grand Ole Opry and the Smokey Mountains, and spelunking one dreadful day through two miles of claustrophobic caves. After months of cycling, I run the ubiquitous hills around Morristown with spectacular ease. I cook for our hosts and the steady stream of friends who circle by the house. Finally, Jack's pain sends him to the University Hospital in Knoxville, an hour away. This time the doctors won't quit till they find answers, and a week before Christmas, the answers come.

There's absolutely nothing wrong with Jack's knee: the pain is coming from rogue nerves. The cancer is back, and it's metastasized into his spine and his lungs. And into more lymph nodes than we ever knew existed.

The doctors schedule spinal surgery for the next day. There's no time to process this stunning development, and I enter a bubble that cushions me from what's ahead. The bubble keeps me functional; it keeps me from falling apart. It swaddles my heart like giant bandage, like swaths of lumpy bubble wrap secured with rolls of duct tape: impenetrable. It covers me for years. But all that cushioning comes at a cost, a very high cost, with interest that will accrue for decades to come.

15

Without You

————— ≈ —————

A year before the Tennessee diagnosis, Jack and I had an intense, one-minute conversation about death: personal death, not the concept of death. It was a crisp, dazzling December day, and we'd stopped at a bridge while skiing beside the frozen North Saskatchewan. Jack's face had the same stricken look as the day he'd found out the cancer was back. There was no preamble.

You know, there's a chance I might not make it, he said. *There's a chance the chemo won't work. I might actually die…*

For a brief and terrible moment, the prospect of life without Jack swamped my heart. It was like falling into a bottomless pit; it was unfathomable. My words rushed out as if they'd been waiting in the dark for centuries.

If you die, I told him, *I'll die with you. I'll lie down beside you and kill myself. I could never live without you.*

I wasn't exaggerating. Jack pulled me close as we imagined this outcome, cleaving to each other as if death were already pulling us apart.

There was nothing to say. He didn't try to dissuade me, nor did he try to convince me it would be worth staying alive for a life without him. I knew if the tables were turned, we'd be having the same conversation, the mirror-image of this bone-chilling talk.

This was as far as we'd let ourselves go. It was the first time we'd spoken the words aloud: *Death. Dying. Without you.* And even now, with Jack's delicate, invasive surgery looming, we agree without words that we still won't talk about personal death again.

To be close to Jack through the surgery and beyond, I find a place to stay in Knoxville, a dreary student dorm room in busing distance from the hospital. It's Christmas, so the campus is deserted, and the tiny, khaki-green cubicle, empty but for a set of narrow, stripped bunkbeds and two plastic desks, looks and feels like a prison cell. It's a comfortless room, and it's where I'll spend the loneliest Christmas of my life.

The surgery takes hours, and afterwards the nurses whisk Jack into Intensive Care, where he lies in limbo for many days. While he slumbers, I also lose track of time, aimlessly wandering the hospital corridors while I wait for the ten-minute ICU visits that I'm allowed, and dreading the chilly hours awaiting me in the dorm room at the end of each day. None of Jack's Tennessee friends are around; they're away with family, celebrating a happier season.

The weather is pure gloom, relentlessly dark and rainy, and I bus between the hospital and my sleeping quarters in despair. Jack is tormented by dreams of demons entering his quarried spine. It's small comfort to hear from a nurse that other spinal cord patients report similar visions. So horrifying and realistic are these nightmares that he weeps in the telling. In all the years I've known him, I've never seen him so weak and afraid. He's like a terrified child, yet I'm not allowed to climb into his gurney to comfort him.

I'm frozen, unable to think about our future or what could happen next. Jack is hollow-eyed, checked out, and when he finally leaves the ICU, he resembles a shrunken old man, unable to walk. The doctors did what they could, but the tumor was a tricky one, entwined around his spinal cord like a sticky octopus, and they offer no prognosis, another warning sign my blunted mind dismisses. Almost overnight, Jack's gone from cycling three thousand miles to needing two people to gingerly lift him into a wheelchair, and the pain that's finally left his knee has exploded throughout his ravaged body.

Our Tennessee trip is over: the doctors recommend immediate transfer to the cancer hospital in Edmonton.

It's all a blur. Somehow, I manage to box our bikes, pay for air tickets, and get us to the airport. Jack is in pain the entire way. We land in Edmonton on an impossibly cold and sunny January day, 40 degrees below zero. But the faces that welcome us at the airport blaze with love and boundless support: It's Blair, still devoted to Jack and me, despite our betrayal, and Gwen, so emotionally bonded to both of us that she's almost a triplet. They lift Jack into a warm, running car, and we're off to the hospital, again.

16

Sleepwalking

———～———

J ack is relieved to be back with his original oncologist, a father figure and friend, and back in the care of his former hospital. It feels like home. The pervasive smell of cancer still lingers in the halls, but the rooms are bright and the nurses, for the most part, are angels. Without asking, without any extra medical insurance, Jack is given a large private room, the best room on the unit, which includes a fold-out cot for me. It's as if the hospital has been waiting to roll out the red carpet. There's a kitchenette down the hall where I'll fix my mini-meals, and the room is big enough to host at least eight visitors at a time. The room is tucked in a corner where our festivities won't bother other patients, and none of the nurses enforce visiting hours, nor do they fret over how many friends are streaming through.

And the stream is steady. All of our Edmonton friends show up, bearing food, books, natural cancer remedies, and portable mini-parties. They're exactly what Jack needs, what I need, but I'm still in my bubble, still numb, and still refusing to consider that this next round of treatments could also fail. Jack's in the bubble with me. Without discussing the flip side, we've convinced ourselves that staying positive is the key to a cure, so we won't contemplate any other outcome, ever. Instead, we're still talking about Guatemala, about making our way to Florida and carrying on with our trip, about my learning Spanish and Jack's plans for medical school. We're sure if we imagine wonderful things, wonderful things will follow. Likewise, if we deny death's existence, death does not exist. On good days, Jack can shuffle a few steps by my side without his wheelchair; how hard is it to imagine he'll be flying soon?

And so, the next four months unfold. I'm with Jack around the clock, except for an hour in the afternoons when I leave the hospital to run twenty-four therapeutic laps around the perimeter of a covered hockey arena. Living in the hospital becomes normal, and we spend peaceful hours between treatments and visitors, playing Scrabble and snuggling on the bed. Scrabble is good; it means Jack can concentrate for longer periods of time, that he has a life apart from his sickness, and that his competitive spirit—always a match for mine— is still alive and well. In fact, after recovering from the trauma of spinal surgery, his mind seems sharp as ever, and friends who come to encourage us are amazed at how his signature joy, even under such dire conditions, ends up energizing *them*.

In late March, I rent a nearby basement suite so we can start spending weekends outside the hospital. It's a dark little nest, with a tiny, windowless bedroom. Our friends give us space on these retreats, and Jack sleeps the days away while I lie beside him, reading or daydreaming. We play the waiting game: if we can simply stay the course, simply do what the doctors prescribe and remain optimistic, the monster will be slain.

Jack's father, now living in California, flies to Edmonton and joins us at the hospital. John Sr. is a bona fide shyster, a disbarred lawyer with secrets we can only guess at. When Jack was ten, his mother died in a suspicious house fire, and Jack, suddenly bereft of the parent he adored, grew up convinced of his father's complicity. There were troubling inklings, and Jack's suspicions never lifted. But that topic has always been taboo. John Sr. copes with Jack's illness by harassing the hospital staff, pushing everyone to do more for his golden, first-born son of promise, his perpetual all-star, who's lost his hair, his muscles, and his ability to walk more than a few feet at a time. His father's agitation unsettles us, and I'm relieved when he finally gives up and goes home.

A friend gives me a chunk of Afghani opium to help me sleep. But I'm already sleeping: I'm sleepwalking through these numbered winter days, alive to Jack but blind to what's staring me in the face. He's shrinking into a skeleton; his face is gaunt, and his broad shoulders and strong legs exist only in memory. Not only that; he's reading an overtly Christian book by Malcolm Muggeridge called *Jesus Reconsidered*. Was Jack reconsidering? This should be a sign, but I miss it. Even more obvious is the title of another book that rests on the bedside table: *On Death and Dying*, by Elizabeth Kubler-Ross. I see it, but I don't. (Who set it here? Did he ask someone to bring it? Does Jack ever read it? These questions surface years and lifetimes later.)

I miss all these signs, every blatant one of them, while waiting for our wonderful life to resume. As impossible as it seems, it never occurs to me that Jack could be dying. The bubble is like opium, a potent and persuasive liar, and I let it bewitch and benumb me.

On the last day of April, Jack's oncologist comes to our room and pulls a chair next to the bed. He sits close to Jack, cradling both our hands in his. He's crying, which is not a good sign; he's always so composed, so calm. His voice is shaky.

I don't know how to tell you this, but all your tests are back, and it's not good news. In fact, it's bad news: the treatments aren't working. There's no sign of remission. This cancer's so aggressive, it's spread everywhere, and there's nothing left for us to try...I wish there was, but there isn't. I'm so terribly sorry...

He pauses a moment to let these words sink in before continuing.

There's no point in your staying at the hospital anymore. It's time you went and did whatever you need to do with the time you have left. I think you should go home today – you don't have much time.

We wait for the punchline. It comes.

Realistically, I'd say you have three weeks left, at best...

My heart goes into freefall, and then the bubble swaddles me again. This time, the words get in, but the feelings are still trapped.

The nurses have already prepared Jack's end-of-life medications, so it doesn't take long to pack our few belongings and check out. He leaves the hospital the same way he came, in a wheelchair. I roll him into a bright spring afternoon, the sunshine a mockery of our death sentence, and we drive to the river valley. Without words, we head to the same spot above the river that witnessed our decision to be together, less than two years ago. The truth we've been running from has crashed on our heads, and we cry a river. But we still can't speak. How can we possibly articulate such anguish? An inescapable wedge is forcing us apart. It's as if we're reaching for each other across a canyon, sucked in opposite directions by powers beyond reckoning. The bubble's sprung a leak, a giant gash, and the unthinkable has slithered in, squeezing my heart like a python.

But now Jack finally speaks, and perhaps he *has* been thinking the unthinkable, after all: it seems he's already given thought to his final days. It's too late for a bucket list, but he does have a three-step, end-of-life plan.

After we cry ourselves out (an hour, a lifetime?) he shares his wishes. First, he insists, there'll be no funeral. He wants to gather all his friends and host a farewell party—soon, within the next few days. He wants to personally say goodbye to each friend and to eulogize *them*, not the other way around. Then he wants to fly to California and spend a week with his father and brothers. His third wish is to spend his final week in Phoenix with his oldest friend, Peter. We'll buy return tickets, Edmonton to Los Angeles to Phoenix and back. And that's it. There's no fourth wish, no wishful thinking there'll be time or energy for anything more.

At least these plans give me something to do. There are people to call, flights to book, and bags to pack. I'm efficient and mechanical, and the busyness is an analgesic: if I were to stop and think of what I'm prepping for, I'd shatter beyond recovery.

But there's an urgent, timely conversation that eludes us. Jack's impending death puts all the focus on him, and rightfully so; he's staring down the barrel at twenty-one quickly vaporizing days. As the cancer patient, he's obviously been the center of this whole wretched journey, and as the caregiver, I've learned to put my own needs and fears on hold. It's years too late before I finally realize what I forgot to ask, and he forgot to broach. Given the circumstances, it's an obvious question, but perhaps the bubble can be blamed for this lapse, too.

The question is this: *What about Marilyn?*

I forget to consult him, my life, my compass, my advocate. I forget to ask, before it's too late, *What about* **me** *for the rest of my life?*

What will I be, where will I go, how will I live, what will I **do***, once you're no longer here?*

My life dovetails with Jack's, until it won't.

At least forty mourning celebrants attend Jack's farewell party, held in someone's carpeted, unfurnished living room where there's enough room for everyone to circle Jack, seated cross-legged in the middle. There'll be no feasting and drinking tonight, but the room is awash in love as Jack addresses each friend in turn, recalling the course of each friendship and sharing his favorite memories. In a last-ditch miracle, he's radiant and seemingly pain-free, filled with a supernatural energy that carries him through the evening. The room is alive with the Jack we all love: cracking jokes, poking gentle fun at himself and his friends, and bringing out the best in everyone. There's a time to rejoice, even in pain, and this night is all about rejoicing in his greatest treasures, these diverse companions who've colored and shaped his years in Canada.

Relationships and connection: nothing matters more to Jack. The Gang is all here, of course, and scores of other dear friends, including Clive and Paula, Roy (who saved my life so I could meet this second death) and Minna (his angel wife, who delivered us from hypothermia). Saul, the Silver Fox, is with us, and so are all the friends we've met through him, and even a couple of Jack's former girlfriends, who've never stopped loving him, even if they've moved on. Because that's Jack: easy to love, and hard—no, impossible—to forget.

Maybe the room holds fifty. I'm not counting, and I'm barely listening; I'm scrunched in a corner, hunkered in my bubble, which must've sprung another leak, because now I'm weeping enough to drown us all. Arms reach out, condolences are whispered in my ear, but I can't be reached. Jack waits to share his thoughts about me last, and I know these are words I need to hear, words that might carry me through the days and years ahead, but I can't take them in. My body weeps, but my core has left the room. When he's finally done, the room is silent. No one has ever been part of a night like this.

I wish I could have stayed.

17

Subterranean Lake

The next morning, we fly to Los Angeles. Jack's father and youngest brother are living in Santa Monica at the Marina Del Ray, on a small catamaran of suspicious provenance. The sun-drenched marina is crammed with too many boats slowly rotting in the heat, and the catamaran's interior is dark and claustrophobic. It stinks of overripe fruit and fusty laundry and foul sewage. Within minutes, I'm queasy with a nausea that lasts the whole week. It's an unkempt bachelor's space and a den of thieves: a dozen credit cards, all embossed with strangers' names, are scattered on a sticky burl table, and tepid, half-finished drinks leach into the varnish. I can't believe people live like this—rocking sickly on the water in such tight space.

Jack, floating in morphine, is oblivious to all of this. After the farewell party, he drifts into sacred, lonely waters: the place he must go to prepare for death. I've lost him. For days he drifts in and out of lucidity, receding into a hazy second childhood, brought on by his father's proximity, before drifting back into opioid dreams. I leave him in his father's care and take long, agitated walks along the boardwalk, hating Los Angeles, hating the boat, and hating, most of all, this sudden, drug-induced abandonment. When the heat becomes too much, I wander through air-conditioned grocery stores full of lush California produce, but the smell of the catamaran and impending death renders all food revolting. I want to fly away, to escape everything and sink into my own opioid dreams.

Jack's father refuses to accept his son's death. Desperate for an eleventh-hour cure, he begs us to take Jack to a clinic in Mexico. Even Jack, in his dream state, knows this is a fool's errand, but we go; for me, at least, it means a day away from the boat. His father drops me off at a beach in La Jolla to wait out the appointment. It's my first and only chance for solitude, away from the hordes in Santa Monica. The beach is almost deserted, and I bask in the sun-lit ocean and the soft, enveloping sand. Being immersed in such beauty unleashes a flood of profound joy, but the moment troubles me: my lover is actively dying, and it's too soon to release myself from his suffering. Nevertheless, the moment is transcendent, and this strangely timed joy seems like a sacred infusion, granting me something I'll need for later on.

The clinic turns him down, of course, and we drive back to the marina in silence. Jack's father, faced with this final wall, shuts down. The rest of the week evaporates into emptiness. I'm not sure what this hollow visit with his family means to Jack, if he's registered much of it, or if his profound withdrawal is a way to cope with his father's inability to *be* with him. Both brothers, too, are emotionally distant; even Jerry, once part of his inner circle, has turtled in to protect himself.

I'll see his father many, many more times in the years to come—but only in my dreams. He returns in an oft-recurring nightmare as an enabling trickster, with Jerry in tow, stealing Jack away from hospital under cover of night and whisking him away from me into a second, secret life. These dreams of betrayal and treachery are the worst, by far, of all the post-death dreams waiting to haunt me for decades to come.

Week two is gone. We fly to Arizona on an evening plane.

In Phoenix I picture eggs frying everywhere—on sidewalks, cars hoods, park benches—and wonder if anyone's tried making pancakes on their driveway. Every surface sizzles with stockpiled heat. I remember Jack's description of his first winter in Edmonton, of mapping out every warm doorway on campus and ducking in for minutes of relief from the arctic air as he ran from class to class in his skimpy Arizona jacket. I picture him out of breath, ruddy-cheeked and exhilarated by his new northern home, and my heart dies another hollowing death.

On a map, our cities lie in an almost straight line from north to south, or south to north. I think about destiny, and the decisions and twists of fate that perfectly landed us in each other's lives. I think about Jack's childhood here, about the motherless boy with the shadowy father, the boy who loved baseball and tennis, deserts and canyons. I watch him briefly come to life again as he reconnects with Peter, his first best friend, and they reminisce between bouts of pain and pools of morphine. My heart breaks with tenderness and I stay near, but in the background, giving them space to relive their boyhood together. The heat compels us to stay indoors all day, and only after 10 pm, when frying an egg might take five minutes instead of two, do I slip outside to run the fragrant, empty desert streets.

It's dark when we leave Phoenix, nearing the eleventh hour: exactly three weeks since the doctor's 21-day deadline. As we board for this final trip between the two cities that shaped Jack's life, I'm suddenly crushed with fatigue, with the stress of nursing Jack's emaciated, pain-riddled body, and with the months-long effort of keeping my emotions at bay. I've barely eaten during these two weeks, sickened by the decay in the catamaran and depleted by the heat of Phoenix, and suddenly I'm ravenous. Flight attendants wheel Jack to his seat and he floats beside me, still as death, spectral as a corpse. It's a wonder he's allowed onto the plane. I sense alarm and concern from passengers across the aisle, but I ignore them; all I want is my next meal.

Once we're airborne, a stewardess brings me a dinner tray, but just as I'm pulling the silver lid off the plate, Jack starts gasping for air, his toothpick arm grasping my wrist for rescue. I cover the food without tasting it, but I'm angry, not compassionate. I want to eat. I don't want to deal with a crisis. I want, for once, to think only of myself and not to think about sickness, pain, or the next plunge into decrepitude. I want to be left alone with my plastic airplane food. I want to eat everything on my tray, and then, while Jack sleeps without appetite, I want to finish everything on his tray, too.

These traitorous thoughts will torture me for years.

Someone— maybe it's me, or maybe it's one of those concerned passengers, looking on—alerts the flight attendant, and now she's giving Jack oxygen from a dangling mask. *A plane is a good place to be oxygen starved,* I think, as I sit in my bubble and wait for Jack's breathing to stabilize before I can decently lift the silver lid again. The food is still warm, but it tastes like sin in my guilty mouth. Still, I scarf it down. I'm an animal, selfish and wired for survival.

Soon after midnight, when we finally land in Edmonton, it's déjà vu from last January, minus the freezing cold: Blair and Gwen are waiting in the terminal (so aptly named) to carry us home. They gently wheel Jack to the car and lift him into the front seat, and we drive through the warm prairie night, cradled in their care. I feel like I've been around the world in a leaky dinghy since I last saw them. We speak softly, intimately, in harmony with each other and with this sliver of the night.

When we reach our basement apartment, we don't go in. Jack wants to sit on the back steps and look at the stars. He's lucid again, but fragile, childlike. The four of us sit like a single entity, arms around shoulders and waists. Blair is laughing, happy to be with Jack again, even like this. Gwen, ever attuned, is absorbing Jack's pain, and she's the one who insists on taking him back to the hospital when he struggles again to breathe. Since getting in the car, I've handed over the reins, and I let her lead the way.

We're back at our second home, the cancer hospital. It's somewhere around three a.m. when Jack's face is cupped with an oxygen mask and he's whisked away to the third floor. I'm relieved he's back in care, and I linger with Gwen and Blair for a few more minutes before crossing the lobby to the elevators. But before I can press the elevator buttons, an unfamiliar nurse blocks my way. She's not letting me in.

Go home, she orders. *Go and get some sleep. You're exhausted, you've just come back from a long trip—you need to take care of yourself.*

She sees my stricken face. *Don't worry; we'll take good care of him.*

This is the first time I've been forbidden to stay with Jack, and the first night since his lonely stint in the Tennessee ICU that I haven't slept beside him. I plead my case, arguing that I lived at the hospital for four months, that I need to stay with him, that I've *always* stayed with him. But there's no one else around, the lobby is deserted, and she's the boss.

Go home and get some sleep, she repeats, steering me towards the exit. *I'll check on him during the night, and I'll phone you in the morning before I get off shift. You need to go home, sweetie, and get some shut-eye!*

I bristle at her words. She's treating me like a child, or like a patient's distant relative who doesn't know her place. She doesn't know me or Jack, or how the doctors and nurses have always honored our relationship, or that I'm next-of-kin. But I'm so very, very tired, too tired to argue any more, and so I go.

Back in the windowless basement room, I fall into a stupefying sleep, only to be awakened three hours later by a ringing phone. It's the nurse, getting off work, keeping her promise to call.

I'm just getting off shift, she says. *You might want to come in soon.*

But I'm deliriously tired, and sleep sucks me back to the ocean floor. Do I dream? I think so, but they're messy, tangled dreams, and next thing I know I've come up for air and now it's 10:40, almost four hours since the nurse called. I remember her message and scramble into last night's clothes, then run to the hospital. It's 11 a.m. A different nurse sees me heading for Jack's room and she intercepts.

I'm sorry, she says. *Mr. Metheany passed away about an hour ago. Do you want to see him?*

What I want to do is strangle the nurse who ordered me home and had mildly suggested this morning that I *might want to come in soon.* My rage is ferocious, colossal, so huge it obliterates any other feelings. I stand in the hallway weeping tears of rage while the nurses take turns consoling me. None of them defends the night nurse's actions, but their unspoken censure makes no difference. She's the one who barred me from being with Jack when he needed me most, and nothing, ever, will restore what her stubborn arrogance has stolen from me.

I call Gwen from the nursing station phone, but she's already on her way to the hospital.

When she reaches the ward, I'm still shaking with fury. Jack's doctor has found me and drawn me into his office to offer heartfelt words that bounce off my howling pain. I see grief in his eyes, too, but his words spin like pebbles in a cyclone as I keen with a savage mixture of loss and rage, unreachable.

I haven't yet entered Jack's room. It seems pointless; he's gone, and I'm terrified of seeing his empty shell. Gwen and I stand outside the closed door, and she pulls me into her arms. She's mother and sister, twin and fellow orphan. Neither of us wants to see what's waiting behind the door.

As we weep, my anger gives way to something else: fear. Fear of waking up, perhaps, or of letting myself think about Jack's final moments, inexplicably alone. Where did he think I'd gone? My mind resurrects a winter memory of standing with him in a vast, snow-blanketed field, miles from the nearest human lights, and looking up at a billion stars as he described the cosmic loneliness he'd felt while walking alone, earlier that evening, under the same night sky. He'd felt profoundly insignificant, an ephemeral, meaningless dot in the blaze of infinity, and the desolate feeling had overwhelmed him. This memory sears me. He shouldn't have been alone in his final hours; he needed me like the tide needs the moon, and after two years of almost constant togetherness, I'd chosen sleep—for a few wretched, pointless hours—over being with him. *I'm* a wretch, most wretched of them all. I deserve to be left behind.

These thoughts will undo me if I let them stay.

But the body must be viewed. Reality must be squared. We enter the airless room and Gwen holds my hand as we stand beside the shrunken, tiny bundle he's left behind. I can't think. My mind refuses to process what I'm seeing, to record the scene for any future closure. His ashen face is a blank, his body a mere heap of blankets. Now is the time for last words, for tearful apologies, for final declarations of love, and for communion with his spirit, which surely hovers in the room awaiting something from me. But it's useless; consumed with guilt and reeling from shock; I cannot speak or absorb a single impression.

Now is also the time to confirm that death has come: that this, in stark reality, is his dead body, that he was alive in this emptied package for almost thirty sunlit years, and now he's not, nor will he ever again. But my mind is having none of it.

We're with the corpse for barely a minute when Gwen, sensing my distress and struggling with her own, urges me to leave the room. *Enough,* she says. *Let's not remember him like this.*

And so, I don't.

I learn, too late, that in most cultures the living sit with the dead for many days, reckoning with truth. They grapple head-on with grief by tending to the corpse, by washing and perfuming the empty limbs, by dressing it for the last time in carefully chosen garments, by decking it with silver and gold and relinquishing all to the grave, but not before letting the tended body speak from the centre of the mourning room, where its utter silence, absolute stillness, and unmistakable odor, insistently wafting through the blanket of too many flowers, serve to convince even the most resistant survivor that death has truly displaced the departed.

They are gone.

I learn, too late, that there are vital reasons for going through the rituals of funerals and memorials, and that ignoring these rites of passage, even to honor the wishes of the deceased, comes at a heartbreaking cost.

All this ageless wisdom I have yet to discover.

In the ignorance of youth, in my breathless fear, I stood next to Jack's corpse for sixty frozen seconds, and the whole time my mind was racing the perimeter like laps around a hockey rink, blanking out the truth. I couldn't *see*. He wasn't there, in his body or the bed, and nothing truly registered. Or if it did, it registered like a leaf falling on stone at the bottom of a subterranean lake.

Like Peter's triple denial of Christ, I'd failed three times during the course of Jack's final day on earth to do the kind thing, the right thing, and the wise thing. And as often as I'll let these blighted memories surface, I'll be haunted by shame for years. Not only that; along with these failures of love and wisdom, I've dug my own psychic grave by failing to begin the grieving process with a firm grasp on Jack's death. My soul hasn't connected the dots on Jack's demise, hasn't conceded that he truly, actually *died* in that hospital room on May 22nd, 1978.

For a very long time, my dreams will replay the day's events as a grand deception. Instead of dying, my dreams insist, Jack escaped; he fled, he *ran away* from me under cover of night, leaving a body as fake as the dummy I left in my childhood bed at fourteen, intent—and successful—at hoodwinking the pitifully left-behind.

18

The Map

I spend the afternoon of Jack's death on my bike, coursing through the sun-flecked river valley and reverently crossing the iconic High Level Bridge, a memory-laden landmark from nearly every chapter of my life, before coasting into the manicured gardens of the Alberta Legislative Building. It's a glorious summer day, ahead of the northern calendar; the gardens are bursting with blossoms and the air feels like silk. In the course of a few hours, I've moved from anger to shock to elation, and I feel Jack's spirit soar beside me, released from his body of pain. *He's free, he's been set free!* This certainty fills me. The walls his illness raised between us, the suffering I couldn't fully share, and the profound loneliness of facing death at 29, have tumbled down. He's with me again, more fully than he's been since the day of his last surgery, five months ago. I allow myself to enter my body again, at least partially, and then I let my body sink into the garden's lush, emerald-green lawn where I lie on my back and smile at the sky.

This whelming joy stays with me, baffling my friends. I should be grieving, pulling in and processing my profound loss. But perhaps I *have* been grieving, albeit subconsciously, for the past five or six months. I'm like a soldier, stoically completing my stint before collapsing back into myself and my humanity. My heart's been bound with invisible knots. But now that we're both been sprung from the cancer ward, I've recovered Jack's spirit and he's inside me now, safe from further pain and harm. I wrap him in my love and hold him tight. Relief surges through me like a drug, and although I have no plans, no future beyond this moment, I'm blessed with an unexpected ladle—a fragrant, overflowing ladle—of peace.

A week after Jack's death, I get a call from the mortuary to pick up his ashes. They're packed in a square white cardboard box, and they rattle like pebbles and sand in heavy dust. I pick up the box and feel nothing, no connection with these contents, leading me to wonder if they've given me a random mixture of burnt cadaverous leftovers. Who'd be the wiser? After strapping the box on my bike carrier, I ride downtown to meet a friend for lunch. It feels weird to carry the box into the law firm where she works, but what if someone were to steal it? Even if the ashes aren't really Jack's, I'd feel guilty for my negligence. The box goes with me into the office lunchroom, and I vacillate between placing it on the table or next to my feet. My friend finally notices.

What's in the box?

It's Jack.

Her face is a blend of shock, dismay, and compassion, and only in writing this do I see the joke: Jack in a Box.

She wants to know how I'm doing *—Fine, okay, I don't know* – but we steer clear of gruesome topics (ashes, crematoriums, and endings).

Whatever its contents, the box is mine and I'll have to come up with some sort of plan for it, later. For now, it's merely a bother, albeit a creepy one. I still can't put the words *Jack* and *death* in the same sentence, even in my head.

It's the same week. I've given notice at the basement apartment—the only time in my life when a mere one-day notice is enough—and it's time to pack up. Between us, Jack and I own so little. Apart from his bike and his banjo, all his belongings fit in an army-green footlocker that's followed him from place to place since he first left home for college. The chest is half-full of things he deemed worth keeping. I take out the contents and arrange them on the floor around me: some well-read books, the recorder he used to play before bedtime, a few articles of clothing, a packet of postcards and letters, a movie poster of Cary Grant being chased by an airplane in *North by Northwest*... and not much else. I decide to keep the books, the recorder, and the banjo. I'll give the bicycle to someone who'll love it as much as Jack did—possibly Blair. For reasons I can't remember, I decide to not keep any of his clothing. Perhaps keeping Jack alive means getting rid of all evidence of his death, and the simple clothes he wore in his short-changed life—his soft shirts, blue jeans, and beloved Adidas—will always conjure up the body that's missing. I make these decisions quickly, instinctively, perhaps afraid to linger and fall headfirst into grief.

I've forgotten what I did with everything I let go.

Jack traveled light, in every sense, and my own possessions are equally spare. I'm not a shopper or a spender, and before the bike trip we'd divested ourselves of nearly everything we weren't taking with us. The only goods I've added since then are the second-hand winter clothes I bought when we returned to Alberta in the throes of January.

A folded roadmap falls out of the footlocker as I prepare to repack it. I spread it out on the floor and see it's a map of western Canada and the US, with a hand-drawn yellow line tracing a route between Edmonton and Phoenix. In black ink, another line follows the yellow line from Phoenix to Boulder, Colorado. I know immediately what I'm looking at. It's the map Jack used on a solo bike trip a few years before. He'd been riding from Phoenix to Edmonton, but after contracting hepatitis, he'd been forced to abandon the trip in the Colorado Rockies.

The roadmap changes everything. In an instant I know what I'm meant to do next: finish the bicycle trip for Jack. I'll start riding in Alberta and fill in the black ink all the way to Boulder. It feels as perfect and inevitable as anything I've ever done.

But as certain as I am of my new direction, I'm terrified of travelling solo by bicycle. I've never imagined *being*, to say nothing of *riding*, without my joyful, competent, inspirational partner by my side. This is radical new thinking, and I'm well aware of how much I relied on Jack to keep my bike and my morale well-tuned. He was my travel guide and my protector, knowing how to plan and pace a good day's ride, how to find the perfect place to sleep each night, how to keep us on budget, and how to glean great tips and local yore along the way. Even more, he knew how to squeeze every minute of pleasure from the day, and his unflagging zeal carried us lightly through each hour. In fact, I couldn't remember ever feeling afraid on my travels with Jack, apart from the ghastly hours we spent spelunking in the Tennessee caves and the weeks of worrying over his knee pain. Even then, his joy and grit had kept us going.

But bicycle touring alone will be a different kettle of fish, and it takes only minutes to compose a list of every scary thing I can imagine befalling me, riding solo into my future.

This was my list.

1. **Bears.** I was going to be in bear country for the whole trip; they'd be a constant, lurking presence wherever I camped. In fact, on one hiking trip a few years back, a bear and her cubs had loped across Blairilyn's pup tent, shredding it to ribbons. (We weren't in it at the time. But an hour earlier, we *had* been.) I'd be spending at least eight or ten hours every night in my tent, alone—not that having a partner could prevent bears, but I'd feel less vulnerable with a brave man beside me. Every summer, fresh horror stories about bear attacks circulated among campers like Hollywood gossip. There was no end to the dreadful ways that bears could maul and dismember you. So, bears.

2. **Bike repairs.** I'd never been interested in mechanics (my eyes glazed over when being instructed in anything more complicated than a hammer and nail), and I hadn't mastered fixing a flat tire, let alone a malfunctioning derailleur. Jack, on the other hand, had been a consummate bike mechanic. One of his favorite books was *Zen and the Art of Motorcycle Maintenance*. I'd read it, too, but I'd skipped over all passages about actual repairs, and always preferred to study Jack's hands while he tended to my bike. (How could I focus on greasy chains or calipers when his beautiful hands were on display?) What would I do if my bike broke down

in the middle of nowhere? What if my unmaintained bike flew apart while I was careening down a mountain?

3. **Headwinds and Morale.** I hate, have always hated windy days, and biking into pummeling headwinds is torture. With Jack ahead, smiling and waiting for me to catch up— usually with a joke or a wry insight I could ponder for hours—I could persevere through the worst of winds. Plus, at the end of any windy day, there'd be the cheering prospect of simply being with Jack. Without him, harsh headwinds might tempt me to pull off the highway for good.

4. **Getting Sick. Or Flattened by a Logging Truck.** I wasn't *planning* on getting sick, but things would be grim if I were to sicken in the middle of nowhere. Once I left town, no one but God would know where I was from week to week, let alone day to day. Cell phones didn't exist back then; *in the middle of nowhere* meant exactly that, and letters sent to Gwen would only tell her where I'd been. And what if I got hit by a logging truck or a train? Who'd be there to scrape my sorry remains off the pavement for identification?

5. **Inclement Weather.** Yes, it was almost June, but weather in the mountains is always a crapshoot. Mountains can be fickle. I love the Rockies on sunny days, but when heavy clouds and rain sock in, the same crags bring me to despair. Whatever the weather, the only way out of the mountains is through them, one gloomy mile at a time. How would it feel to pedal alone through freezing fog and rain? Who would warm me at night if it snowed?

6. **Loneliness.** I was counting on Jack being with me in spirit, but what about those moments when his physical absence would tear me apart? Could I persevere through the canyons of grief that

lay ahead? Would memories of riding and camping and sleeping with Jack completely undo me? If I let myself cry, would I ever stop? I couldn't contemplate this fear for more than seconds at a time; it was like peering into a roiling volcano.

7. **Bears.** This was my first and ultimate fear, landing twice on my list. In truth, I could do nothing to prevent *any* of my fears from manifesting, and even though all the others were far more likely to happen, being mauled by a bear was something I'd let myself imagine too many times. The terror was unfathomable, but somehow I'd let my approximation of it get deep in my psyche.

I *wasn't* afraid of people attacks, of rapists or serial killers or crazy truckers who'd gleefully drive me off the road out of pure, impersonal malice. To me, the universe was essentially a friendly place (except bears). And I wasn't afraid of getting lost or of lacking the stamina to ride, unless I got sick; I could read a map and I'd already clocked a three-thousand-mile trip with Jack.

Reviewing the list emboldened me. Embarking on this trip would not only test my mettle but could be a qualifying test for the rest of my life. If I could complete this journey, I was confident I could handle anything else life might throw my way.

This final thought cemented my decision. Completing this trip was the perfect way to prove I could survive Jack's absence and move forward. And even if it was a bold premise on which to stake my future—who knew what greater challenges lay ahead?—I was already convinced that Jack's death would be the greatest loss of my life, and that surviving it would shape me as much as sharing in his life already had.

Besides, there was no other door in sight. What else could I do? Look for a job and rent a room? That certainly wasn't what Jack would do if the tables were turned. He'd be off chasing *me*. Making this trip would be the ultimate way, the *only* way, to channel his spirit of adventure and imprint its essence on me.

Because that's what I wanted most: to emulate his adventurousness, his love for people, nature, and travel, and make him proud of how his life had utterly transformed mine.

Still, I wasn't confident I'd go the distance, and new fears assailed me as I started assembling my gear. Was I making a huge mistake? What if I absolutely *hated* traveling alone? In that case I needed a way out, a *gracious* way out, so I added a generous loophole. The deal was this: I *had* to stay on the road for at least two weeks, no matter what. *No matter what!* But if, after fourteen days I was utterly miserable, I'd let myself off the hook without guilt or shame. This provision seemed fair and reasonable, though I hoped it wouldn't come to define me.

Once I'd committed to the plan, preparing for the trip was simple. I renewed my passport and cut my hair, though why I chose to cut it then is a mystery. Perhaps the gesture was a subconscious way of severing the months I'd spent obliviously watching Jack die, months that in retrospect dismayed me. How had I been so blind? What had I been thinking? The stylist chopped my elbow-length hair to my shoulders; this was shorter than I'd specified, and almost too short to pull into a ponytail. I went home and wept for the first time since Jack's farewell party, profoundly ashamed that a bad haircut, rather than his death, had triggered such despair.

Only later could I see how this breakdown wasn't about my hair, but about how fragile I was: much too fragile to begin processing the grief embedded in every pore. I could weep only for smaller things. The haircut had punctured a little hole in my bubble, where my strongest emotions lay buried beyond conscious reach, and some of my grief had broken through. But only a little, and only briefly; this was all I could handle. My grief reservoir would stay underground, perfectly hidden and almost forgotten, swelling with years of new sorrows till the day it all surfaced and capsized my life.

But that's another sadder and much later story.

In the spirit of new beginnings, I threw out my thrift store wardrobe and splurged on new clothes for the trip, nothing expensive, but each piece carefully chosen, since I'd be wearing these seven items *ad infinitum.* Here's what I bought:

1. 1 pair of the flattest-rolling jeans I could find.

2. 1 pair of denim shorts with cute red satin trim

3. 1 green-and-white striped tube top

4. 1 navy-blue tank top

5. 1 red-and-gold twirly hippie skirt

6. 1 pair of strappy, off-duty navy-blue sandals

7. 1 flannel plaid shirt (navy, white, and red)

I already had my cycling shoes, my running shoes, a windbreaker, a sweatshirt, a sun visor, and a poncho; also a bike lock and a tool kit. The back carrier would handle my little yellow tent, the silky green parachute, a thin blue sleeping mat, and one down sleeping bag. Into the double panniers went a tightly-rolled towel that doubled as a pillow, and also a flashlight, a bowl, a mug, a single set of cutlery, and a jackknife. My modest toiletry bag carried a razor, a comb, a toothbrush, sunscreen, and another bottle of the 18-in-1 Castille Soap that had scrubbed Jack and I clean from Thunder Bay to Tennessee. This time I chose the almond scent instead of the peppermint.

Since I wouldn't have my beautiful mechanic with me, I knew I'd need his tools, as well as the illustrated bike repair manual I found among his books but making room for both meant leaving something out. Our tiny propane camp stove got the cut. I'd be camping in vast tracts of mountain parks and wilderness, so there'd be plenty of wood for camp-fires to cook my veggie stews. The last thing I bought was a large can of tomato juice; emptied of its contents and fashioned with a bent wire handle, it was my new, all-purpose cooking pot. I strapped it last onto my loaded bike, where it would bounce behind my sleeping bag, getting blacker and more seasoned with every night away.

19

Concentrated Storm Track

M y journey began with a compromise (a portent of things to come), but it was a concession I could imagine Jack making, too. Getting through the first leg of the trip, from Edmonton to southern Alberta, would be dispiriting at best: a long slog on a busy highway through bland, featureless farmland. I figured we'd both put in enough bicycle miles in and around Edmonton to justify a route adjustment. Simply put, I didn't want to be foundering in the slough of despond by Day Three, so I boxed up my bike and took a Greyhound bus to Lethbridge, in the southwest corner of the province. This dry, windy city would be my starting point.

The first challenge reared its head before I'd even unpacked my bike. Within a day of arrival, I was ambushed by a virulent cold with a full roster of symptoms, including overall aches and pains and a completely blocked nose. Cycling requires a lot of oxygen, so being limited to mouth-breathing was going to be a problem. I also had a fever and a sinus headache. For two or three days I stalled my departure, but when it seemed the symptoms weren't budging, I figured I'd try sweating them out.

It was time to start riding. I loaded my bike and rode south, towards Waterton and Glacier National Parks, woefully short of energy and handkerchiefs. Within minutes of hitting the highway, it became clear that Lethbridge might be one of the windiest cities on the planet—and indeed it is, based on its proximity to the Rockies and a concentrated storm track that pumps out daily wind speeds of 30 – 90 mph. This was a particularly high-speed wind day, and the relentless, buffeting head-winds soon reduced me to tears, followed by a rising fury I channelled into pedalling even harder.

Why on earth had I chosen this route? Sheets of mucus poured from my nose, and I was pummeled all day by a dire mix of sun and wind that burned every inch of exposed skin and chapped my face from the eyes down. There was no shelter along the way, no place to escape the wind, and not a minute of respite, and the hours dragged as if I were cycling in place. Of course, I was the only fool cycling this hellish wind tunnel, watching metal-bound cars with air-sealed passengers zip by without a hair out of place. Day One, Part One exceeded my pre-trip apprehensions: I couldn't imagine a worse cycling experience, unless it involved a runaway logging truck and rabid bears. Even then, either of those disasters would've mercifully knocked me out of my misery.

It was provident to make that fourteen-day pact with myself; without it, I'd have turned my bike north and let the wind blow me right back to Lethbridge.

It was also good that I couldn't see beyond the next mile. The head-winds and head cold were just the overture. As if summoned by the tempter himself, my listed fears were queuing up, impatiently waiting to confound me.

By nightfall I made it to the National Park and limped into the first campground, willing to pay the government nearly a full day of my allocated budget for the privilege of setting up my tent on a lumpy patch of gravel. Another compromise! But it was late: the sun had dropped behind the peaks and the temperature was plummeting. I was beyond exhausted, so tired that I collapsed in my tent without eating. There was a young couple camping next to me, a head-over-heels couple who kissed and joked in their fairy circle like Jack and I had, and I could hear them laughing and making dinner just a few feet away. Loneliness. That was Number Six on my list of fears, but I hadn't dreamed it would hit so soon. I felt hollow and gutted, wondering how deep the pain would spread if I let myself feel. Even blunted by my swaddling bubble, the loneliness was worse than cycling through the wind tunnel.

And then it snowed. Actually, I was too busy shivering in my partnerless sleeping bag to realize it was snowing until the tent roof sagged in my face and I crawled outside to investigate. In my eagerness to dive into my tent and disappear, I hadn't tightly secured the tent fly, which was a huge mistake. Snow was piling on the netted roof windows, deflating the tent like a punctured dirigible. And by now it was too late for adjustments; even if I could see enough in the dark to reattach the fly, I'd get even colder in the process, and then I'd be flirting with hypothermia. All I could do was crawl back in my icy burrow and wait for this sleepless night to find morning.

All of this might've been sufferable if I could breathe through my nose, if my face weren't aflame with sunburn and windburn, if my lips weren't cracked and raw, if I weren't shaking with cold. And if I'd had some dinner in my belly, and if I didn't have to see those lovebirds in the morning, whose healthy bodies, I knew, were warmly entwined in their joined sleeping bags. Everything happening at once felt awful. What was Fear Number Five again? Oh yeah: Inclement Weather, especially inclement weather in the Rockies. I was flying through the list in less than twenty-four hours, and the only thing missing was a hungry bear. Languishing in my capsized tent, deflated and weak, I was prime pickings: a bear could roll me up like a crepe and start chomping on my ice-cold feet. I might not even care.

Morning was delivered like a newspaper sploshing an icy puddle. Just as I'd dreaded, the mercurial Rockies, lurking in fog and no longer majestic, had turned against me, sullen and oppressive. Yesterday's scorching sun had vanished, and the day promised nothing but further misery. Still, all I could do was pack my soggy gear and head deeper into the mountains.

But I couldn't just slip away without a final twist of the knife. As I was leaving, the lovebirds emerged from their tent, chipper and rested in their fleecy camp underwear, and invited me to share some coffee. I accepted, though I could scarcely bear to look at them, and I'm sure I talked about Jack before cycling away. This, it turns out, was how I would present myself to nearly everyone I met. I wasn't a carefree 22-year-old girl riding a bike through the States; I was a half-shell who'd just lost her fiancé to cancer, who was defined by his absence, by the crater he'd left behind. He was the absolute best part of my life, and I wanted everyone to know what was visibly missing, to know this amazing spirit who rode with me, mystical and fierce. He was my strength, and I the ghost, the emptied one.

Before leaving Edmonton, I'd left Jack's ashes (or whosever they were) at the base of an unmarked tree in the river valley. It was an intentional distance from the sacred spot where we used to meet: I didn't want his ashes mixing with sweeter memories. The white cardboard box held a dusty, heavy-duty plastic bag full of grey chunks and crumble, impossible to connect with my beautiful Jack. I'd intended to hold a private ceremony, to say profound things and mindfully sprinkle the ashes, but my heart had recoiled at the contents and instead of a ritual, I'd simply upended the box and walked away. The contents meant nothing. The box went into the nearest trashcan.

Now I vacillated between a keen sense of Jack's presence, especially while riding, and the deep knife of his absence, mostly at night, when I longed for his arms around me. This was much more than a bike trip: it was a quest, an attempt to close a broken circle, to re-enter a closed chapter and find an alternate ending. It was the hardest thing I'd ever done, but also the easiest and perhaps only way to stay close to Jack. It was running away, and it was coming home. It was potent time alone, day and night, when I let my thoughts flit between reveries and the pleasure of an empty mind.

But once the sun blazed through the clouds and the mountains unthawed, it was also a stunningly scenic bike tour, and the rhythm of riding sixty to eighty miles a day through breathtaking landscapes carried me in a tranquil space. By the time I reached the middle of Glacier Park, my body was strong and ready for the twenty-six-mile ascent on Going-to-the-Sun Road, followed by the twenty-six-mile swoosh down the other side of the Continental Divide.

Suddenly there were other cyclists on the road, mostly hyper-athletic men, and my competitive spirit clicked in. I was queen of the big ascents, and I loved glimpsing their astonished faces as I churned past chiseled, lean riders bent over their streamlined bikes. I certainly didn't fit the super-biker mold: I didn't own a bike helmet and my only concession to professional biking apparel were my clip-on shoes. My grey Apollo bicycle was a nondescript ten-speed, basic and low-end, lacking a granny-low gear, and loaded with dusty, mismatched equipment, including the blackened hobo tin that swung like a tail behind me. Thus girded, I beat most of my competitors to the top.

But the descents were different. I didn't share the testosterone or the reckless gene that impelled these hard-core cyclists to zoom downhill without braking. No flying over handlebars for me! These mountains harbored tight curves and distracted tourists, wide-open cliffs and cement barricades. I coasted, and sometimes I braked; I tried to absorb the scenery as it whizzed by. My competitors beat me on the downhill, but by now I suspected I was miles beyond most of them on the pleasure spectrum.

20

DIY for the Newly Bereaved

———————⁓———————

A few days into my trip, I've left the national parks behind and fallen under a different spell: riding rapturously through wide golden valleys flanked by cobalt blue mountains in western Montana. The sun is faithful, my cold has run its course, and I've stopped worrying about my list of fears—with the exception of bears. Indeed, bears still lurk in my psyche as I struggle each night to fling a small rucksack of food into branches beyond their reach. Who am I kidding? I'm short, with a lousy throw, and I waste energy by attempting to lasso branches either too high or too weak to hold. Besides, I wonder, won't my little carton of yogurt dangling from a tree simply entice them to the *real* dinner treat—me?

I've heard enough stories of campers being attacked in their tents to know this fear is rational, though statistically I'm far more likely to be struck by lightning, maybe even twice. As I throw the rope and fail and throw again, I ponder which would be worse: to be eaten alive and picked clean by carrion, or to lose only an arm or a leg and perhaps live to tell the tale. The latter seems unlikely; most bear attack survivors seem to make it by dragging their bloody bodies to a pick-up truck, where-upon they drive (miraculously, with one leg) to the nearest hospital and henceforth onto the front page of their local newspaper. And most of these stalwart souls make no concessions to avoid future attacks. They're hard-core nature lovers, outdoorsmen, hunters with a healthy respect for wildlife. I, of course, don't have a pick-up truck to crawl to in the event of an attack, so I won't be counted among these survivors, giving news-paper interviews and showing off my scars.

On the other hand, I never worry about people attacks. I've become adept at finding perfectly hidden camping spots near lakes and streams, where I wash my clothes and skinny-dip before sunset and dinner. This is one of my favorite parts of the day. After hours of riding, my body is sumptuously tired, and the river bathing is a wonderful and necessary rite. Once I'm rejuvenated and almond-fresh with Dr. Bonner's miracle soap, I'm a happy woodland creature, hanging my river-rinsed clothing on bushes or rocks and building my little nest for the night.

But after night descends and I'm in my tent, the bear fears return. One night, perhaps a week into my two-week trial period, I'm camped along an old logging road, far from the nearest town or gas station. For once I've managed to get my rucksack up a tree that's at least twenty feet away from my tent. It's probably midnight and deadly quiet when something brushes the side of my tent. I'm instantly awake, adrenaline surging through my veins, and there's more noise, something's moving around, crackling the underbrush, *circling my tent!* I'm paralyzed, unable to move my arms or legs, to roll over or cover my head in a final, futile act of self-preservation. My body's flooded with fear. *This is it. The bear, the bears… they're finally here.* By now I'm picturing not one bear, but two, possibly three, circling my tent and debating who gets first lunge.

And now there's a new sound: the sound of a zipper opening—the zip of a pannier pocket on my bike, just six feet away! *Bears don't zip: they claw! They rip! It's a person, an intruder, a thief….robbing my saddlebags?* Even in my terror this scenario seems absurd. I have nothing of value except my passport and a few travellers' checks. And bike tools. Why would someone follow me all the way up this desolate mountain road to steal a few bike tools? Then I think: *Someone plans to rape and murder me, and he wants a souvenir before he starts! He's looking for my underwear!*

Over my thudding heart, I hear the sound of rummaging, digging around. More zipping, or rather, unzipping. Frozen in fear, I wait for a knife to slash through my useless tent door, but the rummaging goes on. Time expands as I struggle to move even a finger.

I finally break through the paralysis and feel for my flashlight. The tent door feels far away—I'm lying with my head in the opposite direction—but I manage, in short, jerky spasms, to shimmy my sleeping bag around so I'm facing the door. I'm shaking like an unbalanced washing machine, barely able to hold the flashlight. *If I can just unzip the tent flap three inches and peek out…* My body twitches and seizes with fear, but eventually I get my eyes and my flashlight to a crack in the door and catch the intruder red-handed.

He's scattered my stuff all over the forest floor.

It's an enormous raccoon. The beam of my flashlight bounces off his glassy eyes and for a moment he's paralyzed, too. Then he tries to stare me down. And then he waddles back into the darkness, mission aborted.

It takes a while for the adrenaline to wear off, but by morning, the terrifying episode seems hilarious. I check through my stuff. He didn't take my passport, my checks, or my tools, but he did steal something he must've needed: my emergency candles.

What a dummy. He forgot to take the matches.

A day or two later, I'm riding through a cluster of close mountains, with barely a car in sight. The forest on every side is thick and deep, deep green. There are climbs, plenty of them, and my legs feel strong and invincible. It's a hot June afternoon, but every climb is followed by a delicious, breezy descent. I'm happy to have found such solitude, happy to commune with Jack and let my mind float as I ride without distractions.

And then it happens: Fear Number Two. Midway up a long uphill slope my bike seizes, and I fall sideways into a cement barricade overlooking what appears to be a bottomless drop. A quick inspection indicates the problem is not as simple as a slipped chain; something is dreadfully wrong, and it involves my derailleur, whose name and inner workings represent to me the most inscrutable of mysteries. Suddenly the sun seems unbearably hot. I have no food, barely half a bottle of water, and a tool kit I've barely met. Propping my ailing bike against the barricade, I pull out the bike repair manual I've been meaning to read and try to ignore my panicky heart.

It takes a while to focus, to orient myself to the technical words and diagrams, and it's clear this will be no quick fix. Leaning against the barrier, I empty the kit and arrange the tools in a semi-circle before me. Page one. There ought to be a primer for doofuses who haven't learned the names of tools beyond hammers and screwdrivers. A book for stranded neophytes stuck in the middle of nowhere. A DIY guide for the newly-bereaved, haplessly traveling with ghosts, fears, and magical thinking. But there isn't, so I press on. The pictures are helpful; maybe I can make this work.

Two hours later, I *do* make it work, at least enough to get my bike operative and over the next several hills before a truck finally appears on the lonely road, and I flag the driver down. By now it's getting dark, and I'm afraid my bike will seize again and leave me stranded for the night. My rescuer drives me beyond the first gas station and into the next small town, which, providentially, has a bike shop, an impossibly tiny one that might exist just for me. I'll get my bike professionally tuned in the morning and probably for free, since I'm traveling solo and wearing the cute denim shorts with red trim. It's going to work out, after all.

But the greatest victory is my new-found skill: I *can* learn the art of bicycle maintenance, at least enough to earn some respectability among the bike touring subculture. As the trip progresses, I become adept at fixing flat tires and at removing my chain every week for a cleansing soak in a dime's worth of gasoline, usually while I'm doing my weekly stint at a laundromat and waiting for my silky green parachute to spin clean. I'm not exactly *studying* the bike repair manual in my time off (I prefer to study maps), but at least we've become friendly.

Still, the tests are not over. One morning as I cycle, hitting my stride after a breakfast of bananas and yogurt, I'm suddenly struck with a felling wave of weakness and nausea. Forced to pull over, I huddle with my map by the side of the road, hoping to find a place of refuge nearby. But even if there is a gas station or a rest stop within the next few miles, I can't ride any further. In a daze, I drag my bike into the nearest clump of trees, set up my tent, and crawl in. The sickness intensifies. Shivering like a nearly-drowned kitten, I cry with fever and a searing loneliness. It's nearing noon; the hot sun presses on the roof of the tent, and I picture myself from above, a quivering speck in a yellow dot on a vast planet, lost from sight and bereft of human contact.

And then: a genuine miracle. When my anguish becomes unbearable, I feel the weight and warmth of Jack's body cradle me, spooning me as he did on countless nights, his arms a shield around me, his face nestled in my hair, his breath soft upon my neck. I hear his steady, soothing heartbeat, and his love fills the tent with peace. The visit is so real, so comforting, that I simply accept his presence and fall into a velvet sleep. When I wake up several hours later, the fever is gone, and my heart is full.

I haven't even hit the two-week cut-off, yet most of the fears on my list have reared their fearsome heads and been routed — or at least subdued. I've dealt with illness (twice), headwinds, snowstorms, loneliness, night intruders, and breakdowns. Even my dread of bears has been tamped down, thanks to Rocky Racoon and my new awareness that not every bump in the night is a death knell. Not that I'm any less vulnerable to bear attacks, but still: I've decided to stop letting invisible bears rob me of peace. I may as well worry about being hit by a logging truck, yet I haven`t let that fear hold me back. Surely the divine covering I feel, the umbrella of protection I almost take for granted, doesn't exclude bear attacks from its policy.

A newfound confidence floods me. *I can do this,* I realize. *I can handle whatever comes my way. I can go as long as I want, as far as I want, wherever I want. And I want to keep going and going and going…*

And then, the best realization of all: *I'm having fun!* Strangely enough, I hadn't imagined actually *enjoying* my quest; this was meant to be a serious life test, not a vacation.

In spite of the challenges, or maybe because of them, I'm thriving. I've fallen in love with Montana, with map reading and navigation, with waking up to new scenery every morning, with discovering fresh beauty around each bend of the road. At the start of each day, as I cycle my first five or ten miles, I send up a simple request for the one thing I want that day – perhaps to camp at a lake with a sandy cove, or have a friendly conversation, or find a store with ripe bananas and fresh tomatoes, or stumble across a book that's worth reading. And every day these prayers are answered. I don't ask for mighty things, but the One who's looking out for me invariably delivers, and for that I'm always grateful.

One evening, still in Montana, I'm browsing an old-fashioned general store in search of dinner (the basics: potatoes, tomato juice, carrots, and peanuts-in-the-shell) when I notice a sign for a barn dance that night and decide to go. It starts in an hour. Back at my makeshift campsite, I dig to the bottom of my panniers for party clothes. So far, I've had no occasion to wear my swirly hippie skirt, but now I pull it out, along with my navy-blue tank top and strappy sandals, and head back to town. It's a balmy, starry summer night, perfect for a dancing in a hay-scented barn.

The dance crowd appears to be mostly well-acquainted locals from nearby ranches and towns, and I drift around the outskirts of the hall, apparently sequestered in a no-contact zone marked *outsider*, before spotting two guys at a table who look like outsiders, too. Soon the three of us are sharing beers and taking turns on the dance floor. It's the first time I've danced since the night the Hovel closed, and the most sociable I've felt in months. My new friends are Allan and Phil, both teachers from Seattle, who've been leisurely camping their way across Washington, Idaho, and Montana. Between song sets, they describe the pristine rivers, mountains, trails, and hot springs they've visited, along with the paucity of traffic and other campers. It all sounds amazing. I'm hooked.

We dance till the barn shuts down, then say goodnight. When I return to my tent, I pull out my flashlight and map for a closer look. I've fallen in love with Montana's Bitterroot Mountains and don't want to leave. If I head west from here instead of south, I'll get more of these untouched, mid-range mountains and all the perks my friends have mentioned: hot springs, seclusion, and just enough tiny towns along the way to keep me fed and watered. And if I keep going, I'll reach the Pacific Ocean. I flash back to the transcendent hours I spent at the beach in La Jolla, waiting for Jack's futile medical appointment in Mexico to finish, and my mind is set: West it is, and to the sea!

Plus, Allan has given me his number in Seattle. We talked easily that night, and before parting, he used a cool word to describe what he thinks we have: an *affinity*. It's enticing to have a destination with an actual person in port, especially one who'll be surprised and delighted when I show up. As far as he knows, I'm still enroute to Colorado.

Later, I'll wrestle with how casually I scrapped my original plan of completing Jack's trip. Did it matter if I made it to Boulder? In some ways, changing my route seemed dishonoring, after all, I was supposed to be following the hand drawn yellow line, yet Jack also delighted in spontaneity and being open to the winds of fate. And now that I was in the flow, traveling solo the way I imagined he had, my final destination seemed inconsequential. I knew Jack would be proud of what I'd already accomplished, of how I'd imitated his resilient spirit and found my own. Now I was ready to venture wherever my open map beckoned.

After all, that was how Jack had traveled his entire brief, amazing, and unconventional life.

The westward route is as pristine as Allan and Phil had described, and I pedal through Idaho and Washington at a tranquil pace, marveling at the endless, rolling mountains, and amazed that someone's named a town in a blistering corner of Idaho *Moscow*—a hot, baking town, the most un-Russian place I can imagine. I feel a comforting connection to these forests and valleys; unlike the Rockies, the blanketed Bitterroot and Cascade Mountains are breathtaking without being overwhelming. I feel safe, at peace in these valleys and mountain passes. Even the weather is temperate and calm, at least till I reach the scorching high desert of eastern Washington, and suddenly find myself in landscape that resembles the lifeless, pocked face of the moon. Even this, for a brief time, is beguiling.

Most of the time, I feel luckier, fitter and far more attuned to the sights and smells of my surroundings than the passengers rushing by in air-conditioned cars. Bicycle touring is the ultimate way to travel: You can clock a good distance every day at a speed that lets you interact with nature, people, sky, and whatever else grabs your attention along the way. At the right pace, you'll slip into a meditative space that dispels worry and negativity. You can sing all day, or write books and letters in your head, or let your becalmed mind effortlessly carry you back and forth in time. You'll feel your lungs, heart, and muscles strum with vitality. At night, you'll sleep the best sleep of your life; by day, you'll breathe the freshest air (provided you stay clear of cities and big highways) and learn the joy of eating to fuel a happy body. Life is immediate, close, just the right size. You can ride as fast or as slow as your body dictates, and, when you stop for the night, be as lazy or exploratory as you please. Best of all, you can do all this on a shoestring budget, so several hundred dollars will carry you far.

But there *was* one day during this interlude when I felt like a fool for opting to travel by bike. That was the blistering hot afternoon I cycled above the canyon of the Wawa River, looking down on scores, maybe hundreds, of rubber rafters and tubers making their way down the same course to the sea, but languidly, floating in the cool waters of the river and flanked by the shade of its steep canyon walls. This time they were the ones who got it right, and I the idiot, courting heat stroke, sunburn and dehydration as I doggedly pedalled above them, steeped in a rare fit of envy.

But that day was an exception, and the green in my heart dissolved as soon as the sun started its western slip and dusk turned the cooling highway pink.

21

Entangled

W hen I reach Seattle, Allan is as surprised and delighted to see me as I'd hoped. We spend the first evening at his house, hot tubbing with several out-of-town friends who are also spending the night. I end up sleeping in Allan's bedroom, partly by default and partly by choice. My longing to be cuddled leads to heartbreaking sex, and I'm not expecting the cathartic emotions that follow. I need too much, and this schoolteacher I barely know can't possibly provide it. Still, I decide to stick around to see where things go. I've recklessly thrown my heart at him, as well as my body, because I've never learned how to separate the two.

Allan suggests a backpacking trip, a five-day immersion into the coastal mountains together, and this seems like a way to be close, to find some of the emotional connection I've been craving. But I end up more empty than full: we have some good moments, interspersed with moments when I want to run away. But where can you escape on a wilderness backpacking trip? This disconnect is not his fault. He treats me gently, as if I'm a battered child, but I'm entangled in my longing for

Jack, and Allan's failure to be who I really want only stirs my emptiness. By the time we hike back out, the relationship has run its course.

I phone Gwen in Edmonton, my ever-devoted friend, who offers to meet me in San Francisco. She knows I need her: someone who knows me so well, who deeply loved Jack and watched my relationship with him unfold from its inception, and who knows how much I've lost, how much we've all lost.

To get there in time, I plan to hitchhike to California with my bike, but Allan, always kind, offers to drive me. Still, the only way I can bear to spend twelve more hours with him is by getting high. His presence is fraught now with personal reproach; I'm appalled at how quickly I landed in his bed, how quickly I moved, or tried to move on, from Jack. Somehow, somewhere, I find some LSD to take on the drive down; such tickets to escape are available whenever I need them, though I can't remember now how I found them. I drop the acid as soon as we get in the car, and let Allan deliver me safely to Gwen.

My friend is more than a breath of fresh air: she's a wind of renewal. We explore San Francisco on foot, hoofing miles between its fabled markets, parks, bridges, and piers. We talk for three days straight, only stopping to stuff ourselves with fresh seafood and French bread. We've also made plans with Jerry, Jack's youngest brother, who's bringing the dreaded catamaran to meet us; he wants to take us to Catalina Island. This is a good and terrible plan. I don't know how I'll handle these recent reminders of Jack. But when Jerry arrives, he's cleaned up the boat, and the stench of decay has faded. The credit cards, too, are gone from the burl table.

I spend most of my time on deck, avoiding memories of being with Jack in the hold, of watching him slip away from me in a morphine haze. The ocean air is warm and intoxicating, and Catalina Island in 1978 is exotic and sparsely populated. But Jerry's physical resemblance to Jack unnerves me. I can almost find Jack in Jerry's embrace, and this confuses both of us. The days are haunted by Jack's absence, but we cannot speak of him directly. He's the link between all three of us, and he's close, yet achingly out of reach. In the end, it seems we're drawn to the same coping strategy: we drop acid together and spend a surreal day hiking the scorched hills of Catalina.

This is the last time I'll ever see Jerry. His perilous attraction to scamming, to scoring quick money so he can live for months on a beach in Maui, will land him in maximum-security prison before the year is out. He's a little bit like Jack, and a lot like his father.

After Gwen and Jerry leave, I decide to head north on my bike through northern California and then along the Oregon coast. Within hours of leaving the city, I meet Frank, who's biking in the same direction. Frank looks like something hatched in a wheat field: he's utterly organic, from his flaxen hair and glowing skin to his gunny-sack shorts, homemade sandals, and the bag of sprouts he's growing on the back of his bike. He preaches the gospel of purity: a raw food diet and strident eschewal of all things processed, packaged, and normal. I learn this about him right away. But he seems harmless enough. We agree to ride together for the day and see if our paces match. They do. At nightfall, we pitch our tents side by side and share a campfire. Of course, I'm the only one using the fire to cook, and Frank continues to preach as he masticates a gloopy concoction of oats, nuts and seeds, soaked in water and sun-percolated all day on the back of his bike.

Frank's personal life is as unadulterated as the wild grapes we pick along the way. He avoids all contaminants, including women, citing a painful breakup several years back. That's fine with me. He's my first riding companion since Jack, and even though we're both tentative—each day is a test, we're on a trial basis—we eventually commit to an open-ended riding partnership, no schedule and no strings attached. He's a very safe choice: I know I'll never be physically attracted, because something about his squeaky-clean body scent, to say nothing of his extreme food doctrines, turns me off. As for Frank, he seems to view me as a project or a possible convert (my body is *almost perfect,* if only my bottom were *just a little slimmer,* he tells me, after cycling behind said bottom for several hours and sizing me up), but for him my body measurements are about objective aesthetics, not sex appeal. After a few days, he lightens up on preaching and accepts the obvious: I'm in great shape and excellent riding condition, despite my cooked vegetables and morning coffee.

We've both been dreaming about cycling through ancient redwood forests, and as we pedal the inland route through Northern California, the trees get bigger and thicker. On a splendid summer afternoon, we ride through the continent's largest, oldest trees: the Avenue of the Giants. I feel sorry for the deprived tourists who drive through the Avenue in cars, missing the dappled, scented, slower absorption that Frank and I enjoy. It's the moment in our travels when I'm most in synch with Frank; we both know everything about this afternoon is perfect, and we can't stop grinning and raising our arms as we ride.

When we get to Oregon, it's warm enough to sleep on the beach under the stars, until the night we reach Astoria and nasty weather sends us to a motel. This turn of events is so out of character for Frank that he becomes unhinged. We go to a diner and he orders *pasta,* not salad, and then buys a bottle of wine to drink in our room. Something tells me this is a bad idea. I haven't touched alcohol for weeks, and for someone as distilled as Frank, the wine will be poison. But, as is my typical wimpy way with men, I go along with it. It takes only a glass or two to awaken his long-dormant sex drive, and I spend the next two hours scooting around the room and fending him off until he finally throws up in the bathroom and passes out.

In the morning, he's deeply ashamed—for the pasta as much as the passes—and can barely meet my eye. Our companionable, uncomplicated partnership is over. We part ways quickly, without exchanging hugs, addresses, or even last names.

And this changes my direction. Because Frank is riding north and I'm afraid of crossing paths with him again, I turn around and head south. This time I'll take the coastal highway all the way back and follow the California coast to Baja.

At least, that's what I'm *planning* to do.

The next leg of my journey features the letter P. Shortly after parting with Frank, I meet a cyclist named Peter from St. Petersburg. He's as placid as Florida is flat, but pretty to look at, and companionable. Our paces match. We share a campfire and, then a sleeping bag. I can project whatever personality I want onto him, and his passivity absorbs and reflects it back. It's a strange interlude, a petit-romance with a cipher. We pedal the spectacular coastal highway towards Petaluma, distant and close, loving and detached. Pleasantly, the nights and days with Peter pass: fourteen in all.

In Petaluma we meet another cyclist named Paul. Paul is a physical, passionate, possibly bipolar man. He's also eighteen years my senior. Paul proposes we all go to a dance that night, and we do. I dance with Peter, and then I dance with Paul. Peter is languid on the dance floor, but Paul dances with a crazy, kinetic energy and we are perfectly out of synch. He is not my type, will never be my type, but I like his potent energy. The three of us spend a second day together, and we get to talking. Paul wants to pedal the desert from the Bay Area to El Paso, Texas, where his sister lives. I decide I'd like to cross the desert, too, and visit the other Peter, Jack's old friend, in Phoenix. Cycling the desert, a whole new world for me, is suddenly feasible with a riding partner. Peter stays the course, south instead of southeast, and rides off without me. Not gladly.

Goodbye, Peter. Hello, Paul.

The two of us cycle back up the coast to Paul's place to prepare for the desert trip. He lives in the hills above Gualala, a tiny dot on the map about 130 miles north of San Francisco. Paul is a self-employed carpenter, a lumberjack, a fisherman, and a frustrated musician. He's built himself a three-story redwood chalet with band-sawed lumber and stained-glass windows, much of the material recovered from building relics and the rocky coves below Highway 1. He's also converted an old camper into a split-level treehouse tucked into a redwood near the house.

Paul is a cross between a Highlander and a Viking; he's muscular and agile, with a full beard and flowing auburn hair that encircles his bald pate. His blue eyes are sad and perceptive, childlike and ageless, reflecting his life so far, a saga of mixed and thwarted dreams. Like the nascent projects resting in his yard—driftwood, burls, bottles and other treasures salvaged from the sea—his mind teems with possibilities, tangents, and projections. Perhaps I'm the next project. I sense all this, but I don't go running for the hills.

After all, he's not my type. And he's so much older, almost my father's age.

It takes time for Paul to get ready. Meanwhile, there are nights in the treehouse under the stars. There's hot, sweet cinnamon tea and candlelight; buttery fresh mussels from the ocean and the Grateful Dead after we've eaten; long conversations and slowing down. There's a foot massage that doesn't stop at my feet.

And just before we're ready to leave, there's a phone call. His mother has been diagnosed with Stage Four cancer. Instead of heading straight to the desert, we'll cycle to Marin County to visit her and Paul's father first.

In the course of our relationship, Paul and I will end up cycling the 130 miles between Gualala and San Francisco many times. But this is my first visit to Paul's childhood home, where a booby-trapped relationship with his father still lingers. Paul is forty, his father in his seventies, yet the conflict feels ageless and intractable. His mother's illness has heightened the tension. And then there's the girl Paul's brought with him: his father is incredulous. I look sixteen, not twenty-two, even younger than Paul's teen-aged daughters. It's my first exposure to how our relationship will be perceived by almost everyone we meet. Paul is nine inches taller, almost twice my body weight, and, despite his vigor, seems to visibly carry the cargo of a lifetime in every pore. I'm a young Dorian Gray, my sorrows still hidden. As a couple, we probably look like an abduction in progress, and if we'd been traveling in the age of cell phones, sightings of possible kidnapper and missing teen would've lit up hotlines wherever we went.

But Paul's mother, fragile and translucent, looks into my eyes and loves me. *Paul and Marilyn,* she intones, *Marilyn and Paul.* She seems relieved that her son has found a sweetheart, a companion, someone to be there for him after she's gone. She clasps my sun-browned hands in her pale, dying ones, and gives me her benediction.

But she's not finished with life just yet; there'll be some last-ditch chemotherapy, just in case. Everyone hopes for a miracle, Paul most of all.

Go, she tells us. *Take your trip across the desert. Enjoy yourselves! I'll be fine.* We believe what rests easier on the heart, and cycle off.

As we head from the sea towards Stockton, the coastal green melts quickly into brown and gold. With every mile, the road takes us deeper into arid farmland fed by wide irrigation ditches, dark little rivers that tempt me to abandon my bike and plunge in as the heat rises, and then the road climbs into fragrant golden hills adorned with emerald cotton-woods—perhaps my favorite scenery. We ride into Yosemite National Park, not yet overrun by tourists and trailers, but home to summer-long hikers and hippies.

We spend a few days hiking with the hippies before cruising out of Yosemite and into the Sierras on Paul's fortieth birthday. Forty seems ancient to me, and I spend much of that day riding behind Paul, contemplating his bald spot, burnished by the sun, wondering how I've landed with a man nearly twice my age. I'll wonder that often. On this day, however, my thoughts towards Paul are tender. Before long we're clearly in the desert, joining the dust-cracked trucks that service scrappy, sun-baked towns—Visalia, Bakersfield, Tehachapi—squatting in the desert like sullen stones.

In Barstow, we have a bitter argument—over what? —and part ways, only to turn back and reconnect before we've lost each other for good in the tumbleweed wasteland. In fact, we argue often, pulling and resisting each other, though looking back I can't remember what triggers these spats.

Our connection is like the desert, beguiling and dangerous, beautiful and harsh. We spend balmy, peaceful nights under the stars, only to be attacked on other nights by vicious red ants that slip into our saddlebags and torment us for weeks. We wake to clear mornings, in love with the purple desert as we brew our cowboy coffee and watch the wasteland come alive, only to hate it by noon as the sun leaches the color from the hills and the lift from our bones. By evening, the sizzling roads begin to cool, and we swerve to avoid large clusters of tarantulas that scuttle across the highway at witching hour. The spiders are exotic, of a piece; the desert is mysterious and beautiful again.

Perhaps it's the desert that's tearing us apart. More likely, it's my ambivalence over being with Paul in the first place. I do and don't envision a future with him, but he's a romantic dreamer; he's written me into the next chapters of his life and we're in deep. My thoughts of Jack are packed away, like emergency supplies in the bottom of my panniers, silently awaiting my return.

Like most escapist long-distance cyclists, we avoid all major highways, taking the slower routes along backroads and blue highways. In the desert, these byways are empty of cars and commerce, except for the occasional truck and far-flung gas station. The longest of these stretches is an eighty-mile slice of nothing between Twenty-Nine Palms and the next water tap, a tiny dot on the map marked *Rice*.

That morning, we start the trek early, loading as much extra water in plastic milk jugs as our bikes will carry, and trying to not think about distance or thirst. If unlimited water was available, I'd drink many gallons a day; I sweat that much. By midday it's pushing 103 degrees; I take off my shirt and ride topless, attempting to let every possible inch of skin feel the hot breeze my movement is generating. We see two cars that day. The precious water we're rationing gets hotter and hotter as the sun steals back every sip we drink.

By early evening, we reach Rice: one working gas pump and a decrepit white shack posing as a gas station. At least there's a water tap here, with more tepid water before it finally runs cool. We're parched and exhausted, but proud of ourselves, and an acknowledgment of our accomplishment, a simple pat on the back by an appreciative observer, would be nice. We get nothing. The leathery proprietor, lone inhabitant of Rice, curls his lip and spits before commenting on our journey.

That's nothing, he drawls. *Why, I been so thirsty once, I drunk water from a cow pie!*

He spits again, then shuffles back inside his shack and shuts off the lights.

At last, there's an oasis. We reach the Arizona border and find plenty of water at man-made Lake Havasu, where we camp for two days to soak ourselves in its cool blue waters. London Bridge has been dismantled and replanted here, but we don't visit. We're here for the lake. The sun and the water knock me out, and as I sleep on warm slabs of granite, Paul takes black and white photos of me lying face down on a towel. I'm as brown as a succulent raisin and perfectly proportioned. Frank, I'm sure, would approve of my tanned svelteness.

We make it to Phoenix. It's been five months since Jack's final night on earth, the night we flew from his desert city back to Edmonton. I don't call Peter until the day before we arrive; I'm anxious about introducing Paul, my new partner, to Jack's oldest friend, and especially so soon after Jack's death. As I expect, Peter is skeptical of my new relationship, and throughout the first day he keeps shooting me quizzical looks. But by the second day, Peter and Paul are laughing like good friends, and a week later, as we're leaving, Peter gives me his brotherly blessing.

He's nothing like Jack, he says, *and that's a good thing. I couldn't take it if you were trying to replace him. You never could, we both know that. But Paul's a good man— I like him. He's got a lot of character, a lot of insight, and he's interesting.*

I take this as a good sign and resolve to stop fighting with Paul, if I can just get a handle on those sneaky triggers.

From Phoenix we ride south to the Wild West town of Tombstone, Arizona. Jack would've loved this slice of history, and maybe he *did* spend time here, years ago. Being in his home state immerses me into Jack's recollections of early days, and I try to connect the scenes he shared with the surreal landscape we're cycling through. I want to see more of it, maybe head north to Flagstaff and the Grand Canyon, but this is a shared venture, and our fixed destination is El Paso.

We head further south, lingering for a week in Bisbee, an old mining town near the Mexican border that's been resurrected by an infusion of hippies and artisans. The tourists haven't found it yet. We make instant friends and go dancing, and for a few days we imagine casting our lot among these fellow eccentrics and joining their hermitage. Our age difference doesn't bother anyone here. The town's been carved into the hills, a series of narrow footpaths dotted with tiny patios, potted cacti, and colorful pottery. It makes me think of burros, llamas, and the Peru I have yet to reach.

Paul finds a shortcut on the map, an off-road alternate that follows an arm of the San Pedro River for a while. It's impossible to resist the prospect of finding water in the desert. We trade the paved blue highway for a dusty sand track full of sheep's head thorns. There's no one, not a car, not a soul, along this stretch. But after a few days of too many flat tires, we're dismayed to see that the river, a last-leg trickle at best, has vanished altogether. It's too sandy to pedal our bikes, but also too late to turn back, so for two days we walk along the cracked riverbed, dragging our bikes through piles of billowy sand.

On the second day we come across basins of soft, black, slippery mud in the parched riverbed, like huge bowls of silky chocolate pudding. Casting off our dust-baked clothes, we jump in the mud and spend the afternoon slipping, sliding, and rolling around like baby seals until we're spent. Luckily there's a tiny trickle of fresh water nearby, the last lickings of the expired San Pedro, and we take turns rinsing the mud off our bodies, one mucky inch at a time. This afternoon is lightning in a bottle, a once-in-a-lifetime fiesta, and surely we're the only people on earth lucky enough to discover this velvety mudtopia, miles from everywhere.

Further down the riverbed, our luck turns, or maybe it holds. The next afternoon we're lying on our stomachs, half-hidden by thin willows, consulting the map before pitching our tent for the night. Suddenly there's a gun over our heads, and a fat, surly man attached to it. He wastes no words. *F***ing wetbacks! What the f*** are you doing on my land!*

We're too stunned to move. There's no one else around, no witnesses, and this guy is seriously xenophobic. Two bullets and he could climb back into his pickup truck and disappear. But my sun-bleached hair—and Paul's startled blue eyes— must tip him off: We're not illegal Mexicans, but something far less credible. After a closer look, he backs off without a word and drives away, leaving us collapsed over the open map. Thank God we're not refugees: it would've been *Adios,* with barely a trace of our passing once the vultures finished picking our bones.

We leave the mystique of Arizona for the plain roads of southern New Mexico. This desert seems scrubby, monochromatic, and tedious. Maybe it's just the route we've taken. Or maybe we've already seen enough tumbleweed and desiccated roadkill to last a lifetime. We push ourselves to ride longer and faster; now the journey is grunt work, and Paul is anxious to see Susan, his sister in El Paso. They've never been close, but now, with their mother dying, he thinks they ought to try.

The El Paso we end up visiting has neither charm nor mystique. Susan lives on a dreary, sun-bleached military base, and she's the prosaic and conservative opposite of her brother. She also seems a bit slow. She's much older than I, but she reminds me of a little cousin, latching onto me with a transparent fascination that embarrasses Paul. We spend a day across the border in Juarez, where I eat the worst Mexican food of my life as we're serenaded by braying mariachis. It's my first and only visit to Mexico.

When we get back to Susan's from Juarez, there's a message from Paul's father: the chemotherapy has failed, and their mother is declining fast. We ought to get back there, pronto. Susan can't—or won't—make the trip now, but we'll deliver her love in the rented car that whisks us back across the desert in its hard metal shell.

22

Stem, Seeds, and All

I t's way too soon to be back on a cancer ward. As we enter, I'm assailed by the familiar smell of sickness mixed with disinfectant and over-steamed hospital food. I want to run; I don't know if I can do this again. But Paul needs me, and so I will. I push the panic down.

His mother is feather-light, numinous, and strangely joyful. She's a believer, but I also sense a disappointment in the way her life's turned out that readies her for heaven. Paul's father, on the other hand, is locked in a grim psychic fortress, walled off from everyone. He's angry, aloof. It's not his mother or father who'll need carrying, but Paul, still wrestling with childhood demons and terrified of being left alone with his cantankerous, impossible to please parent.

And so I wait again for death. Each time we visit the hospital, Paul's mother is closer to the angels, farther from us. Paul and his father bicker and spar over nothing and everything. We stay at his parents' house, where he and I sort through cupboards and organize his mother's kitchen, stuffed with the clutter of thirty years. In the process, we uncover hundreds and hundreds of empty, stacked Cool-Whip containers stashed not only in the kitchen but throughout the house. We stuff them into jumbo garbage bags, incredulous at his mother's bizarre hoarding. The Cool Whip gives Paul a perfect target for his rage. All those gallons and gallons of fake, chemical poison: How could they *not* have killed her?

She doesn't last long. This time there's an actual funeral in a church, with hymns and a convoy of cars to an actual gravesite, followed by glutinous casseroles and jellied salads: all the things Jack refused to let us do for him. I wonder, as I will for years to come, whether overruling his final request would have given me even a little closure. But I don't think it would have, as I was deep in my bubble, guarding my heart, even before he died. And I must still be in it, because the grief swirling around Paul's family doesn't trigger my own avalanche of grief. My avalanche will come, but not for a long, long time.

After the funeral, I'm compelled to stay. How can I leave a shattered man, reeling from his mother's death and his father's rejection, especially in the grip of a gloomy northern California winter? At this point, I'm convinced I've been brought into Paul's life for this very purpose. He *needs* me. Besides, his mother's haunting words won't leave me: *Paul and Marilyn, Marilyn and Paul.* How can I betray a sweet, dead woman's dying wishes, knowing her son has no one to fall back on? There's no discussion. We move back to Gualala and look for ways to earn grocery money and fill the silent, rainy hours inside Paul's lonesome coastal outpost.

The house is an extension of its builder: a wonder of hardscrabble creativity and craftsmanship. Every foot of it was built by hand and fuelled by grief—the way Paul's traveled life—and it's a remarkable amalgamation of salvaged beams and redwood. The ceilings are high, the rooms expansive. It smells of wood smoke and forest. But there's barely any furniture, no radio or TV. There's no sofa, nothing soft except the mattress and two pillows we share on the third floor. Most of our time is spent in the kitchen, where we make coffee and soup on the wood stove. The entire second floor is empty, except for a few boxes of old books and magazines, and in the chilly afternoons I wrap myself in an old blanket and dig through the boxes for something to read. *Stranger in a Strange Land*, *Desert Solitaire*, stacks of the National Geographic magazines I've missed since reading in my grandparents' basement as a child. When I finish the contents, I start over.

Paul's lot is halfway up a steep ridge that climbs darkly from the ocean, and the house is camouflaged by giant trees. Other homes hide in the forest, scattered along the gravel road that winds from the highway to our quarters and on to the top of the ridge, but they're like distant forts, silent and self-contained. People move here to escape the hustle of California cities, to escape *people*. We could be anywhere on the planet, stuck inside these empty rooms, nursing our private griefs.

I still have some travel money waiting for me in a Canadian bank, but we're living hand-to-mouth, the way Paul's lived since he gave up a business career, his *Brooks Brother's Days* he calls them, to follow his inner rebel. He's a huge Edward Abbey fan, and would probably be happiest blowing up dams and pipelines in the name of eco-terrorism. Some days he finds local work, building decks or chicken coops, and I tag along, passing him tools and nails as he decries the evils of corporate greed and Cool Whip. But most of our income comes from fishing, and fishing becomes my great escape.

Every morning I fix binoculars on the sea from our third-floor window, hoping for one thing: no whitecaps. Whitecaps mean wind, and wind means no fishing; a stormy sea could easily swamp our aluminum rowboat. There are more white days than blue ones, and on no-go mornings it's only the promise of coffee that gets me out of bed and into the hours waiting to be filled.

Fishing days are purposeful. We climb into Paul's red pick-up and drive to town for fish bait—a plastic tub of slimy calamari—and a bag of unshelled peanuts. Not far from town, there's a secret, unused cove where we launch the boat. Paul rows us past Sea Lion Island, an enormous splodge of brown rocks resembling giant turds, where we linger to watch hundreds of fat, barking sea lions lolling on the rocks or rolling in the deep. But these are their fishing grounds; we need to find our own. We row out farther.

Once we think we've found the spot, Paul baits the hooks—because the calamari repulses me—and after we catch our first small sea bass or snapper, he cuts off its head to use as bait for larger fish. While we fish, I munch on peanuts, tossing the shells overboard and waiting for the next *thunk* of a pulled line. The fish surrender themselves from the seabed like adults in a children's game of hide and seek. Most of them are fat and fleshy. On a good day, we catch a dozen.

Paul loads the calamari, but I clean the fish. There's something primal and satisfying about scaling and decapitating clobbered fish before slicing them into tidy fillets and sliding the final product into clear plastic bags. There's a dog on Paul's property, and she hovers nearby as I slit the fish from end to end, scooping the guts into a metal bucket. Afterwards I'll boil the heads and entrails just for her. We sell the fillets from door-to-door, three dollars a pound. Paul drives me round to our regular customers, the other hermits in the woods, and I knock on new doors seeking more. I'm the official face of the company now, and sales are up. It seems we're the only local fishermen.

We eat some of our catch, but I'm even more partial to the deep purple mussels we scrape off sea rocks and drown in garlicky butter. I also sauté thick, black seaweed with onions, carrots, and soy sauce, make yogurt in jars near the stove, and grow sprouts in big pickle jars by the kitchen sink. These provisions, along with homemade soup, form the basis of our diet for months on end.

After months of cycling, followed by the physical inertia of waiting for Paul's mother to die, I'm restless, inside and out, and I take to running a steep red clay trail that climbs a mile and a half to the top of the ridge, often running it twice in succession. As winter progresses, the muddy trail gets slippery and treacherous, but even on rainy days I run. The workout, the deep breathing and tough push to the summit, keeps me sane.

To deal with his grief, Paul has taken to nightly drinking and piano playing. He's loaned his piano to a neighbor down the road and now he borrows it back, hammering at the keys in the shed where she keeps it, and downing a bottle of wine. If I walk ten minutes up the road, I can hear him. He's a tortured soul, a phantom of the opera, and the feverish playing unsettles me. I've also never had a boyfriend who drinks alone, and this, in itself, is scary. I refuse to drink with him, hoping to discourage the habit, but this only leaves him with more for himself. At least he's an anguished drunk, not a mean one.

To fill the days, I start writing daily letters to Jerry, Jack's brother, incarcerated in Chico for crimes he won't disclose. It's a two-mile walk to the post office, mostly through forest and then along the highway into town, and I walk it quickly, hoping each day that the box won't be empty. There's usually a fat, meandering letter awaiting me. Jerry's writing reflects his state of mind: disjointed, fanciful, obscure. He shares next to nothing about prison life, and neither of us writes of Jack—at least, not directly. The correspondence must be saturated with loss, but we don't see it: we're both running from our pain and amusing each other with whatever humor we can distill from our trapped, shadowy half-lives.

The months drip by. Paul and I attempt to socialize with neighbors, but it's awkward; our blatant age difference puts people off, and we stop trying. Or maybe our psychic pain is too visible. By May, I'm drowning in sadness and pointlessness, but frozen in place; I can't envision a way forward, a way out. So once again I drop some LSD. I take it on a brilliant summer day by the hidden banks of the Gualala River, where I can swim and sprawl in the sand, completely alone. The trip is good; it brings me back to myself, back to the girl who was enjoying her bike trip, riding mindlessly with low-maintenance Peter, before falling into this latest vale of grief. I decide it's time to start riding again.

When I tell Paul my plans, he latches on: Maybe we can ride together to Alberta. He's always wanted to go to Canada (doesn't everyone?), and now he proposes we go and meet my parents. I say yes, because I don't want to hurt him or spark a scene, but inside I'm screaming. He's woven me into his future, but I can't meet him there. I have to get away.

A few long day rides will get me ready for touring, solo or not, so I start with a thirty-mile loop to Point Arena. It's a hot, hilly slog after months of not riding. I'm resting in the shade on Main Street, munching an apple, when I spot two cyclists with loaded bikes lounging on the other side of the street. I wave and cross the road, cyclist to cyclist.

Hey, where're you riding? Where're you from?

Both guys look miserable, and they eyeball me like I'm a freak. Something's up—or down—with these two.

Um, to Washington?

Yeah? And where'd you start?

They glance at each other to see who'll deign to talk to me. The brown-haired guy wearing wire rim glasses musters a thin smile.

Los Angeles. But we're from New York. What about you? You're taking a little ride around town?

He glances across the street at my uncool, luggage-free Apollo bike, propped against a street pole. Over the winter, Paul decided to repaint the frame, and now it's hunter green, and even less impressive. Both cyclists have mistaken me for a local, and (I'll learn later) a fifteen-year-old at most.

I press on.

Actually, I'm on a day ride from Gualala. You must've passed through there today; that's where I've been living lately. But I'm getting ready for another bike trip, probably to Colorado. I haven't really decided yet, but I've already ridden a lot of the coast.

I watch their faces slide from disinterest to attention. The other guy, who's sporting a long black ponytail and cornflower-blue eyes behind bookish spectacles, stops staring into space and gives me a closer look.

Yeah? Where else have you been?

And so we do the bike talk. I tell them about the east coast trip with Jack, and my forays in the northwest, and about the desert trip. And about this strange, souring relationship I need to leave. When I finish, ponytail guy—whose name is Ron—asks for my apple core and pops the whole thing—stem, seeds and all—into his mouth. It's a weirdly intimate act.

They tell me about their trip so far. About fighting headwinds all the way up the coast and hating it. About getting so sick of each other they're both ready to pack it in. How this trip's been nothing like the adventure they started planning two years ago, and about the discussion they were having when I interrupted: how they were going to find the nearest Greyhound station, box their bikes, head back east, and possibly never speak to each other again. And then, of course, more bitching about headwinds and how utterly miserable bike touring has turned out to be.

It's true: riding the Pacific coast from south to north is the much harder way to go. It's a pity no one told them this ahead of time, but this is the seventies, when bike tips come by word of mouth or not at all. I talk about the best riding I've done so far, through the stunning mountains and valleys of the northwest, and speculate on riding east through Oregon and beyond. And within minutes of meeting, we've hatched a plan. We'll all change course and start a whole new trip together.

This is the plan: Ron and Jeff will battle the wind a few more days and wait for me in Eugene. As soon as they get there, they'll send a postcard to General Delivery at the main post office, telling me where to find them. Meanwhile, I'll make the break from Paul and get there right behind them. They agree to wait a set number of days and if I don't show, it means I've changed my mind. But I'm not going to change my mind. Making urgent plans with riders who are counting on me is my ticket out.

I ride back to Gualala and tell Paul my plans, intimating we could still reconnect at some indefinite time and ride on to Alberta. I have no romantic designs on my new riding partners, having merely found a quick, time-sensitive way to get out of Dodge. Paul is disappointed, but he's just found some long-term carpentry work and needs the cash, so our nebulous plans will have to do. Besides, even in the throes of his own misery, he probably knows it's time to set this thrashing lovebird free.

I start organizing my gear, but within hours of our discussion, I fall suddenly, dreadfully ill. For two days I languish on the third floor, feverish and weak, unable to formulate a coherent thought. Still, I'm aware that I'm late for my rendezvous and that my rescuers will leave if I don't make it in time. It seems I'm doomed to die or remain trapped forever in this house of grief.

On the third night, the sickness lifts and I scramble to leave in the morning. I'm spent and pale and utterly determined to go. Paul agrees to drive me sixty miles up the road to make up for lost time, and we heave my loaded bike into his pick-up. Along the way we spin a comforting fantasy of cycling the Canadian Rockies in the fall, softening our breakup into a brief hiatus. When we reach the drop-off point, Paul parks the truck and leads me into the woods. He wants to make love one last time. With equal measures of pity and guilt, I surrender, but my mind is already sprinting towards Eugene, trying to catch up.

The next few days are rough. After months of living in the redwoods, I'm not used to the highway sun, and by the time I reach Eugene I'm aching with sunburn and road fatigue. My fingers, clenching the handlebars as I cycle against time like a madwoman, are red claws; my back howls with pain when I finally disembark. But I've made it. The deadline was yesterday, but I'm hoping Ron and Jeff will have sensed I'm on my way and waited an extra day.

But now there's a bigger problem: it's Saturday. I was counting on the post office being open all day, but it's closed till Monday.

I spend two dejected days roaming the streets of Eugene, hoping to catch sight of my new friends. Where do I even start? They could be anywhere in this college city. My sunburn howls and I'm hollowed from overexertion. In my weakened state, it seems imperative to find Ron and Jeff, as if I've never cycled solo before. I'm like a lone playing card, loosened from the deck and worthless on my own.

I'm at the post office as soon as it opens on Monday and the postcard is waiting for me, along with the address they promised. Ron and Jeff write that they've met some locals and plan to stay with them till Friday morning—three days ago. I get directions from the postmaster and race across town, hoping against hope they're still around.

On a leafy green street, I find the little bungalow, and *hallelujah!* There they are in the front yard, loading their bikes with the same glum faces they wore in Point Arena, until they look up and see me, and now they're grinning and hooting my name: *Marilyn!!* We're hugging and jumping around the yard, and I tell them about my strange sickness and the closed post office, and how badly I hoped they'd still be here. Ron tells me how Jeff kept wanting to leave, and even this morning was pushing to hit the road early, not expecting me to show, and how Ron had thrown the I Ching three times over the past three days, each time getting the *same hexagram, the Marrying Maiden*, and how this so-called *coincidence* was mind-boggling, because there are 64 possible hexagrams in the I Ching, and the odds of getting the same one even *twice* in a row are slim. Jeff confirms this is all true, that he watched Ron throw the sticks and get the Marrying Maiden each time, and he admits to being astonished yet faithless in the face of uncanny oracular evidence. As

Ron intuited, I *was* on my way, and now we're all delighted to hit the road together. It's clearly meant to be.

And the magic continues. Together, the three of us have great chemistry, and we're in high spirits as we cycle across Oregon, and I'm thinking this might, in fact, be my favorite state in the Union so far. The weather is perfect, and there are natural swimming holes and warm, secluded places to camp at the end of each day. Ron and Jeff are singers, and at night we sit around the campfire and teach each other rounds, stopping from time to time to share a single pipe of apple-scented tobacco. By day we catch trout and forage for wild strawberries, fiddleheads, and mint. We crack each other up. It's the most childlike I've felt in years, maybe ever, even with the pipe smoking.

Ron and Jeff are Brown University alumni, and they're both following a guru from India, a Baba somebody-or-other who's coming to New York in late July to meet his American disciples. Their plan is to gradually wend their way back east in time for his visit. I've dissolved the bad blood between them and transformed their journey, and now they're convinced I ought to meet Baba, too. Since I haven't been able to shake their miraculous account of the Marrying Maiden turning up three times, I figure there must be something deeper going on. Ron tells me about being in India with Baba, and his face glows. The grainy looking photo of an unkempt Indian senior doesn't speak to *me*, but Ron is sure that when I meet Baba, I'll *know*.

Somewhere in the middle of Idaho, my relationship with Ron turns romantic. Now we're sharing my tent, dancing to Muzak in the aisles of small-town grocery stores, and nuzzling each other at every rest stop. Naturally, this changes our group dynamic. Jeff has a girlfriend in New York, and after a week or two of watching us moon about, he decides to end the trip and fly home to his sweetheart. We'll catch up with him in New York.

My relationship with Ron is fresh and buoyant, and I'm completely taken with this whimsical boy-child, perhaps because he's the complete opposite of Paul. Now everything is song and dance, no longer Sturm und Drang. After my dark winter in Gualala, I'm starved for pure light-heartedness, and singing and dancing with Ron feels like salvation. We ride on to Wyoming and into the wonders of Yellowstone National Park.

But illness seems to follow me around. We're barely in the park when we're both stricken with rivers of diarrhea and stupendously foul gas that smells weirdly floral. We forego camping to stay in a youth hostel, near to a toilet, and after our billowing flatulence fills the bunkroom, the other guests wordlessly give us an entire dormitory to ourselves. We're both too sick to be embarrassed, at least, not for long; it's impossible to stop farting. Somewhere along the way, maybe in Idaho, we must've drunk contaminated mountain water and contracted giardia, also known as beaver fever. But we don't know this yet. All we know is we're stinky, runny, and weak, too weak to explore the geysers and canyons of Yellowstone. After a few days of extra sleep in our private dorm, we get back on our bikes and head east. At this point I'm closer than ever to Colorado, but once again I'm not going to make it to Boulder.

I'm feeling better—still flatulent, yet physically stronger—but Ron is rapidly losing weight and stamina, so we decide to hitchhike from eastern Wyoming to Wisconsin. Several obliging truckers deliver us from point to point, and from there we cycle the rest of the way to New York.

I'd forgotten about the humidity in the eastern seaboard, how cycling on hot days feels like wearing a rubber suit and pushing through pea soup. Already I'm missing the Northwest, as well as my once-romantic and whimsical partner, whose illness has morphed him into a peevish exposed nerve. It's understandable; he feels like crap.

In Michigan, we lose each other on the road for an afternoon and it's almost permanent; we're navigating an unavoidable stretch of busy, snaking highways that concoct multiple ways to separate travelers. Suddenly alone, we each loop around for hours before finally winding up at the same café. It's fate again, or serendipity, and if we hadn't finally landed in the same place at the same time, we'd have been separated forever, because we haven't exchanged any contact information or considered making a contingency plan. We haven't even exchanged surnames. My ambivalence towards Ron softens; we shed some grateful tears and ride on.

Two weeks before Baba's arrival in Brooklyn, we make it to Albany, where Ron lives alone on the fifth floor of a brownstone walk-up. His amoebic colonizers are thriving and he's a zombie, sleeping all day with the curtains drawn while I wander the city like a misplaced tourist, wishing I'd taken a different turn out of Yellowstone. When I return in the evenings, Ron rouses himself to eat a bowl of lentils and brown rice before falling back to sleep.

Strangely, we don't take him to a doctor, even though he's clearly wasting away; perhaps he doesn't have insurance. Staying with him is like living with a somnolent turtle, and he barely notices when I ride off one weekend to camp near some waterfalls. Even this getaway is dispiriting; I can't escape the oppressive humidity, even near the falls, and I loll in my tent like a corpulent worm in a sweat lodge. The only thing keeping me in Albany is the commitment I've made to meet Baba.

That, and my inner Florence Nightingale.

When the day arrives, we bus to New York City; it's finally time to meet the great guru. After all these months of heightened anticipation, he's waiting for us in a nondescript building on a typical Brooklyn street. Jeff is here, and there are a dozen other disciples awaiting their turn in someone's apartment living room. Baba, ensconced in the master bedroom, will determine how long each follower's private session lasts. Ron can scarcely contain himself; he's missed his guru, his second father and savior, and he's convinced Baba will instantly recognize me as one of the elect and pull me into his inner circle.

Despite the buildup, or maybe because of it, I'm double-minded, most of my energy consumed by hating Brooklyn in August and wishing I were anywhere but here (west! west!), yet curious to finally see the enlightened one. When our turn comes, Ron leads me into the bedroom and kneels, then prostrates himself before a tiny, wrinkled man who resembles a giant prune on an orange cushion. Baba looks right through me; I don't even register as a sentient being. Instead, he glares at Ron and starts yelling at him in Hindi. Ron is dumbfounded, speechless. After a minute of yelling, it's over. A man in white robes whisks us out of the room. Ron's been waiting two years for this moment with Baba—this brief, puzzling moment—and he falls to the floor in despair.

The man in white translates for us. *He says you are very, very sick,* he tells Ron. *He says you need to leave right away and go see your mother. He says don't come back here until you've seen your mother.*

Ron is a reluctant son but an obedient disciple. We leave immediately for Rhode Island, where Ron's querulous, widowed mother lives alone, resenting nearly everything her only child does.

Ron's mother is as alarmed as Baba to see him, but not by Ron's ghastly appearance. In fact, she doesn't seem to notice her son is ill. No, she's alarmed by *me*: the first girl Ron's ever brought home to mother. She regards me in my little denim shorts and tank top, braless and brown-skinned, sun-bleached and unpolished. A hippie chick.

Nothing we say mollifies her; she's convinced I'm a 16-year-old runaway who's seduced and bewitched her foolish son. I guess I could show her my passport and set the record straight, but I don't bother. She's a plump Jewish termagant, and I watch her tear into Ron for past and present transgressions, for leaving her and for taking up with me. I'm baffled that Baba, in his divine wisdom and foresight, has sent us here.

But everything changes a few days later, when she invites friends over for a dinner party and I volunteer to plan the menu, shop for ingredients, and cook. Her friends are so delighted with the food (and me) that suddenly I'm a 22-year-old culinary genius and meeting me is the best thing her son's ever done, apart from graduating from Brown. She invites more friends over to dine on my food and marvel at my skills, which include spirited dinner conversation, a change from the recycled gossip they're used to. Not only that; without her awareness, I've almost converted her to vegetarianism.

Meanwhile, Ron's getting paler and thinner, and he tortures himself over the Baba meeting. He queries me with endless loops of unanswerable questions: *Why was he so angry? I've never seen him angry before! I used to be one of his favorites! Why was he so angry? Why did he order me to my mother's? Why did he ignore Marilyn? Why was he so angry...?*

After two weeks of this, I want to run away. I'm not in love anymore; I'm appalled, again, at where I've ended up, hovering over this ailing man-child, now barely a shadow of the blue-eyed, pony-tailed young

Romeo I met that sunny California afternoon. I still have enough money in the bank for a flight to Edmonton, which beckons like a bastion of peace and sanity, not to mention my city's pleasant summer climate, which never reduces me to a sweaty rage.

But how can I leave this wretched man behind? This is what Ron wants to know, and he wears me down with wrenching appeals to take him with me. Another boyfriend wants to go to Alberta and meet my parents, something I'd never suggested to either. In the end, compassion overrules my common sense. He's clearly wasting away, his once slender body now skeletal, his pale skin nearly transparent, his blue eyes now saucers over gaunt cheeks and sharp cheekbones. It's not Ron's fault that he's sick and possibly dying; we both drank the same sparkling, tainted water in our halcyon days, trusting our eyes over common sense, and even his overbearing mother won't help him deal with the consequences.

Poor child.

I cave in and buy two tickets to Edmonton, both of them one-way.

Once again, Gwen is waiting to greet me at the airport. I've written her rhapsodic letters about Ron, pre-Wyoming-days, and I'm shocked by *her* shock as she visibly struggles to reconcile the haggard wraith leaning on my arm with the glowing descriptions I'd sent her months before. I can still see traces of the monkish young man who looks like he stepped out of a pre-Raphaelite painting, but to Gwen he's a grotesque, raven-haired scarecrow.

I suddenly realize how bizarre it is to have left Edmonton on the heels of Jack's death, only to return fifteen months later with another emaciated man leaning on me for support. Nevertheless, Gwen delivers us to my parents, who have graciously agreed to house us while Ron sees a doctor. This invitation is a big deal: It's the first time I've slept at my parents' house since the night I ran away at fourteen and swore I'd never come back.

This time, my folks are troupers. They welcome Ron as if he's a regular new boyfriend meeting their regular daughter's normal family. In the morning, they shuttle us to the doctor who delivered me and my brothers into this world, my mother's physician for most of her life. I haven't seen Dr. Shandro, who also happens to be my mother's second cousin, since my I broke my left foot dancing on a rickety homemade stage with Laura, but he's expecting us, and he's already prepared a morality lecture for me. He pulls me into his office to deliver it before greeting Ron. His sermon has a single point: I shouldn't be having sexual relations with any boys until I'm properly married. He will attend to Ron, but not approvingly.

After my morality shamer examines Ron, he makes a quick phone call and sends us directly to the hospital. There's a bed waiting for him, and intravenous drips and blood work to be started. This is when we learn the word "giardia." My body has managed to process and kill most of the organisms we unwittingly imbibed, but Ron's body hasn't, and he's in bad shape. He's going to need at least a week in hospital on a drip for treatment and rehydration, and plenty of time afterwards to recover his strength. The amoebas invading his body (and those still flitting around mine) will be eradicated by many weeks of treatment with Flagyl, the go-to medication for giardia.

Ron is a stellar patient, soaking up the nurses' ministrations with the thirst of a mother-poor child. When he returns to my parents' house, his nausea is gone, replaced by a voracious appetite. This disturbs my mother, the queen of portion-control, who's had no experience feeding bottomless troughs (they weren't allowed in our family), though to her credit she usually bites her tongue over his multiple helpings.

In between meals, Ron and I hop on the nearest bus in search of more calories: He's an eating machine. My mother is also unsettled by Ron's practice of lifting his plate of food over his head in silent prayer before eating, and even more unnerved by the Baba shrine he's set up in his sleeping quarters, my brother's former bedroom. Out of earshot, she quizzes me about the garlanded photos, the fruit offerings, and the cones of incense I've persuaded him not to light, although their musky fragrance still pervades the room.

I don't know what to tell her. I don't share about meeting Baba or about the Marrying Maiden, or even about my secret misgivings, and I'm careful not to eat an apple in front of her, lest Ron dispatch the core—stem, seeds, and all—after lifting it heavenward. This might push her over the edge. She's being amazingly tolerant, for once, but I know her newfound patience is wearing thin.

Now that Ron is walking around and out of immediate danger, I don't know what to do with him. Since our time in Providence, he's regressed to the emotional level of a six-year-old. He's ever petulant and whiny, and maybe the illness has unmasked his true nature. On one of our food outings, he throws a temper tantrum on a busy street corner, pulling bills out of his pocket (my money, on nebulous loan) and scattering them to the winds. As I'm scrambling to retrieve them (money, after all, is money), he screams louder and throws his glasses to the pavement, shattering them, along with any hope of salvaging our relationship. This is the final straw.

I'm sending Ron back to New York on my rapidly dwindling dimes. It's another financial hit for me, but he won't leave unless I actually put him on a plane. I ease him into the breakup by playing the citizenship card: *How can you work here? You need to make some money. You're illegal. Maybe you can go back and look into getting a work permit....* I don't offer to marry him, which would be the quickest route to a visa, although we talked about marriage early on, back when we were dancing in the aisles and prone to foolish conjecture. Ron knows he's disappointed me, though not how ridiculously and irredeemably. I'm trusting he won't get the visa, or that he'll finally realize, when his future letters go unanswered, that this bird has flown.

You'd think by now I'd be the queen of breaking up. But no; I'm the queen of creeping-out-backwards-with-a-big-fake-smile-and-a-slew-of-empty-promises. There ought to be some kind of prize for champion heart-breaker wimps like me.

But Ron has one last trick up his sleeve, one final ploy to wrest some sympathy from me. The night before his flight, he sneaks into my father's wine cellar and downs a bottle of potent blueberry wine. Wispy, recuperating Ron, now 130 pounds on his 5'8" frame, who's still taking Flagyl, verboten with alcohol, and who never, ever drinks, can't handle it. At five in the morning, my father finds him under the rumpus room pool table, passed out in vomit, and he gently lifts him to the car and deposits him at the airport.

My father deserves bonus points for his tact in this episode. He lets me sleep right through the drama, and when I finally wake up at 10 a.m., the vomit, the bottle, and the boyfriend have vanished. I never see Ron again, but eleven years later, he sends me a poignant letter, praising my patient love and wondering if we have a second chance.

23

Even Goddesses Get the Blues

———— ≈ ————

Once I've dispatched Ron, finding a place to live and replenishing my bank account take precedence. I head back to the university for both. Within days, I've landed a job as head cook at one of the student union cafés, as well as an interview at a grad housing co-op called The Muse. I'm not a grad student, but lots of my friends have been, and I figure I'll fit in. If nothing else, my cooking skills should garner interest.

The Muse is one of ten houses comprising the student co-op, and perhaps the most international among them. Over a no-frills dinner of stir-fried veggies and brown rice, I interview for a rare and coveted empty room. The housemates take turns cooking supper; tonight's insipid meal turns out to be standard fare at the house at least three times a week. I'm introduced to this evening's featured cooks: Colin, from Wales, who resembles a ginger Oscar Wilde and is as cynical as he is tall, and his English sidekick, Dave, who's a foot shorter and, unlike Colin, seems to have retained a shred of goodwill towards man, if not woman. I meet the others. Gisela, from Germany, a Teutonic Mary Poppins—practical, no-nonsense, and blunt. Heather's a radical feminist earth goddess who shares a room with tender-hearted Paul, from Ottawa — a city east enough from Edmonton to seem borderline exotic. Mark and his girl-friend Annie, both Australians, live in a basement room next to the one I hope to rent, and are described by their less-driven housemates as obses-sive students who surface only at mealtimes. It's true; they make a brief, business-like appearance before disappearing downstairs to study. They certainly don't fit the Aussie stereotypes I know.

Rounding out the roster is Edward, Paul's angular, outspoken friend, also from Ottawa, who came months ago for a short visit and hasn't got-ten around to leaving. I'll soon learn that he spends most days reclining on a sofa in the oversized kitchen with a day-long pot of tea, serving as The Muse's witty and tireless commentator. Edward's excessive chatti-ness makes me suspect he's gay (he isn't), and he has the most startling, cornflower blue eyes I've ever seen. He's not a paying tenant, but his vote, either for or against me, will probably count more than the others. He might seem uselessly unemployed, but he's a crackerjack at cutting through pretense, and everyone knows it.

This dinner is all about appraising me. After we've eaten and I've been questioned and scrutinized and sent off to await their verdict, the household will dissect my pros and cons and cast their votes. It's a bit nerve-wracking; I'm not sure what kind of housemate each interviewer is looking for.

The women are concerned I'm not a student and seem a tad threatened by my newly single status, but as soon as my cooking cre-dentials come up, everyone relaxes. It turns out there's a cold cellar in the basement full of enormous zucchini (they harvested a bumper crop in the community garden, and no one wants to see it wasted), so they've added an inviolable house rule that every dinner must include several pounds of it, preferably not in the guise of soggy stir-fry or another loaf of cloying whole-wheat zucchini bread baked with too much honey. I promise creativity. I mention my cleaning credentials—more positives. I'm also happy to volunteer extra hours at the food co-op to cover their busy student schedules. Plus, I've got biking stories, romantic and otherwise, to share with these thesis-curbed world travelers. By the time we're sipping our Celestial Seasonings tea, I'm confident I've scored points with everyone, with the possible exception of Colin, who seems like he'd cast a negative vote for anyone other than himself. The next morning, I get a call, and the room is mine.

It's another basement room. I paint it a deep hunter green with white trim and cover the floor with a crimson Oriental rug. Now it's a room that wants to be shared.

Apart from the weeks after Jack's death when I slept alone in my yellow tent, this is the first time I've been single in seven years. Perhaps I should value this chance to grow on my own for a season, but I don't. I feel empty—achingly, perpetually empty, like an hourglass full of holes. Nothing fills me. I lie on my bed for hours, listening to torch songs and circling close to thoughts of Jack, but not so close that I trouble the sleeping waters of grief. I'm longing, pining for him, but I can't acknowledge this impossible yearning by name, or I'll shatter completely.

Still, I know that no one can replace Jack—all my short-lived substitutes have made this clear—and I feel cheated, robbed of the one relationship I'd craved and dreamt of all my life. He alone fit my body, heart, and mind so perfectly, my true earthly counterpart. How can I live with less, knowing what I've known? There's also a deep mine of anger lodged in my heart, but I'm not ready to admit, let alone excavate, it. For now, the anger sleeps, a bitter landmine. Instead, I cry with Linda Ronstadt as she laments her shattered heart, broken like a wheel, unmendable and sinking on a ship out in mid-ocean. Like Linda, I'm a victim of love, a *prisoner in disguise,* trapped in utter brokenness.

I'm no stranger to finding myself in lyrics. The day I met Paul, I heard Jackson Browne's *Fountain of Sorrow* for the first time and knew I'd found my life's theme song before the end of the second chorus. I was that girl, knowing the hollow sound of her own steps in flight, wearing a brave smile betrayed by the sorrow in her eyes. But the lyrics that haunt me now, playing over and over on my turntable and in my head and telling me how I *really* feel, are from a Karla Bonoff song, *Only a Fool Gives a Heart Like That*: She sings about giving it all and getting nothing back, and somehow these words evoke my deepest pain.

Of course, I *did* get something back—so very much, when Jack was here—but now he's gone, and I feel like a victim of his truncated life. Even worse, a victim of *Jack*: he disappeared in a flash, taking my future with him. He left without saying goodbye. He filled me up, fuller than I'd ever dreamed of being filled, only to leave me empty, stranded on a highway in the dark. I'd looked to him for everything, for love, purpose, encouragement, direction, and joy, but when I needed him most, when the love of my life, my heart's temple, was suddenly gone, my comforter was nowhere to be found.

This, in fact, is the cruelest aspect of my grief: whenever I let myself feel his absence, it's to Jack that I automatically turn. And that gap, that crater, feels like falling into a bottomless, hidden canyon, tumbling into a void. His twice-felt absence is a double, twisting knife: he isn't there to catch me, to pull me in with the only comfort I need, the only love that can heal me. He's gone.

Worst of all, he took most of my heart along with him—all the best parts—and left me with a damaged sliver, a sliver so embedded with grief it seems permanently grounded. A punctured, aching sliver, useless to carry me through the rest of life.

I lie on my bed and let the lyrics probe me like a doctor pressing broken bones: *Does this hurt? And this? What about here? What happens when I press over here?*

I want the pain to stop; if I let myself feel for more than a few seconds, it sends me through the roof, then down the bottomless canyon. But I also want someone, an expert in these matters, to validate its scope: *pervasive and acute, statistically off-the-charts.* I want him to wince in compassion as his fingers press wider to gauge its extent. I want him to look me in the eye as he uses the term that best describes its heartbreaking magnitude: *exquisite.*

But I can take only a morsel of exquisite pain at a time. After baptizing my room in sorrow, I start spending more time upstairs, joining Edward on the kitchen sofa after work. It's another frigid Alberta winter, and snow piles at the windows as crystalline days plunge into dark by four p.m. We brew more tea, stretch our legs on the coffee table—his long and looping, like a giraffe's, mine short and restless, always twisting and folding—and talk for hours, bantering, teasing, debating, and inevitably circling back to our favorite topic: analysing our quirky housemates and the rest of the co-op community. Edward has a wicked sense of humor, and mine comes back.

Word spreads through the ten co-op houses that there's a new girl at The Muse, and suddenly the house is inundated with gentlemen callers. At first, I'm unaware these are calculated visits. I figure it's normal to have all these male grad students making the rounds, dropping by in the late afternoon when I'm off work and trying to cadge an invitation for dinner. But Colin and Dave enlighten me. *They're a bunch of hungry wolves,* they tell me, *sniffing around at fresh female meat.* It's not an enticing metaphor. But I accept some offers for coffee dates, film nights, and moonlight skates, and none of these wolves turn out to be predators. Nor are they boyfriend material. I become good friends with three of them – my skating buddy, my film buddy, and my coffee shop buddy. The only mutual chemistry is with Edward, my kitchen sofa buddy, and one night we spend hours debating whether or not to take the next step. After talking in circles till three a.m., we decide not to jeopardize our cerebral relationship with sex. It's the right decision—though we'll revisit the question later. I'm living chaste as a nun, at least outwardly, though not by choice.

Too many late nights jeopardize my job, however. After burning one too many pots of soup (three in the course of one sleep-deprived week), I get a call from the manager, informing me of plans to cut my wages in lieu of the scorched soup. *I thought you were a professional,* she scolds. *I thought you'd be better than this. I just can't have you serving charred soup.* It stings, but she has a point.

My heart's not in it; I'm distracted and dreamy, disengaged from my tasks. I resign on the spot and decide to try waitressing. Before the week is out, I'm serving waffles and coffee at Uncle Albert's Pancake House, a cozy corner restaurant redolent with the warm smells of buttery syrup and bacon. Waitressing suits me; I get to move fast and make people happy simply by showing up at the right moment, coffee and loaded plates in hand. It's a lot more fun than monitoring pots and griddles in a hot kitchen, and the tips are great.

To supplement my earnings, I take on a catering job for a New Year's Eve party. Dale, my coffee shop buddy, offers to help. He's brown-eyed and bearded, earnest and devoted. After withdrawing $400 from my account, we load three grocery carts with supplies, but when it's time to pay, the money's gone. Frantically, we comb the supermarket aisles and the heavily snow-banked parking lot, searching in vain for the wad of cash. It's December 29th. Everything goes back on the shelves, and we spend an anxious hour weighing our options. I've got just over $200 left in the bank, so we drastically modify the menu and start over: we'll serve cheaper food and fool the senses with plate appeal. Hopefully, the music and the alcohol will also cover the difference.

It works. No one seems to notice that the menu's been pared down. Our duties over, Dale and I hit the dance floor to celebrate. I'll break even, barely. Still, we made it work, and we're bopping to the music like spring bunnies when Dale suddenly pulls me in for an open-mouthed kiss. I'm caught off guard and push him off like I'm fending a shark. The hurt in his eyes slays me—I realize, too late, that he's fallen for me, hard— but it's no use pretending. He's like a brother, a close and comforting brother, but never a lover.

Four months later, as I'm bundling my oversized parka to donate to Goodwill, I notice a strange lump at the back, along the bottom hem. I probe the pockets and discover a hole, then rip it wider to pass my hand through. And there's the lump: twenty $20 bills in a fat, rubber-banded roll. I've made a profit on the party after all. And I see that sometimes lost things *do* come back, given time. They're just not always the things we really, really want.

I'm faithful to my promise to volunteer at the whole foods co-op on behalf of my housemates, and that suits me, too. I get to weigh and ring up earthy products in paper bags as I dispense recipes and my growing knowledge of all things vegetarian and natural. The co-op is woodsy and warm, filled with bins of organic root vegetables, buckets of tofu, honey, and hand-churned peanut butter and burlap sacks of colorful beans and seeds. It's the hub of Edmonton's counterculture now that The Hovel's gone, and the walls are plastered with handbills for concerts, New Age practitioners, workshops, ride shares, and communal housing. It's a great place to meet kindred spirits.

This is how I meet my next boyfriend, Pravesh. One day this stranger shows up at The Muse's back door, inquiring about something posted at the food co-op. The next day he shows up at the store while I'm bagging mung bean flour. Or maybe it's the other way around. At any rate, we meet twice within twenty-four hours, and the sparks are immediate and insistent.

He's a constellation of triggers: the same height as Jack, with soft brown curls, a fine-boned face, and the blue eyes I keep falling for. He's a film-maker from Quebec who speaks rudimentary English with a sexy French accent. He's forty years old, like Paul, but he's a lighter, younger forty—at least outwardly. He's also a sannyasin, like Ron, except unlike Ron's censorious guru, Pravesh's master is Baghwan Shree Rajneesh, the guru of child's play and free love. In short, he is a tantalizing blend of innocence, maturity, boyishness, simplicity, and spirituality, and all of these things, as well as his recent arrival to Alberta, make me want to explore and protect him. He's like a fairyland sanctuary, sparkly and mysterious, yet somehow familiar.

We both read the same handbill about an Easter weekend workshop on Rebirthing, a New Age process designed to revisit and expunge the buried trauma of birth, thus freeing the soul to pursue greater self-actu-alization. Or something like that. I'd been thinking of going, wondering if a complete reboot might be my next step on the path to enlighten-ment. When Pravesh (that's his sannyasin name, the only name he uses) decides to go, I get off the fence and commit. It seems destined, some-how, as if the workshop and this strategically placed stranger are keys to the next stage of my journey. I just *feel* it.

Still, I tell myself to take things slow. After five months of unhappy celibacy.

As if.

To be honest, I've never been so strongly attracted to someone I've just met. Which doesn't necessarily mean it's written in the stars.

The retreat pulls me back into the world of Professor Saul, the Sil-ver Fox, who's gone from holding karma-cleaning sessions in the house where Jack and I lived to hosting weekend retreats at his coun-tryside property. The last time I visited his estate, the poplar forest surrounding his buildings was so full of gorging, writhing tent cat-erpillars, I could hear them chomping through the shredded canopy like a bad science fiction movie. This time, it's too early for caterpil-lars or spring, and I tromp through soggy piles of snow between our lodgings, the kitchen, and the circular gazebo where the sessions take place. Twenty or so spiritual seekers have gathered to be rebirthed, and almost all of the exercises will be conducted in pairs. Without a word or a moment's hesitation, Pravesh and I partner up.

The facilitators guide us through a smorgasbord of mind erasers: silent and noisy meditations, face and body massages, humming and chanting, dancing and shaking, screaming and crying. With each exercise we lose whatever mild inhibitions we had coming in, until we're finally instructed to re-enact our (forgotten) journeys down the birth canal, thereby unearthing our soul-restricting baggage: the terror we've repressed at being expelled from the all-nourishing womb and facing the first of a lifetime of rejections. After two days of breaking us down in preparation for the ultimate meltdown, it seems to work. The close quarters, the long hours, and the ego-expunging exercises pulverize us until we're all writhing on the scratchy blue carpet like vocalized fetal worms, sobbing and spent. The life application from this astonishing group catharsis is left for us to figure out. It all feels Very Significant.

And of course, the intimacy of being rebirthed into each other's arms propels Pravesh and I into deeper intimacy before the weekend is over. We find a quiet bedroom on the premises to hold our own retreat. I must have seen it coming, but maybe not so fast. When it's time to leave the retreat, he follows me home to my hunter green room with the crimson carpet and my hungry double bed.

Back at Uncle Albert's, a distracted customer collides with me while I'm delivering a fresh pot of coffee, scalding my chest and possibly prompting my move from the pancake house to a downtown, upscale pizza parlor, but the faux-Italian restaurant, housed in yet another basement setting, depresses me so much that I switch careers again, and take a job delivering utility bills for the city.

This new job involves mapping out a new route each night (we cover the entire city in the course of every month), hopping on various buses in the morning, and walking six hours with a heavy sack of bills until the bag is empty. The week I start, the temperature dips to 40 below, but I'm so thrilled at the prospect of getting *paid* to *walk* that I don't care. Besides, I know all about long walks in arctic weather: the longer the walk, the colder the air, the more purifying the experience. Before layering up and leaving the house each morning, I stoke my inner furnace with a tall cup of strong tea and three capsules of hot cayenne pepper. The pepper does a slow burn as I churn through the neighborhoods and peek into windows. I'm getting paid to walk!

When I meet Pravesh, three months into my new job, I get a delightful, unsolicited bonus at the end of each workday. He turns out to be an excellent and tireless masseur, happily tending my tired muscles when I get home. Our relationship is a heady mix of sensuality and serenity; the hours we spend together float lightly, and we never argue. He's found his lodestar in meeting my needs, which is a new relationship dynamic for me. Jack was ever caring and attentive, but he also had a wide, rich circle of friends and interests that intersected mine like a Venn diagram. Pravesh died to his former life when he became a sannyasin—he won't even talk to me about his years with the National Film Board, or reveal his discarded birth name—and now he lives to serve: to serve *me*. I am the sun to his moon, the Dulcinea to his devotion. At first, his attentiveness is intoxicating, especially after months of lonely nights: I'm starved for touch, and this man can't stop touching me. Suddenly I'm a pampered goddess. But even goddesses need intellectual stimulation, too.

It's not that Pravesh isn't intellectual; I knew he could be. After all, he'd been a documentary filmmaker for years. But in his devotion to Rajneesh, he now downgrades the intellect and embraces the world of empty-mind sensuality. We talk, but the talk is of Rajneesh and India, of becoming like children (now that we've both renegotiated the birth canal and are in our spiritual toddlerhood) and of forsaking *doing* to simply *be*. Quite frankly, I'm a dreamer *and* a doer, a Practical Annie who thrives on getting things done. The concept of simply *being* instead of doing sounds paradoxically aspirational, but some nights it sends me running upstairs to plumb my under-stimulated intellect with Edward.

Edward is still around. He waits in the kitchen like a Cheshire cat, intently watching my whirlwind romance unfold. He's been studying me for months, since the beginning, as he studies everyone he deems *interesting*, and this is one show he doesn't want to miss. He seems to know something I don't, but holds his cards close. Pravesh, perhaps wisely, is wary of Edward, and Edward keeps a cool, amused distance. The two men couldn't be more different.

To my dismay, my attraction to Edward is growing. And I want a fuller relationship with him.

One of the values espoused by Rajneesh is emotional transparency, and so, in a spirit of painful obedience, Pravesh encourages me to explore my feelings about Edward with him. This is agonizing for both of us, and weird. Upstairs, Edward and I are also analyzing my dilemma. I think I'm in love—with Pravesh. So why am I more strongly attracted to Edward than ever? It's bizarre to be having these mirror-image talks on two floors, my heart on display like Exhibit A, poked like a touch-and-see demonstration in a children's museum. I feel like a trapped mouse between two cats: one cat sly and patient, the other sadly resigned to letting the mouse decide.

I'm not even sure what Edward ultimately wants, but he's not playing hard to get; he's simply leaving the decision up to me. He's ready if I am.

Further complicating matters is another Rajneesh tenet: to achieve true freedom, you do whatever scares you most. I suspect the guru's chief reason for espousing this nonsense is to encourage unconstrained sexual experimentation among his devotees, but Pravesh holds fast to its essence. If I'm afraid of having two simultaneous relationships, he tells me, I shouldn't view it as natural resistance to an inherent taboo, but as an invitation to personal growth. *Go there.* This idea of conquering fear with action has worked for me in the past—by jumping headfirst into my solo bike trip, for example—but when it's applied to the sphere of relationships and morality, even I can see it's fraught with folly, or danger, or both.

What terrifies Pravesh is the prospect of freeing me, in the midst of our relationship, to pursue a romance with Edward. So that's what he's convinced he must do. He spends hours trying to persuade himself and me that if I'm wrestling with such strong feelings, my spiritual growth *depends* on his sanctioning and my undertaking this experiment. Not in the same bed, of course, but under the same roof, and inside the same quivering, skittish, and deeply conflicted heart.

I teeter on the brink of polyamory for weeks. No one can make this decision for me, and it's as if a circus crowd is collectively holding their breath while I hyperventilate in full view on the platform above. I'm a child of the sixties, a disciple of the seventies, but this leap crosses an invisible line that terrifies me to the core.

I'm only 24, I think. If I'm doing stuff like this now, what will I be doing by the time I'm 35, or 40? Where will I end up if I let all the boundaries dissolve?

These thoughts must spring from a higher source than the usual counsel I keep. For starters, I never think *that* far ahead. No, such warnings must come from God, who's rescued me from unseen bears and near calamities, recurring despair and soured relationships. I'm well aware that *something* greater than my own strength or wits has carried me thus far. And in spite of my New Age leanings, I'm convinced there's one true, personal God who's been watching over me, at least since Jack died. His umbrella of protection feels as real as the fears I'm trying to outrun. Feeling God's *love* for me is still out of reach, but I see undeniable evidence of an invisible shield, guarding my life on every side, even as I keep putting my heart in danger.

These thoughts— that a jaded, rueful, besmirched Marilyn is waiting down the road if I don't change course—give rise to panic and a sudden switch to my default mode. *I need to get away,* I tell myself. *I need to pack my bike and leave all this behind.*

But I'm a pushover. Pravesh mopes and wheedles me into letting him join me on my escape, at least for the first two weeks. If there's a codependent gene in me, or even a stupidity gene that blinds me to unhealthy patterns and keeps landing me in the same soupy waters, I haven't discerned it yet. Once again, as I'm instinctively running from unsustainable dilemmas, I cave in and compromise.

Cycling together is a fiasco. Pravesh isn't in bad shape, but he's a terrible riding companion, stoically enduring but never enjoying the rigorous mountain climbs and their dividends: breathtaking vistas, mental clarity, and invincible thighs. It's like riding with a ball and chain. I can't help comparing him to all my previous riding partners who, despite their foibles, shared a passion for cycling, camping, and wilderness. For Pravesh, it's merely a means to an end—keeping me close—and in the end, it completely backfires. Ten days in, he's exhausted my goodwill, and in the middle of another frustrating afternoon, I banish him for good. He cycles off like a forlorn ghost, his orange sannyasin clothing flapping in the wind, and I'm tempted to feel guilty before reminding myself that tagging along was his idea, not mine. This was supposed to be *my* flight from difficult decisions, not his attempt to be something he's clearly not.

I learn later that Pravesh hitchhiked back to Edmonton, where he refused to leave my bedroom at The Muse. This does not sit well with my housemates, who already find him strange and unrelatable (most of them are practical doers, like me). I wonder if he and Edward ever talk, and I picture my tall, observant, almost-boyfriend lounging on the kitchen couch, waiting to see what the cat will drag in next.

But at least I'm free and back in my beloved riding states, Montana and Idaho. This time I have no route, no destination, and no social agenda. I want only to clear my mind. I ride the most secluded backroads and hide myself at night, avoiding people and conversations. I'm following different routes and, unlike my virgin solo trip, there are no patent tests this time around; there's nothing to prove. Almost by default, I've achieved that elusive state of being-here-now: riding purely for the sake of riding, with no plans beyond the next hill and the next campfire.

But my mind swirls with existential questions. I'm thinking about gurus and sannyasins, about living small and finding a reason to live, about the I Ching and mixed messages and destiny, about the many paths to truth and how the more paths I explore, the more lost I seem to be. I'm thinking about the spiritual glimmers I've had, all the transcendent moments on LSD and mescaline over the years, about my near-death experiences and the tantalizing pull I feel to the other side, and about all the spiritual seekers I know, and how no one, *no one* really knows what happens after death, though I'm convinced the answer to *that* question is the absolute key to life.

The thought that I'll never know what lies beyond the grave until it's my turn to cross over brings me to despair, because I'm desperate to know where Jack is. On this leg of my post-Jack odyssey, he's moved further away, beyond my conscious reach. I still won't let myself think directly about the life I'm not living with him, but his spirit haunts the locked chambers of my heart.

So I ride like an orphaned widow, my life in tatters behind me. There's nothing ahead but the road. And spirituality, my most likely ticket out of living a meaningless life, has sent me down a rabbit hole.

When my mind wearies of such profundities, I wonder how long I can keep riding aimlessly, and whether I'll ride this way forever.

24

Stranger in Paradise

I'm nearly invisible, a hermit slipping into tiny mountain towns for provisions before melting back into the scenery. On this trip, I've mastered the art of avoiding entanglements and even simple conversations by hanging a psychic curtain around me, the fierce cloak of *do-not-disturb*, and it's working well. So I'm definitely annoyed when a dozen or more resting cyclists, scattered along the side of the highway with their sag wagon, block my way as I'm attempting to zoom past them. It's a mountain ambush. They wave me over and somebody yells. *Hey! You! Come and have some lunch with us! We insist!*

Insist indeed. They've made it impossible for me to do otherwise.

I pull over and see that lunch is being served by the side of the road: stacks of plain Wonder bread sandwiches on paper plates and orange Kool-Aide from the bowels of a huge plastic dispenser. The leader of the group, a squeaky-clean youth leader type, zeroes in, waving a half-eaten sandwich. It appears I've been ensnared by a church group on a bike tour.

I'm turned off by the unwholesome lunch and the too-wholesome vibe emanating from the group. Besides, I'm not hungry. But their tone-deaf leader misses (or ignores) my cues and presses on. He's setting an example for the flock.

What's your name? Marilyn? Marilyn, come and share some lunch with us!

It's clear he's not going to let me pass until I've supped with them, so I agree to eat half a processed cheese sandwich. Road toll, I guess. Someone hands me a paper cup of lukewarm Kool-Aide. And then the leader does this: after extending a sandwich in my direction, he abruptly pulls it back and bellows, *Marilyn, do you know the gospel?*

Now it's clear I won't even get the stupid sandwich without hearing an evangelistic spiel, but I'm not having it. Reaching past him, I grab the plate out of his hand and pull it close before answering.

I know the Gospels, I huff. *Matthew, Mark, Luke, and John. Good enough?*

My hostility hits him in the face like a wet towel. End of discussion. I chomp through the unwanted sandwich in four bites and the group releases me; no sale today. Mustering a half-hearted apology, I hand back the untouched Kool-Aide, then reclaim my bike and the road. They can have their hokey religion, their bologna sandwiches and orange sugar water. I want none of it.

It's a jagged interaction. But hopefully the perceptive among them learned something from the two of us. There are ways to share your faith, and there are ways to never, ever adulterate the gospel. Don't dangle a carrot or a sandwich in front of a sensible person and expect a receptive audience. Manipulation and crass incentives only sully a message that's already hard to swallow.

Three days later, I'm still stewing over the sandwich incident. The road has carried me to a little mountain town called Thompson Falls, where I cruise the side streets searching for a place to clean up. That morning I'd sent up my daily prayer request for a hot shower and a much-needed shampoo at the end of the day. This town looks big enough to have a community swimming pool, but I can't find it. I'm stopped on a quiet corner, chugging water and enjoying the shade, when a faded blue pick-up truck pulls up. The driver is a blond, bearded, junior mountain man with a wide grin. He exudes clean living and bonhomie. His first word to me is probably *Howdy*.

His name is Scott. He points me towards the town pool, and we fall into easy talk about mountains and Montana. He tells me about a private spot near the river, a few miles out of town, where I can safely camp. And then he asks if he can join me later for a campfire. He looks as harmless as apple pie, and I figure a bit of company after weeks of self-imposed isolation won't kill me. If nothing else, I can pick his brain for great hiking trails and hidden hot springs. I say yes. He'll be there after dusk.

I wish I could recreate the conversation that night, as we poked at the campfire with blackened sticks and watched sparks pop in the dark, but I didn't actually *hear* a word Scott said. As soon as I realize he's an evangelical, my mind converts his words to dribble. For hours we debate the merits of Jesus Christ over the superior truths of reincarnation and all-paths-flowing-into-one-with-the-universe. The sandwich episode has soured my already-cold disposition to Scott's message, and though I regard myself as supremely open-minded, I am, in fact, supremely *closed* to an entire world religion. To me, Christians are under-evolved, unenlightened, and woefully dull. I feel sorry for them and have little respect for their spiritual ignorance, their shiny sincerity, or their ultra-conservative lifestyles. But tonight, I'm up for a good argument. Our conversation is less a debate than two simultaneous sermons, each of us preaching to ourselves as our lofty arguments bounce off the other's perfectly closed mind.

Eventually we run out of words and firewood. Scott stands up, brushes off his jeans, and makes one final appeal. *Will you come to church with me tomorrow? Please? Just once, to check it out? You might really like it!*

Of course I won't. But I genuinely appreciated his company and thank him for coming. Maybe, I declare, with more time to grow and experience life, he'll see the light. I certainly hope so. I wish him well and wait for him to drive away before dousing the embers with water from a nearby creek. So long, passing acquaintance. I'll be well past Thompson Falls by the time Scott is making his way to church.

The next morning, I awoke to the steady thrum of rain on my tent. The patter of rain on the tarp at night—if my tent is pitched high and dry—could be as soothing as a lullaby. But rain in the morning meant the day was off to a bad start, especially if I was camped far from the nearest town and had nothing fresh to read. There were hard-core riders out there—clocking insane daily miles and missing all the scenery—who rode through downpours without a second thought, but I refused to ride on rainy days, except to zip to the shelter of a nearby restaurant, laundromat, or library, if anything was near. Even then, I'd throw on my poncho and walk from wherever I was camped rather than splosh through puddles and torrents on my bike. But this morning I was too far from town for a quick trip in, and the rain was coming down hard. I'd have to wait it out.

I was anxious to get moving, to get a cup of coffee at the nearest café and get back on the road, hopefully putting in a good day even with a late start. Watchful as Noah, I waited till the rain slowed to countable drops, then unzipped the door and looked out. The mountains had melded into the sky; it was gray and overcast, impossible to tell where the sun was or what time it might be. Noon? I never traveled with a watch, but it felt like I'd been trapped in my tent for hours. Whatever book I was reading wasn't holding up. The sky looked ominous, but birds were beginning to chirp: maybe the clouds would dissipate soon. Birdsong was usually a good sign. As soon as a snippet of sun broke through the gray, I started packing.

Twenty minutes later I was stopped at the first gas station, still on the outskirts of town, sipping the coffee I'd been craving and readying my bike for the day. The sun, helped by a brisk wind, was winning the war in the sky. Suddenly I heard someone shouting my name.

Marilyn! Marilyn! Hey! Over here! I'm over here!

What? Directly across the highway there's a little white church, and there's Scott, gussied up in a button-down, short-sleeved shirt and tie, with a thick black Bible in the crook of one arm. He's yelling my name and waving with the other arm like I'm lost at sea and he's the lighthouse. And it's five minutes to eleven. Church is about to begin, and what are the odds that I'd be standing here now, of all places, and he'd be right across the road and... Darn it. I guess I have to go.

I'd been thinking a lot about synchronicity lately, and to me this is no mere coincidence: it must be a mandate from God. Not that I'm thinking of what his greater purpose might be. It's just clear that I'm meant to cross the street and go inside. I'll attend the service, and then I'll leave. At best, it will set me back a couple of hours. And boy, oh boy, will this ever make Scott's day!

It's the first time I've been in a church service in over a decade, and I'm dressed like someone who's *never* gone to church: skimpy shorts and a cropped tube top, one-quarter of my entire biking wardrobe. To say I stand out is an understatement, but Scott seems thrilled to have me at his side, and I stop comparing myself with the demure, cotton-skirted women in the congregation or worrying about my exposed skin. I'm just a little chilly, is all; it doesn't occur to me that my bare midriff and tanned legs might distract the menfolk.

There are maybe fifty worshippers crowded into the wood-panelled sanctuary, all conservative to the core. They're not holy rollers or slain-in-the-spirit banshees, but they're not detached, rote worshippers, either. When they start singing, it's obvious they *believe*, and this makes me cry. I cry because they share a simple faith I'll never have—not that I *want* it, but still, their lives seem simple and straightforward, unlike the circular canyon I'm stumbling through. I assume they all live on the surface of things, that they've never taken the psychedelics or thrown the I Ching or read the books or done the workshops, so they've never felt or seen the things that have shaped my world. I'm so far beyond them, I think, and for a minute I feel sad for them, stuck in their one-dimensional faith without a clue about *real* spirituality, and yet…my tears are getting heavier, and now I'm crying for myself, for the complicated, convoluted life I've been trying to outrun. Or out-cycle. I don't know where I'm going, literally or figuratively, or what I'll do once I get there. There's a huge hole inside me, deeper than I dare investigate, and once I strike this nerve, my buried anguish rises like Jesus from the grave, and I'm crumpled in the pew, convulsing with sobs.

Scott sits beside me, awkwardly patting my shoulder while I cry, and even without looking at him, I sense he's pleased with all this, with my cathartic response to the gospel he attempted to preach the night before. Not that I hear a word of this morning's sermon, either. It's the singing that's gutted me. It's simply being in a little, old-fashioned country church, thinking about my life, that's making me weep.

After the service, Scott steers me from person to person, introducing his exotic potential convert to his friends, and inviting me to join some of them for lunch. I say yes, only because it seems rude to worship and bolt. What's another hour, after all? But I'm aloof, holding myself apart from the group and refusing to discuss the service or my life, wrapped again in my invincibility cloak. It's just lunch, just fuel for the road before I leave this strange little world behind.

By two pm I'm back on my bike and heading west. Scott, of course, has urged me to stay longer, to at least take a Bible with me, but I've declined both offers. *It's been lovely,* I tell him, before shaking him off like a persistent fly. *It's been a while since I've been at church, so it was kind of weird. But it's not for me.*

I'm dying to escape: I've had enough of Thompson Falls and weepy, old time religion.

After weeks of perfect weather, the storm clouds follow me out of town. It's a strange sight: there's blue sky in all directions except directly above, where a flotilla of dark clouds moves in tandem with my bicycle. I try to outride them, but it's hopeless. The clouds sputter and drizzle, then stop, pretending to repent, before giving way to another downpour. I spend the afternoon ducking for shelter and cursing the rain, and by day's end

I've ridden only thirty miles—not nearly enough, but I'm running out of patience. A road sign welcomes me to Paradise: Paradise, Montana.

There's no sign of an actual town, but I like the idea of spending a night in Paradise, and I climb to the top of a high hill where my tent can perch overlooking the valley. From here I can watch the storm come and go, free from the threat of flooding. As I push tent pegs into the drenched, grassy hill, I feel the freighted ions in the air.

This time it's an electric light show. It rains and crackles and roars all night before Zeus runs out of bolts. Then it just rains and rains and rains, for another full day, and I'm trapped inside my tent with a twice-read novel and little else. Whatever provisions I've brought—plain yogurt, crackers, bananas, raisins—need to be rationed. My panoramic mountain view is a slow-moving canvas of heavy clouds, jostling like stupefied cattle on a train.

The irony of being exiled in Paradise doesn't escape me, and by the second day I'm kicking myself for not accepting Scott's offer of a Bible. Not that I'm hungering for the words of life, per se, but at least I'd have something fresh to read. I toss on my sleeping bag as the hours drag, lifting the tent flap to check the sky whenever the rain falters. The storm forces me to stay another day, and by the third afternoon, I'm determined to get out of Paradise and *anywhere* down the road before night falls.

It's nearly evening when I make my break. If I can ride even twenty miles to another camp, I'll feel like I'm getting somewhere. Plus, I need food. I pedal fast, glancing at the pewter sky and trying to outrun the winds stockpiling clouds above me. Thirty miles later, I pull into a solitary gas station to fill my water bottle, check out the selection of stale snacks, and reacquaint myself with the hermit in the mirror.

When I come out, there's a familiar blue pick-up truck waiting next to the gas pumps, and Scott, grinning like Howdy Doody on his wedding day, beaming at me through the open window. Except for my regrets about not accepting his offer of a Bible, I'd almost forgotten him. But he has not forgotten me. His eyes lock on mine like handcuffs. Warm, padded cuffs, but handcuffs nonetheless.

Marilyn! I found you! I glance at my loaded bicycle—easy to spot—and realize he must've seen it from the highway while I was inside. But there's more. He's transported, ecstatic. *I've been praying to find you since you left Thompson Falls and the Lord answered me! It's a miracle!*

By now he's out of the truck and moving closer, his face radiant with divine endorsement. He doesn't even ask how I'm doing, or if I wanted to be found.

In fact, he continues, *I knew I was going to find you, I just knew it! Because I've been praying about meeting someone like you for a long time, and now it's all happening. You need to come back to Thompson Falls with me. And I've already talked to my pastor, and he says you can stay with him and his wife for as long as you want! So it's all worked out!*

I'm as miserable—and alarmed—as he is euphoric, but he seems oblivious, perhaps intentionally. Maybe he knows that seeking verbal consent from me will send him home empty-handed. Or perhaps his joy blinds him to the panic that's befallen me. I look to the heavens, which are primed to erupt any second in another epic downpour. There's just this gas station and me, with miles of open, wet highway in two directions and nowhere to hide. Scott is already moving towards my bike, getting ready to load it onto his truck.

All signs point to this: it doesn't matter what I think. This isn't about some lonely Christian zealot and his answered prayers. This is *God* hemming me in, nipping at my heels like a persistent sheepdog and corralling me into this tiny pocket of Montana. It's divine synchronicity. It's the hound of heaven, and I'm certain, though not pleased, that he's finally tracked me down.

Time's up. Like a thwarted fugitive, I climb into the cab. As we drive back to Thompson Falls, my bike a felled gazelle in the truck bed, Scott tells me more about the hunt. He wasn't actually driving around looking for me; his hardware store manager had sent him on a delivery a hundred miles away, and he was heading home when he spotted my bike. But the praying part was true: he'd been petitioning God for my soul since the day we met. And he wanted to be the one to save it. In fact, he confided, he'd been praying for a couple of years to convert a girl out of a cult and deliver her to the Lord. *I must be the girl,* was the not-so-subtle inference, though he doesn't say it directly.

He does, however, whisper exactly that into the phone when we stop enroute to visit an acquaintance. It's hardly a visit, and I suspect the stop is actually a pretext to use the phone and call his brother in Michigan with his urgent and wonderful update. There's loud, excited whispering, the kind you can hear from the next room.

I'm sure she's the one, he gushes. *She has to be. She's so pretty! And she's Canadian! And she's not exactly in a cult, but she's all into reincarnation and stuff so it's like she is, and she's been riding around with all kinds of weird people, but now she's gonna stay at Pastor Jim's house, and I just know*—and here he almost squeals—*she's the wife I've been praying for!*

His words send a shiver down my spine, not because I think they're prophetic, but because the thought of marrying this earnest straight arrow makes me shudder with aversion. He's not bad looking and he'd be a fine catch for the right person, but his one-setting personality leaves me cold. Still, I can't shake the feeling that God is using this convergence for a higher purpose than answering Scott's prayers for a cult-rescued bride.

I agree to stay for one week, and only one; this is non-negotiable. And I request personal space to do my own thinking. He needs to leave me be. There must be no gospel sandwiches and no personal probing. No preaching. If I could have all this in writing, I'd have it notarized.

Scott has obviously relayed my conditional surrender to Pastor Jim, because once I'm delivered to Jim and Judy's plain-as-toast bungalow, they welcome me with such low-key nonchalance that I know it's an act. They zip-lock their zeal and promise me privacy: a quiet, tucked-away basement room, 24-hour access to the kitchen, and freedom to come and go as I please. They don't even point out the evangelistic books placed conspicuously throughout the house. And this is all good. Even if Scott hasn't conveyed my ambivalence, they surely sense it. I'm a feral cat, lured to a trap that may or may not work. If they make one false move, I'll likely bolt.

Scott also attempts to curb his enthusiasm, having said too much. Fortunately, his schedule prevents us from to spending too much time together; he works all day at the local hardware store. Our week-long routine falls into place. We meet for a 50-minute picnic lunch at noon and hang out in the evenings. The rest of my time is spent reading the Bible and hiking the mountains that cradle the town. Another caveat: he must never ask what I'm thinking, where I'm at, or what changes, if any, the Scriptures are working on my heart. This is a private undertaking between God and me, and as far as I'm concerned, none of Scott's business.

Instead, we talk about Mormons. Scott is obsessed with Mormons, with their dubious origins, jaw-dropping teachings, and celestial fantasies. The polygamous splinter groups are even more reprehensible. He fixates on their culture with the intensity of a former anthropologist turned witch-hunter. In fact, the girl he imagined marrying was supposed to be a rescued *Mormon*. But now that I'm here, with my *pretty little knee bones* (this is Scott's idea of a Christian compliment, referring to my toned legs and spiritualized with a loftier reference to prayer), he's had to revise his dream: I'll be his rescued wife, he thinks, and his helpmeet in proselytizing captive Mormons.

It happens that years ago, for some class or another, I'd also done an in-depth study on Mormons and gotten temporarily obsessed with their strange origins. So, I'm happy to revisit the topic and dig deeper. This way, we can focus on the Latter Day Saints and avoid discussing my personal quest. Fortunately, Scott never tires of discussing his future ministry. This, he's convinced, is why God moved him from Michigan to Thompson Falls. He found the Lord in these gentle green mountains, along with a greater purpose for his life, when all along he thought he was simply moving west for a change of scene.

But my time alone, away from Scott, is really why I'm here. Every morning I rise early and slip out the pastor's back door with a borrowed Bible, headed for a trail. The trails are steep, sunny, and people-free. I spend the hours hiking and reading in the shade and hiking some more, pondering what I've read. Someone must have suggested starting in the gospel of John, because that's where I spend nearly all my time, mostly in the first fourteen verses. The words are simple and profound, pure and unassailable.

In the beginning was the Word, and the Word was with God and the Word was God. He was with God in the beginning.

Through him all things were made; without him nothing was made that has been made. In him was life, and that life was the light of men.

...He was in the world, and though the world was made by him, the world did not recognize him. He came to that which was his own, but his own did not receive

him. Yet to all who received him, to those who believed in his name, he gave the right to become children of God....

...The word became flesh and lived for a while among us. We have seen his glory, the glory of the one and only Son, who came from the Father, full of grace and truth.

John's words—God's words—are searing my soul. The supremacy of Christ is inescapable: he's my Creator, the source of all life, the light of the world, the only Son of the only Father, the one who shows us exactly who God is. They're new words to me, yet they feel as if they've been waiting forever, as if a shadow copy, imprinted on my heart before I ever opened my eyes, has been waiting all these years for its original to bring it to light. It's the truth I've been searching for: a single, immutable truth. There is one God, one holy and perfect Father, and there is Jesus, also God. There is the Spirit, who wrestles with my own. This is the God who made me, who knows me, inside and out, and who comes with light and glory.

The words are honey and vinegar. They challenge every fibre of my life.

But as I read, I'm convinced these words are *truth*, and denying them—trying to stuff the genie back into the bottle—would be the greatest lie of all. However many lies are sleeping in my bed, twisting my blankets in knots, I can't let this be one more.

25

Sea Change

I've found the pearl of great price and I should be dancing for joy, but it's a bitter pearl to swallow. First, I have to admit I've been wrong, that my previous spiritual chases have been worthless: worthless, in that they've led me nowhere, yet precious, because they've led me here. I know I need to renounce all other paths, and this is where I'm challenged most. Maybe I haven't found any ultimate answers during my years in New Age Land, but I'm attached to methods and moments in my journey that I simply don't want to relinquish. I think of myself as the sum of the books I've read, the experiences I've had, and the spirituality I've tasted, and if I let these nutrients go, however imperfect or illusory they might have been, who am I? What was the point of all those small and great revelations if I have to give them up?

Of course, this is exactly the point. I *am* nothing apart from Christ, my Maker: He will define who he's made me to be, and I know what I'm seeking is found in him. But I'm clinging to the old Marilyn, to who I think she is, and I'm afraid to let her go.

I think of Jack's spiritual books waiting for me at The Muse, and mentally rehearse disposing of them, one title at a time. It hurts; it's a letting go of Jack, too, something I'm not ready to do. These books shaped him, and by extension shaped our relationship, along with the music that inspired us, their lyrics sprung from the wells of free love and New Age philosophies. Who am I without them? I've let Carl Jung and Ram Dass and Lao Tzu shape my mind, and even if I'm able to excise their teachings, will their absence make my brain cave in?

And much of it has been instrumental in getting me to this point. Indeed, had I not been immersed in Jung's concept of synchronicity, would I have paid attention to the *coincidences* God was using to draw me in? I think not.

The hardest book to imagine relinquishing is the *I Ching*, not because it espouses a particular worldview—its hexagrams are much too vague for that—but because I like having something to turn to when faced with a dilemma, something that seems like universal wisdom, even if it's ridiculously open to personal interpretation. Maybe *because* it is.

I love laying out the yarrow sticks as I meditate on a pending decision and anticipate the hexagram they'll indicate. Fluid answers to life's fluidity. I like the ambiguity of the *I Ching*, even though I've just been handed clear, incontrovertible truth. It's like giving up Cheetos for a full-on organic feast: I know what's good for me, but sometimes I *crave* that fake orange powder instead of actual protein.

It seems much easier to make the lifestyle changes expected from a guru than to accept the divine supremacy of Christ with all its implications. What would a guru expect? A change of wardrobe and diet, some hours of meditation, a trip to India, accepting a new name—but not a sea change of *everything* on the inside.

But a guru is just another human, just a teacher claiming to be a few steps ahead; this Jesus confronting me is THE SON OF GOD, and I know, without being told, that finding my rightful place in him will require a complete reworking of how I think and live. It's more than a spiritual makeover: it's *dying to self*, to my stubborn, self-serving patterns and desires, a formerly fuzzy concept that's suddenly becoming clear.

It's this narrowing of the path, this cleaving to one Master, only and forever, and forsaking all others, that's making it hard to breathe.

Yet I've been hungering for this. Deeper prayers were churning on this trip, not for swimming holes and sunny days, but to find Truth in this wilderness called life. Even the greatest joy I've managed to find so far without Jack—cycling in the beautiful Northwest—has started to wane, having no clear purpose or endpoint. Life itself seems pointless and cyclical, a message that should've been obvious every time I tossed the *I Ching*. And I know that even if I suppress this new knowledge, extricate myself from my latest relationship disaster, and start fresh, I'll find myself in the same romantic crisis before long: the agony of being lonely in love. This is my pattern, and my inner emptiness is the only thing that seems to stick.

And I desperately want to know where Jack's soul is, if I'll ever see him again. I want answers about life and death, *solid* answers, because I think about mortality a lot, much more, I suspect, than the average twenty-four-year-old. I want a true spiritual path that will carry me through life and not leave me empty—empty-handed and empty-hearted—when I reach my own death. And even if I haven't articulated all these desires and shaped them into prayer, I'm convinced God has deciphered my deepest longings and come through, yet again, with exactly what I need.

But, surprise! I never expected the answer would be *Jesus*, and all the trappings that come along with him: the Bible, the church, and the religion I've been running from since I dropped out of baptism class at the age of thirteen, knowing I was neither ready nor able to go another step in that direction.

So I'm a house divided. Although the divinity of Christ is truth, it's a violent truth: a life-changing, permanent truth. It's also a humbling truth, and accepting it means I have to become a *Christian*. And doing that, actually converting, is the greatest stumbling block of all, because I've yet to meet a Christian I'd want to emulate or hang around. *I just can't relate* would be the kindest way of putting it. Of course, I'm steeped in pride for thinking this way, but the tea bag's been so long in the pot that I can't discern the brew.

Then there's the whole issue of lifestyle. I'm not yet thinking in terms of *sin*, but no one needs to tell me my string of lovers must be permanently cut. I can't go back to Pravesh, which is fine, because I don't want to. But I can't go back and flirt with Edward, either, or contemplate any future romance that involves sex outside of marriage. This is another deep renunciation of self. The string of blue-eyed men who shared my bed after Jack died may have been placeholders, but they filled a vacuum (with varying degrees of short-term contentment) I'm not sure a heavenly saviour can fill. I can imagine an interval of celibacy as I recalibrate my life, but a *lifetime*, if it comes to that? Just thinking about this hurts, and I ache to be enfolded in a pair of strong, manly arms. Does God really expect this of me? Can I do it?

Such thoughts torment me as I wrestle with the Scriptures, my attachments, and the hound of heaven himself. Still, my capitulation to Christ has seemed inevitable since the day Scott spotted me at the gas station and reversed my course. It's not a matter of *if*, but *when*. And even though I'm secretly in awe of the way God has orchestrated events—including the Montana weather— to get my attention, I'll later learn that in this early phase, I'm in the good company of former reprobates like C.S. Lewis: another miserable and reluctant convert, astonished by truth, yet dismayed by its implications.

Scott, of course, isn't privy to any of this. I keep all of it—my nascent faith, my fears, my struggles, and my dread—close to my chest. Instead, we talk about Mormons and Scott's spiritual aspirations, bypassing my own. This is how I want it.

On Scott's day off, we take a long, hot hike to a secluded mountain lake. When we reach the water, I do what comes naturally after a perspirational day of hiking or riding: strip off my sweaty clothes and jump in. I skinny dip not as an exhibitionist, but as a pragmatist; I don't want to hike out in wet underwear and shorts. Scott sits on the rocky shoreline and watches, no doubt wondering how he'll ever rein in this hedonist if she's going to be his wife. Then he throws propriety and his own clothes to the wind and jumps in after me. We splash around in separate circles, eyes averted, until the cold water freezes us out. It's the chastest skinny dipping I've ever done. But Scott is conscience-stricken; it's written all over his guilty face, and later he blurts out his shame. I've led him into lust and unholy behaviour.

Another lifestyle change I'll have to consider.

Sunday rolls around; it's been only a week since my first church service, but I'm already changing—partway, inwardly. This week the church is having a unity service in the city park with all the other little congregations in town, minus the Catholics and Jehovah Witnesses.

As we furtively glance around while singing about being *one in the Spirit, one in the Lord*, I speculate, as people have for centuries, on why the followers of Christ are so divided. As for this ecumenical collection of worshipers, they all appear to be cut from the same cloth. Maybe, I think, it's a matter of architectural preference, each group gravitating to their favourite version of brick and steeple. Maybe it's easier to organize potluck dinners when your congregation fits into the same little building, year after year. After all, this service in the park is a little unwieldy, what with all the tippy rented chairs sinking in the grass and folks jostling for shade, and when we break for a picnic lunch, everyone flocks to their own denominational picnic tables and the interfaith fellowship dissolves. *So much for being one in the Lord,* I think, but don't say.

As day seven approaches, Scott launches a campaign to prolong my stay. I've been expecting this, but I'm unyielding: I promised seven days, and that's it. He's still in the dark about my spiritual progress, though he notices I'm toting the Bible everywhere. This time, when he offers to let me keep it, I say yes. I still don't have a destination, but I have a guidebook.

On the morning of the eighth day, I leave Thompson Falls for the second and final time.

The changes don't stop once I'm back on the road. The compact King James leatherback rides in my handlebar bag, squeezed between map and sunscreen, and I'm conscious of it every minute. All I want to do is read more. I start making deals with myself. *If you ride for two hours, you can stop and read for forty minutes. If you want to read before breakfast, you can ride all morning and take an extra hour after lunch to read more.* The deals increasingly maximize the time I permit myself to read versus the time I spend clocking the miles.

Now I'm all over the New Testament, except for Revelation, which I dip into briefly and decide to reserve for future days. I fall in love with the Sermon on the Mount, and wade into the Epistles, then splash around in Isaiah and Ecclesiastes. I love the poetry and the overlap, the inherent authority and directness in every book. Even in archaic English, the Scriptures fit together like an intricate jigsaw puzzle. It's a massive puzzle, at least 5000 pieces, but the outer edges are taking shape. I'm hooked and dazzled, moving swiftly from intellectual assent to newlywed joy: the joy of continuous discovery and interconnection. I'm no longer worrying over what this newfound faith will ask of me. I just want to keep diving in, over and over, and filling my cup.

Eventually I find myself in National Park territory again, where I reluctantly part with four dollars to camp in a public campsite. It still feels wrong to camp off the grid within the parks, and I don't want to be nabbed by a vigilant park ranger. But this time the camping fee is worth every dollar, taking me full circle to my first night of solo camping, more than two years ago, when I embarked on my quest to complete Jack's trip.

This time, it's not snowing, as it did that first night, but once again I'm camped too close to another head-over-heels couple in love. But tonight, instead of falling into loneliness and despair, I spontaneously reach out to them and share what I'm discovering in the Bible. It's unscripted, unprompted sharing: no gospel sandwiches, no intent to extort a confession of faith, but simply an overflow of joy, as if I've just watched the best movie in the world and have to pass it on. And perhaps because I have no motive apart from this impulse, my listeners respond and ask questions, prolonging the conversation. I'm no expert, and I don't pretend to be. I'm just a lucky prospector who's finally found gold.

The clarity of that moment galvanized me. I realized I'd crossed an invisible line, that I was no longer resisting the message and bemoaning its implications but lapping it up like a parched dog. God's words were changing me, and the changes felt as real and deep as the transformation Jack's love had wrought in me. I also sensed this was just the beginning of a lifetime of change, though I had no idea where God would ultimately lead me. I simply knew he *was* leading me, and that his plans were not to restrict me, despite the narrowing I'd felt in the throes of my resistance, but to *open* my life to greater things, if only I'd let him.

It was a glorious breakthrough.

Where now? I decided to head to my parents' lakeside cabin in the interior of British Columbia, a hideaway they'd built in the years since I'd left home. I'd never been there, but now seemed like the perfect time to surprise them with news of my conversion. They'd be happy, I was certain; my new alignment with Christ would be read as a capitulation to their point of view. This was not how I read it, but that was okay. We had more in common now than we'd had in years, and that was enough. The gospel was a message of peace, after all, and I was ready to be a peacemaker.

My parents were rustics at heart; by choice, they had no running water at the cabin, no plumbing and no phone, and I waited till I was a day's ride away to contact them through a neighbor's telephone. The last forty-five miles up to the cabin followed a steep gravel road, and my father drove down to collect me and my bicycle.

After exploring the property and admiring their handiwork, I shared the plot points of my latest journey: meeting Scott, the rain and the church service and the timing, my empty days in Paradise, meeting Scott again, and the week I'd spent reading the Bible in Thompson Falls. We laughed about Scott's insistence that I was the bride he'd been praying for. As if! And now I was here, closing another circle and no longer a New Age dabbler, but a believer in Christ. We celebrated with little glasses of my father's homemade wine—much improved from the earlier wine I used to smuggle to river parties as a young teen—and a hearty meal on the cabin deck. As I'd expected, both parents, but especially my mother, were pleased as punch. Their runaway black sheep had finally seen the light.

There were four different versions of the Bible tucked in various corners of the cabin, and I spent the next week comparing them and digging deeper. By reading the introductions to each version, I learned there are many old and recent *translations* of the Bible, all derived from the same ancient texts and varying mostly in word choice and syntax, and there are also *paraphrased* versions, which read like storybooks but may end up reflecting some of the paraphraser's biases (although none of the paraphrasers, of course, would mention this). Scott had given me a trusty old King James Version, and while the four-hundred-year-old English was often poetic and arresting, I quickly gravitated to the Revised Standard Version— much easier to understand. I didn't want poetic obscurities or unorthodox syntax, I wanted *truth*, expressed in contemporary English and free of obsolete words and expressions. Later, I'd gravitate to the New American Version, before eventually setting my preference on the New International Version.

But this, of course, was still in the future. For now, I was turning fresh soil, digging deep. I was treasure hunting, searching for glittering jewels, and waiting to see where these promises, pictures, and warnings would ultimately take me.

26

Outer Circle

---～---

The Mix Family was having its first big reunion since migrating to Alberta from Illinois in the early 1900s, and I returned with my parents to Edmonton so we could meet our extended clan. Even on this trip, I was restless to ride part of the way, and my folks stopped enroute for day hikes so I could cycle 40- or 50-mile stretches through the mountains. It wasn't the same as traveling and camping on my own, but I needed the space to think, and my body was grateful for the exercise.

Back in the city, the reunion shed some light on my genetics: I'd had inklings, but hadn't appreciated how *extensively* our family history was peppered with ministers and teachers. Apparently, I came by my aptitude for studying and preaching quite naturally. There were also not a few lawyers in the mix, hence my analytical nature. It turns out we were also related to Hiram Bingham, the American explorer who discovered Machu Picchu in 1911 (who was later mythologized in the character of Indiana Jones), so maybe my restless, wandering spirit extended back to his branch of the family tree. Among my current kinfolk, however, I felt like an outsider, having reached my present state of correspondence to the family's spiritual roots by such an unconventional route, and sensing that another unconventional journey lay ahead. I belonged elsewhere, though I didn't know where elsewhere lived.

My hunter-green room at The Muse was intact but for the ghost of Pravesh, who'd locked himself inside, lamenting the death of our relationship, until the household managed to evict him. I had no idea where he'd gone, nor did I ask. There was no point in tracing him. We were long over.

Edward, too, had finally rolled off the kitchen sofa and moved back east, this time to Toronto. I'd given notice on the room, and I returned for a final meal with my housemates before packing up my stuff. This meal was far more awkward than my interview dinner had been. Over yet another wok of stir-fried veggies and brown rice, I shared my faith story with my soon-to-be former friends. This time, my biking adventures fell flat, crippled by the sappy ending. With the exception of Paul, who would later express an open-minded curiosity, my Christian-averse housemates reacted with silence and then a hasty change of topic. I might have fared better if I'd told them I was converting to Communism or Zoroastrianism. Colin and James, in particular, would have relished dissecting *that* change of heart, but to openly express a faith in Christ was unspeakable.

It was my first taste of being on the other side of the divide, and perhaps exactly what I deserved for years of prideful contempt towards Christians in general, and evangelicals in particular. I wasn't a mocker, at least outwardly, but my kindest thoughts towards Jesus people had hardly been charitable. Now I was seeing firsthand how any mention of the Bible or Jesus could bring conversations with even my most spiritual friends to a grinding halt. Gwen was the only friend who wanted to hear whatever I was thinking, and she eventually found her way back to Christ on her own spiritual journey, not long after I left Edmonton. She was still my most faithful friend, interested in every aspect of my life because she cared about me, no matter where I ventured or what I was contemplating.

I was suddenly doing other things I'd never imagined doing. Now homeless, I moved back to my parents' house and started praying for divine direction. God had brought me to a point where my future lay completely open to new possibilities, yet completely hidden from me. I was convinced there was a *right* path I needed to find, the path to the second big chapter of my life. Seeking this path was the only thing that mattered. I had a roof over my head; I had some money in the bank; I had no debts or obligations or binding ties to anyone, apart from Jesus. The slate was clean, but I had no idea what or how to start writing.

I did have some budding convictions, however. The first was simple: if all this was true—or rather, *since* all this was true—God deserved all of me. Christ was worthy of my complete dedication. I didn't want to be a run-of-the-mill believer; I wanted a *mission*, a way to live that would honor him supremely. Perhaps this meant becoming a nun or attending a Bible college. Perhaps it involved going overseas and serving the poor. I was ready to go wherever he wanted me. But it was essential to get on the right boat.

I also knew that affiliating myself with some kind of church or group was part of the package, though I had no idea which assembly this might be. To this end, I spent my weekends church hunting. On Saturdays I'd pull out the Yellow Pages and plot out the services I'd attend the next day: an early morning service, a late morning service, and an evening one. Apart from the fringe groups I'd heard about and the United

Church (wishy-washy and queasily associated with my upbringing), I was open to almost any place with a cross on the premises.

It was late summer. I was still riding my bike everywhere and thus wearing shorts most of the time, though I knew enough to forswear wearing crop-tops to church. In an effort to dress modestly, I wore knee socks with my shorts and carried a sweatshirt to wear inside. I didn't *own* any church clothes, nor was I prepared to bike across the city in a skirt and heels if I had. Still, most parishioners I encountered seemed more put off than pleased by my sudden, under-styled appearance. I came and left alone to each service. None of the ministers bothered to introduce themselves, unless it was in the handshaking queue afterwards and I was safely headed out the door. I tried sitting near enough other worshipers to make starting a conversation easy, but even when I initiated and wore my sweetest smile, most responders were hopeless at making me feel welcome enough to return.

At one of the oddest churches I visited, the forty-odd members sat in a circle facing each other, while I was left to sit in a lone seat in the cold outer circle, completely ignored from start to finish. In this case, though I felt like bolting, I stayed to the end of their boring, boring service just to see how all-inclusive their shunning could be. They spoke not a word as I headed for the door.

The single exception to this lack of Christian agape was among a cultish group of young, hippie-ish Pentecostals who met in a borrowed church, where shaggy-haired men and women swayed in the aisles and took turns singing long, impromptu prophecies about each other. Here, I was unmistakably love-bombed on every side, from friendly offers for lunch to a bewildering invitation to move that night into the minister's household. It was flattering to finally be wanted, and I returned for a second service just for the smiles. But even with my limited Bible knowledge, I could see that most of their worship was extra-Biblical and profoundly self-focused, not what I was looking for at all.

Over the course of several weeks, I worked my way through a raft of listings in the Yellow Pages, attending churches that ranged from Baptist to Evangelical Free, Apostolic to Mennonite, Four-Square to Nazarene, and beyond. None of them grabbed me, literally or figuratively. But there were still dozens—nay, hundreds—more to sample. Between Sundays, I kept reading and praying, supplementing the Bible with books by C.S. Lewis and other Christian thinkers and writers.

I spent a portion of every day avoiding phone calls from Scott, who called obsessively and was now trying to persuade my mother to persuade *me* to move my pretty little knee bones back to Montana. (She wouldn't, nor would I.) I also spent hours perched on a high stool in my mother's sunny kitchen, weighing what I perceived to be my options, and examining each at length. As I saw it, three of them were viable, and hopefully *one* was the path I was meant to take. My mother listened patiently to my daily analyses, but for once kept her opinions to herself. She was a sounding board—or perhaps I was just talking in her space while she cooked—but I approached this critical juncture as the work of God, and only God could show me which turn was the Right One.

I'd formulated three options.

Option One was to move to India and work with Mother Theresa in the Calcutta slums. This was 1980; Mother Theresa was famous, but not *crazy* famous, and she took on helpers for her work without requiring a full commitment to nun-hood. This would give me time to discern if I was meant to become a Catholic. I'd already written to ask her permission and was awaiting an affirmative response. The strong appeal of this option was being able to dive headfirst into absolute self-denial and service, among the impoverished *dying*, no less. There was also the years-long attraction I'd had to India since wandering into Edmonton's only Indian import store and spying my beautiful dancing doll. However, I wasn't sure whether this was actually a calling from God or just something I'd concocted from a desire to go far, far away and inhabit a more captivating world—as different from Canada, I imagined, as ice is from curry. Still, exotica aside, something in me yearned to help the world's least fortunate.

Option Two was enrolling in a Bible college and strengthening my theology for future assignments. I was leaning towards a college somewhere in Idaho and was midway through filling out the paperwork. All signs looked positive—they'd take me, of course—but I was still awaiting a heavenly confirmation that this was *God's* course for me. The downside of Option Two was imagining life at a Bible school; I pictured a campus rife with gospel sandwichers and hungry future pastors looking for brides, and shuddered. At best, I feared that becoming a Bible college student would require a painful and possibly doomed cultural adjustment for someone like me. Still, if this what God expected, I'd die to myself and go.

Option Three was moving up north to a work camp, where I had a job offer to cook on site and make double or triple the money I could earn in Edmonton. I imagined sequestering myself in a quiet hotel room after the cooking was done and filling the long winter nights with intensive, solitary Bible study, a hefty stack of commentaries on hand. This option would allow me to save money for greater endeavours of faith in the future. My travel funds were dwindling and taking the job could replenish my account while deepening my knowledge, perhaps as much as attending college would. I was, after all, an entrenched self-learner.

Again, the downside was simply not knowing if this was God's plan or simply a justification to earn money and put off making a greater commitment to something else.

Option Four, of course, was the funny one: marry Scott and spend my life rescuing Mormons. When I grew weary of juggling the first three options, I tossed in this colorful ball to jazz things up. What if? But even humorously considering this option was a mere diversion; I could never marry him, however grateful I was for his role in my conversion, and I couldn't imagine God calling me to such extreme self-denial, either. There were limits to which mountains could, or should, be moved. As for Scott, he was holding fast to his dreams, and while I'd completely stopped answering the phone in case he waited on the other end, my mother always picked up, and she stood like a firewall between us. Not that I was in any danger of igniting.

After a few weeks of deliberating, there was no clear winner. A cold and early fall was closing in. One weekend I took a break from church shopping to go backpacking in the Rockies with a couple of friends. The weather was dreadful, and we were nearly blown off the mountain as we traversed the "Skyline" portion of the trail, crawling on our hands and knees along an exposed narrow ridge with nothing but scree and cliff for thousands of feet on either side.

After two harrowing days, we found respite from the elements as we descended, walking three abreast down the widening trail and discussing our lives from the new perspective of having nearly lost them. One friend's life was clearly mapped out: he had a job, a career track, a fiancée, and a car all waiting for him in another city. The second friend's life was sketchier. He'd just finished traveling the world and was on his way back to New Zealand, having brokenly accepted that the love of his life had moved on. The only sure thing awaiting his return was his completed Master's degree; he had no idea what work he'd pursue or who he'd love, or how. But at least he knew where he'd be living.

And then there was me. My life was a huge question mark: I had no ties and was poised to start a whole new chapter—a whole new *book*—but as I discussed the blank page in front of me, devoid of markers or clues, my current state felt like the hike we'd just covered, inching blindly through fog and wind with a terrifying fall into nothingness if I happened to let go. Compared to my friends, and other normal people, my life seemed impossibly open (or blank, depending how you looked at it), but either way, I was committed to this lonely path, trusting God would lead me to *something*. For a few moments, I envied the friend with all his ducks in a row, before remembering I'd willingly shot my own ducks in hope of better things.

When I returned from the hike, two things happened that changed the course of my life forever. One was a phone call from Jess, a friend who'd been close to Jack and me. The previous winter she'd been suicidal and had reached out to me for help, and now she was calling from Montreal, having followed a new boyfriend east. The relationship frightened her; she felt trapped and isolated, and I sensed her new man was emotionally and perhaps physically abusive. Now I had a lasting lifeline to extend: the message of God's love. I shared some of what I was learning. Could I come out to Montreal and see her? Absolutely.

Within the same week, Edward called. He was living near the University of Toronto and taking some classes; one of his courses was an analysis of the Old Testament. My antennae popped. *Edward? Studying something biblical?*

It seemed far-fetched, as unlikely as my taking a course in engineering, but he was the only person among my friends with any connection to the Bible, and I latched onto this news like a blood-starved tick.

If I visited Toronto on my excursion east, we could pool our new knowledge. I yearned to talk with another inquisitive mind, with someone who'd arrived at these foreign shores through similar dark and tangled woods. I'd given up romance in general, and romance with Edward in particular, but now it seemed he might be a link on my new fence, or a torch along the way. It was a tenuous connection, but it was the only real-life connection in sight.

Now I had a two-fold reason to leave my mother's kitchen, site of my circular deliberations, and make a move. I was still praying for God to clearly indicate which option to pursue, and perhaps distance would bring clarity. I'd go by train; allowing for travel time, I'd be gone three weeks. By then, God willing, I'd know what came next.

This time, I'd leave my bike and tent behind. I booked a round-trip ticket to Montreal with a stop in Toronto, packed some clothes, my Bible, and half a dozen spiritual books, and boarded the train lightly, unaware that this time, I was leaving Alberta—and every shred of my old life—forever.

27

Inner Light

———— ⁓ ————

Jack and I had taken a similar Canadian Pacific train three years earlier, as far as the Manitoba-Ontario border, but this trip felt completely different. This time, the distance was a thousand miles further, and the journey seemed endless as the train stopped every few hours for long, silent breaks in lonely outposts. I spoke to no one. I'd decided to fast the whole way, praying for God's guidance in days to come, and hunger, combined with lack of sleep, made me crabby and antisocial. To pass the time, I alternated reading C.S. Lewis' *Mere Christianity* with the Scriptures. There was a passage in Ezekiel that grabbed my attention and I pondered it for hours.

I will give you a new heart and put a new spirit in you; I will remove your heart of stone and give you a heart of flesh. And I will put my Spirit in you and move you to follow my decrees.... (Ezekiel 36: 26-27)

The words *"heart of stone"* undid me. My heart was still shut down, still locked in my impenetrable, grief-proof bubble, even as I struggled to swim beyond it. I still hadn't grasped the immensity of either the bubble or the grief, but I could sense both were starting to calcify into something harder. Deep vaults of emotion lay trapped inside, but I had no idea how to release them or if I'd even survive the process. I longed for a new heart, a heart of flesh that wouldn't be afraid to love without restraint, but the words in Ezekiel declared this ultimate transformation would have to be God's project, not mine.

Whatever it involved, I knew it would be a massive project, and probably devastating.

And I knew I still wasn't ready. But I wanted to be.

As for Jack's eternal destiny, I'd come to fluctuating terms with the state of his soul by holding onto what I knew of his high school conversion, his eagerness to know Christ as a young man, and his wholeheartedness about everything he did, coupled with the strong possibility of a return to the faith as he reconsidered Jesus, along with Muggeridge's book, in his final days. I'd even written a letter to his favorite professor from his former Christian college, sharing the news of Jack's death, the story of my conversion, and my misgivings about the whereabouts of Jack's soul. I believed Jack's teenaged conversion was solid, but his departure from the faith to dabble in New Age thinking worried me. The professor sent me an encouraging response.

God's gracious arms, he wrote, *are long enough to reach across whatever distance Jack might have drifted. I do know that Jack loved the Lord, and the Lord loves him.*

I could torture myself forever, wondering where his soul might be, but focussing on God's eternal love and boundless grace was better than agonizing over the lapsed years in Jack's spiritual journey. However, the horrifying thought that I might never see him again was unbearable, and now I needed the bubble to shield me from the worst feeling in the world, the icy terror that swamped me at the thought of spending eternity in separate realms.

But the passage in Ezekiel gave me hope. God had promised *a heart of flesh*, and I wanted the Spirit to move me in all the right ways. *This might take years*, I remember thinking, *but for now, his promise is enough. When I'm ready for the walls of stone to be torn down and the inner despair to be revealed, it will happen, and my heart will be both tender and strong.*

Meanwhile, I had Jess to encourage. And hopefully, Edward would be ready for a heaping dose of mutual encouragement when I met him in Toronto.

Montreal was gray and rainy, and Jess was in a similar mood, stuck in an abusive, isolated relationship. Her new boyfriend had a dark, frightening energy, and he was provoked by my sudden appearance as Jess' friend and protector. I shared the Scriptures with her while he was at work, but once he got home, darkness reigned. I urged Jess to leave, but she wasn't ready, and a week later I said goodbye and boarded the train for Toronto.

I still wish she'd listened. A few months after my visit, she disappeared, and no one I knew ever heard from her again. She'd been a late addition to The Gang, and even though we knew her well through our shared adventures, no one knew her family origins, except that she hailed from South Dakota. I hoped she'd gone into hiding and surfaced somewhere safe, far from ominous energy and twisted, counterfeit love that held her in Montreal.

Toronto was sunny. Edward met me at the train station on a windy fall afternoon, his blue eyes twinkling with affection and mischief. He was wearing a brown bomber jacket and a bright red scarf—his Toronto look. We walked through ethnic neighborhoods throughout the city, stopping for espresso coffee and baklava, and my lifelong aversion to the-city-everyone-loves-to-hate evaporated. I loved Toronto! A microcosm of the world, it was the most ethnically diverse place I'd ever seen, full of cultural enclaves to explore and ablaze in glorious fall colors. I surged with renewed energy, happy to be in a fresh place with my old friend.

At least for the first few days.

Edward hadn't changed a bit, spiritually or otherwise. He still loved to debate, but now our biggest arguments were over the Bible. The liberal Old Testament course he was taking wasn't building his faith, but rather equipping him with ammunition to shoot down mine. He was as agnostic and contrarian as ever, as verbally dextrous as I'd ever seen him, and completely unsupportive of my new direction. In fact, he was a merciless mocker who thrived on finding ways to undermine my faith and watch me cry as I tried to defend it.

I knew true Christianity was absolutely defensible even if it ultimately rested on faith, but didn't yet know enough to counter his toughest arguments. Edward wouldn't back down or let me change the subject, making our new relationship maddeningly unbalanced. I was staying at his studio apartment on Huron Street, and the tiny room couldn't contain my dismay. After a week of taunting onslaughts—always delivered with a smile on his face—and my own tearful rebuttals, I moved to the YWCA where I could lick my wounds in peace.

My former compatriot was now a thorn in the flesh, and I'd had enough slashing.

But in spite of our arguments and the collapse of a colorful friendship, I loved Toronto so much, I decided to stay.

My mother's sister, who'd moved from Toronto to Montreal, retained a closet-sized studio apartment in Rosedale, an elegant, leafy neighborhood north of Bloor Street, and she agreed to sublet it for a time with the provision I find alternate lodgings on weekends she chose to visit. It was perfectly situated. I set out on foot the next morning and found the best-paying job of my life (so far), waitressing at a ritzy crepe restaurant in Yorkville, where I pulled in generous tips from well-heeled businessmen and tourists. I asked my parents to send my bike on the train, along with Jack's old footlocker, now lightly packed with my own belongings. And I resumed my hunt for a church/group/mission where I could grow and belong.

This time I started with the huge stone churches planted throughout the city center and got briefly caught up in the quasi-mysticism of stained-glass windows, high, vaulted ceilings, and florid organ music. The friendliest parishioners I encountered were at the local Roman Catholic Church, heavily attended by university students, who invited me to an out-of-town retreat the following month. I signed up for the retreat but kept searching. Something was still missing.

My aunt called from Montreal to say she'd be visiting Toronto for Thanksgiving and needed me out of the apartment for three days. Although she'd included this stipulation in our agreement, it stung to be asked to disappear over the holidays. Apart from my new restaurant co-workers and Edward, whom I'd banned myself from seeing, I didn't know anyone in the city. The prospect of spending the holidays at the YWCA depressed me, and it hurt that she hadn't asked to see me. She'd been my favorite aunt growing up, my mother's only sibling and the relative who regularly sat at our family Thanksgiving table, yet somehow, I'd fallen out of favor. Or perhaps she was simply too caught up in her own life to appreciate my loneliness. At any rate, I booked a cold little room at the Y and cried only after I was safely inside.

I spent the weekend in that woeful state of mind, walking for hours through the city and along hidden urban trails I'd discovered, which were turning brown as fall collapsed in decay. The restaurant was closed for four days. On Saturday night, I attended a folk Mass at the Catholic Church, and returned on Sunday morning to a nearby Anglican church that featured massive stained-glass windows, solitary seniors, and a powerhouse organ. I felt like I was in a movie, in a Hollywood version of traditional worship. For lunch I ate a bran muffin and explored Queen Street.

That evening, I decided to start near the base of Yonge Street—the longest street in the world, according to Torontonians—and see how far I could walk before bedtime. Within a few blocks, I started noticing the same poster, replicated hundreds of times on sheets of yellow, orange, and green, and plastered on every available space along the sidewalk: on poles, newspaper boxes, and all over the protective boards erected to conceal construction sites. Over and over, I read the bold-faced, confident pronouncement, strangely illustrated with a floating, open Bible that appeared to be on fire.

The posters said this:

First Century Christianity
First Century Power
First Century Authority
First Century Simplicity
First Century Love
It's Happening Now!

At the bottom was a local phone number, inviting the curious to investigate where and how this remarkable thing was happening. The odd words and the first century concept intrigued me. How could you *not* be curious?

As I walked north along the west side of the street, I was astonished by the sheer number of posters on view. No doubt there were just as many posters bedecking the other side. And how far did they continue? Yonge Street ran fifty-three miles north through the city before joining Highway 11 and proceeding another 1,100 miles to the mouth of James Bay. Where did the posters stop? *Whoever posted them was obviously eager to get the message out,* I thought. *And it must be a huge group to have so much advertising!* I scribbled the phone number into my journal and walked till I was tired. Two days later, I pulled out my journal and dialed the number.

My call reaches an answering machine, still a new-fangled accessory for average folks in 1980, confirming the impression that I'm dealing with a large organization. The recorded message offers no further clues, merely instructing me to leave my number for a return call, but the voice seems friendly, adding this chipper nugget of wisdom before the beep:

And remember! Proverbs seventeen-seventeen! A friend loves at all times!

It's an endearing little touch. I leave my name and number, and several hours later, the phone rings. What follows is this baffling exchange:

Hello?

Hello! This is Henry. How are you today?

Fine. And you?

I'm fine, too. You left us a message.

Um, yeah, maybe. Are you the First Century Christianity people?

Yeah, that's us. Did you see our poster?

Well, yeah, I saw a lot of them. All over Yonge Street, dozens of them. That's why I called.

Great, that's great! So, what can I do for you?

For starters, who are you? I'm just trying to figure out what kind of group you are. Are you, like, Varsity Christian Fellowship or something? (This was the parachurch organization I was most familiar with, and thought might be similar.)

No, no, we're nothing like that. We're non-denominational, just simple Christians, following the example of the early church, and… (Here he goes into greater detail, but whatever he's explaining sails over my head.)

So… you're a church? You have a building somewhere?

No, no building, we're not really a church like that… We're just disciples of Jesus, following the Bible. You know, the apostles' teachings and so on.

For someone engaged in such massive and extensive advertising, he's maddeningly vague.

So… do you have meetings or anything? Something for visitors? That I could attend?

There's a pause, and then: *Hold on—let me check with my partner…*

I wait as a whispered conversation takes place. He's back. *Sorry, okay. Well, tomorrow night Paul's giving a talk on evolution and creation.*

So, can I come? To your meeting? Would that be okay?

It takes several more questions to extract a time and a place. When I hang up the phone, I'm still baffled. Who are these people? And to what crazy meeting had I just invited myself?

It's Happening Now turned out to be two scruffy, bearded twenty-one-year-olds sharing a dimly-lit studio apartment on Maitland Street, in the heart of Toronto's openly gay community. My hosts looked like recent arrivals; the bleak little apartment was barely furnished, apart from a flimsy roll-out cot against one wall and a dozen folding metal chairs arranged in a circle on a shabby beige carpet.

A large flip-chart with hand-drawn diagrams stood ready for the lecture, and six or seven other guests who'd arrived ahead of me were slouched in chairs or sprawled on the floor. Two of them appeared to be passed out or asleep, and all except one—a smartly-dressed Asian woman with perfect posture—looked like street people.

Most of them were Indigenous; one was tragically young, while others looked as if they'd flown past their expiry date and were choking on fumes. It was a *street ministry*, apparently, and Henry and Paul, who looked middle-class and heterosexual and must've landed in this particular apartment block by virtue of its cheap rent and proximity to the heart of downtown, had taken these unfortunates off the sidewalks and into the warmth of their cramped little bachelor unit.

The Asian woman, who introduced herself as Hilary, was around my age and apparently knew our hosts. She and I were the only guests who sat upright and looked at the speaker as he spoke. Paul, dressed in denim bib overalls and a soft plaid shirt, had a sweet country-bumpkin/child savant persona, and his ruddy, boyish face, gamely sprouting a beginner's beard, was earnest as he tackled his subject. I was too distracted by the meeting's strangeness to follow his arguments, but he was obviously bright, and he spoke non-stop, confidently flipping through his diagrams while his listeners dozed, fidgeted, or gazed around the room, trying to process this disparate collection of people and things.

Henry took a back seat. He looked older than Paul; he was taller and broader, and sported a Civil War-era beard (long before this unfortunate look became trendy) and wavy, overgrown hair parted down the middle. He had a distinctive Roman nose and wore odd clothes: a short-sleeved, salmon-colored dress shirt and baggy gray pants. I suspected he'd taken a vow of poverty; he looked as if he'd materialized out of a Goodwill donation bin.

Paul, with his sandals and beads, could've passed as a hippie, except for his manifest innocence, but Henry was impossible to pigeonhole. He was an original: not cool or current and definitely not out to impress anyone, but rather monkish and self-effacing. He seemed deliberately different, as if he'd turned his back on the world without a backward glance. I still wasn't sure what these strange zealots were promoting, but whatever it was, they were clearly all in.

Paul spoke on and on; I retained nothing from his talk, except the strong takeaway that he'd have much more to say on other topics, too.

After the meeting, both men offered to walk me home—I lived 20 minutes away—but Henry asked first. Halfway there, we stopped for a cup of tea. I was curious to learn how he and Paul had ended up on Maitland Street, but once the tea came, Henry asked about me. Suddenly I was talking about Jack, about the impact he'd had on my life and how much I still missed him. This was the most I'd spoken of him in months, and soon I was crying.

If my emotions unnerved Henry, he didn't show it; he was an empathetic listener, letting me cry without rushing to offer empty platitudes. When he finally spoke, he used scriptures, simply quoted and aptly applied, to encourage me. We left the café and he walked me to my door, inviting me back to Maitland Street for their Sunday service. I said I'd try to come. I'd crossed the Anglicans off my list, and the Catholics were awaiting my verdict, after the upcoming retreat.

On Sunday morning I returned to the same little meeting room, minus the visitors. Twelve empty chairs optimistically faced each other, each seat topped with a Bible and a heavy, gold-lettered hymnal. The flip chart had been prepped with fresh diagrams and stood ready to instruct. There was a large pot on the stove, and the room smelled like cheap ground beef mingled with the damp of inner-city mold. Henry and Paul effusively welcomed me. I took a seat and waited for the other guests to show up.

They didn't.

We waited ten, fifteen minutes, while my embarrassment grew. How sad for these young men, I thought, to have planned this service with such high hopes, only to have no one turn up. I mentally rehearsed my exit, wondering how long I should wait before apologizing (for what?) and leaving them to their humiliation. Maybe they'd ask me to return next Sunday, to give them another shot at filling the seats. Would I come back? I wasn't sure. I might be a painful reminder of this week's failure.

But both men were still smiling, and they picked up their hymnals. *Wherever two or more are gathered in my name,* Henry quoted, *I am there among them.* Without a hint of disappointment or dismay, he bowed to pray, and the service began.

Most church services I'd sampled in the previous months lasted an hour. The Pentecostals typically went longer, once the shaking, singing, and prophesying got started, but even their sermons tended to be modest—a half hour at most. Paul's sermon, profusely accompanied by hand-drawn maps and diagrams, was based on the Covenant of Blessings and Cursings from Mount Ebal (Deuteronomy 28 and 29), and lasted well over an hour. He preached directly at me, with occasional glances at Henry, who once again yielded the floor to his partner.

I was beginning to wonder if Paul was the Mouth, and Henry the Hands and Feet (and Poster Guy; he'd confessed to designing, printing, and pasting all those posters). Still, I was enthralled by Paul's lesson, richly saturated with unfamiliar Scripture. When his sermon finally ended, I wanted more.

Not to worry: there *was* more—the service was just warming up. We prayed again. We leafed through the hymnals, trying to find songs we all knew and eventually resorting to Christmas carols and a few Easter hymns. Henry took the floor and preached an extended communion message, followed by a second sermon (or third; I was losing track), this one an exposition of 2 Corinthians 8 and 9, on the grace of giving. Once Henry got going, it was obvious he loved preaching as much as Paul and wouldn't cut corners when opportunity called.

After he'd exhausted the passages (masterfully, I thought), he passed the empty, velvet-bottomed collection plate to me. Moved by the verses he'd read and the pall of poverty haunting the room, I emptied my pockets. I had seven dollars to the penny and plunked it all in the plate, apologizing for the paltry amount and promising to bring more the next day.

Both men looked pale and hungry, and I feared they were relying on Sunday offerings for groceries. As the only visitor that day—and, recalling last week's guests, perhaps the only visitor besides Hilary who'd *ever* have money to spare— the burden to feed these hungry prophets rested on me.

They were grateful. We prayed and sang some more, and finally, as my stomach started audibly growling, the service ended. Now it was time for fellowship. One of the culinarily-challenged men had cooked lunch, and they lifted the lid off the pot to reveal its contents: a sludgy mound of undercooked penne pasta congealed with greasy ground beef and seasoned with… nothing. I was touched but dismayed; I'd been a strict vegetarian for six years, and even if I *had* been a carnivore, I couldn't have choked this down.

But by now I was committed to encouraging my new friends as much as they were committed to their mission. I *had* to eat; it was the Christian thing to do, and two sets of hungry eyes watched me fiddle with a plate as my hosts explained they'd been fasting all week and would only break their fast that night. I nibbled on one noodle at a time, subversively scraping off the meat while gesturing and asking questions in an effort to distract them.

Now the conversation circled back to me. How had I become a Christian, they wanted to know. I put my greasy noodles aside and recounted my travels, the gospel sandwich, Thompson Falls and my Bible reading, and all the synchronicities, miracles, and revelations along the way. I shared about Edward, Mother Theresa and the Bible college, and Scott's delusion that I was his answered prayer. I shared about all the churches I'd visited, the inconsistencies I'd seen and the lack of connection I'd felt with every group. I shared my certainty that God had a plan for me, if only I could find it. It was a long tale, and they listened to every twist and turn, interrupting occasionally to ask for details.

When I finished, Henry looked almost apologetic. He looked me in the eye and spoke meekly. *From our understanding of the Bible*, he said, *a person has to not only believe the gospel and repent to become a Christian, but also be baptized.* He set the words down gently, as if offering me a plate of delicate cookies.

A spark of recognition flashed in my head. This was the vital link that had been floating at the edge of my mind for weeks—the *something* that was missing.

Yes, I said. *I've been wondering about that. I've been thinking about getting baptized at some point, but I don't really understand it yet. I know it must be important, but I thought I needed to find a church first. And that part's been difficult...*

Can we study it out? Henry asked. The rest of the afternoon spread before us, waiting to be filled.

If anyone could show me around the Bible, it would be these simple, unpolished, uncollared lovers of God's word. In just a few hours of worship and teaching, I'd seen how they knew it, loved it, and *lived* it. I'd seen how they cared so much about the lost, the physically and spiritually lost, that they'd walk, even *carry,* them home to this humble room, sharing their donated blankets and budget food, willing to sacrifice comfort and safety for the sake of these cast-off strangers.

And my new friends weren't gospel-sandwichers. The homeless who'd slept in their apartment the night before had opted not to stay for the service, yet they'd be welcomed back, again and again, no strings attached. *Unconditional, practical* love, for Jesus' sake, was pouring out of Maitland Street.

I thought about the hundreds of posters they'd printed and pasted along Yonge Street, enough to grab my attention and pull me deeper into the light of Christ's love. Even if I were the only person to respond to the posters, the only visitor to show up for church, and maybe the only guest with a few dollars to give back, that was okay. It was *more* than okay: it was all part of the plan.

I was baptized that same afternoon. After working our way through scriptures about faith, repentance, self-denial and baptism, the next step was crystal clear. I was ready, and I wanted, without delay, to be united with Christ and share in his death and resurrection. Happily, Henry and Paul were prepared to hasten me into the fold; they'd purposely rented an apartment with an extra-long, extra-deep bathtub and kept a large sack of donated clothes on hand. *Put on lots of layers,* Henry instructed, as he passed me the bag and directed me to the bathroom. *We want you to be well-covered.*

This was for modesty's sake when I emerged, soaking wet, from the warm waters of the tub. In years to come, I'd witness many outdoor baptisms bravely undertaken in frigid air and water and would never regret my simple indoor version. The point was to be fully immersed and to respond in faith, not to worry about what mode the water came in. I'd go on to study the Bible with hundreds of women whose baptisms took place in a wide range of waters, from hot tubs, swimming pools, horse troughs, borrowed baptisteries, and large metal drums, to far-flung oceans, lakes, rivers, and ponds. Regardless of the setting, the spiritual rebirth taking place was the same.

By six pm., redressed in my own clothes and wearing a towel around my dripping hair, I was now their new sister in Christ. Henry suggested taking the Lord's Supper again, now that we were truly united. This time, we skipped the sermonette but added more singing and prayer. My Sunday morning service was turning into an all-day retreat.

And we still weren't finished. My hosts offered another serving of the splodgy noodles (politely declined), and then confessed why they'd been fasting all week. Both men's faces had suddenly morphed from joyful to apologetic.

We're so sorry, Paul told me, *but we've made a vow to God to go to this big metropolitan church where they're preaching some really false doctrine and speak out. We've been fasting all week for boldness. And we have to leave now: their service starts in twenty minutes. Sorry, we hate leaving you here all by yourself, right after your baptism and all...*

He paused to let news of this sudden desertion sink in, and then brightened as he thought of an alternate plan.

But, hey, you're welcome to come with us! You can sit with us and pray when we stand up to preach. It would be great to have your moral support right next to us...

I must've looked as horrified as I felt. He quickly amended.

Or, if you'd prefer, you can stay here and pray...

I was impressed *and* appalled. It took guts to stand up in a congregation of several hundred adherents and oppose what was being preached in the name of God, and I figured if this wasn't purest martyrdom, it was at least impressive folly. Whichever it was, I admired their bravery. But I sure as heck wasn't willing to tag along.

I think I'll just stay here and pray, if that's okay.

It was, and I did; as soon as they ran out to catch the Church Street subway, I got on my knees and petitioned God on their behalf. It was a mini prayer, a baby Christian prayer, lasting less than a minute. Just enough to cover the bases: *Protect them. Be with them. Get them out of there in one piece.* Surely God knew how to manage this venture. I waited a little longer for my hair to dry, and then I floated home.

The next afternoon, Henry showed up at the creperie with a hand-made card. I was surprised; I couldn't remember telling him exactly where I worked, but he'd figured it out. The card was simple and profound. *To a New Lamb,* he'd written on the envelope, with some words of encouragement inside and a verse reminding me I was now in the family of God. *With them,* I suddenly realized.

By reading some posters and walking to Maitland Street, I'd found my way into the heart of Christ and into my new spiritual family: my church and my mission. It wasn't what I'd imagined, this building-less church: no stained-glass windows, no organs, no choirs, and no pews. No priests or liturgies. No *sisters* in Christ, either, unless Hilary returned. *That* would have to change. I was their first convert, their first, very *quick* convert, having undergone the most arduous aspects of my spiritual surgery in the months and years before. But many more conversions would follow in my stead, each rebirth a victory of divine synchronicity.

I finished work at three. Half an hour later, I met Henry at the Eaton's Center, a giant indoor mall at the corner of Yonge and Dundas Street, and started sharing my faith. This became our daily practice. We prayed together, and then we split up and looked for people who seemed aimless, lonely, and perhaps ready for a friendly conversation. The mall was full of loiterers, sad people with empty schedules, newcomers to the city, lonely residents who came to the mall simply to be around others; this was before today's pervasive coffee shop culture, which serves a similar purpose for many. Breaking the ice was straightforward, because I knew how I'd want to be approached and in what spirit: lightly, naturally, respectfully, with a genuine smile, and in sincere, generous goodwill.

My goal, if they were willing, was to talk to them about God and to open the Scriptures together; to be a friend and to stir an interest in finding spiritual truth. If they were hungry and wanted more, I was there to teach—with Henry's help, of course, as I still had much to learn. There'd be no hidden agendas, no gospel sandwiches, and no putting strangers on the spot. Compelled by a new love, I had one desire: to find other wanderers locked inside their bubbles, lamenting lost hearts and dreams, and to gently point them to the only love this world can never sabotage or take away.

It was the least I could do.

Epilogue

The year I jumped into the unsinkable boat of God's love was 1980, knowing his was the one love that would never fade or leave me. For years, this comforting knowledge was more an intellectual certainty than one of emotional completion, but it was enough to sustain me. The mystery of the incarnation, the humble and generous heart of Jesus, the staggering work of the cross, and the thousands of years of history and prophecy leading to the perfect unfolding of God's eternal plan: these were more than enough to feed my soul for years. The Scriptures continue to amaze and suffuse me, though I confess to times I've foolishly tried swimming alongside the boat and have barely treaded water. At my lowest points, I've even questioned God's love and plans for me. But the lifeline has always been there, sometimes out of sight, beneath the waves, but ultimately holding fast.

The healing process, that of turning my heart of stone into a heart of flesh, has taken much longer than any grief counselor would dare imagine. From what I've read, my prolonged grief over Jack lies far beyond the 'normal' spectrum of what's known as complicated or delayed grieving. In fact, working through my bubble-trapped grief encompassed the third and fourth acts of my life, and deserves a separate book and its own telling. I recount the whole saga in my next memoir, *The Box Must be Empty*, relating a much harder journey than the story I've just told.

As much as we long to know our future, it's good we cannot see what lies ahead. Had someone told me the extent and depth of my grief journey, the years of anguish that were waiting and the toll they would take on my future family, I couldn't have borne the knowledge. But the One who formed us knows how much we can handle and at what pace, and he knows that even if I move through life quickly, like that six-year-old sneaking off with her brother's bike, I take eons to process my emotions. There were many layers of buried pain, still throbbing and raw when finally brought to light, which needed a slow and thorough autopsy before being mercifully consigned to the memory grave.

My marriage in 1981 to Henry, he of the distinguished Roman nose and salmon-colored shirts, was of a different cast from all my previous relationships. We were drawn together by a shared purpose and calling, an intense desire to serve others and share the message that had dramatically transformed each of our lives. Our marriage was built on this outward focus and has endured both because of it and in spite of it. Henry has traveled this fraught and wonderful journey with me, as have our two adopted children, now grown, both incredible gifts of God from two different countries.

Along the way, God also fulfilled my dreams to move to India, to meet Mother Teresa, to be a missionary in Africa, to travel the world and to be a *helper* in my life's work, as my eleven-year-old self so wanted to be, before she hit those tragical, terrible teen years and fell off the rails. In fact, the One who formed my wanderer's heart has accommodated my restlessness by settling me in six different countries and sixteen cities to date, with friends, adventures, struggles, and blessings in every short and long-term home. He's continually surprised me, though not always to my immediate delight.

And he's given me lots more stories to tell.

Looking back, it's clear he's been here all along, making sure I'm never stagnant or bored, and for that alone, he is worthy of endless gratitude and praise.

ACKNOWLEDGEMENTS

F irst, my heartfelt gratitude to everyone in my story. Whether your time in my life was long or brief, your impact shaped me and blessed me with a story worth sharing. Rest assured, time and grace have softened any edges, and I'm grateful for *all* of you.

A huge thank you to Kathy L. Murphy, the magnificent Pulpwood Queen, for lifting my hole-punched manuscript from the slush pile and loving my story. You are definitely an author's best friend, and a shiny new angel to add to my glittering collection! I can't wait to meet you in person one day.

Hugs and gratitude to Echo Montgomery Garrett, for echoing Kathy's response to my manuscript, and being a wonderful editor, publisher, supporter, and friend. Your enthusiasm for *Paradise Road* has renewed my heart. I waited months before making contact with Lucid House Publishing. The timing and our collaboration have been perfect, and I look forward to more.

Gratitude for my brothers: To Phil, my Irish twin and fellow artist: Your genuine interest in my writing journey has brought more joy than you can imagine. I love talking craft and analyzing our family together. To Howard, fellow middle child and one of the kindest people I know:

Your love and support are always a huge encouragement. I know you love my writing when you immediately share it with others. To Brian, ever my baby brother: I'm still sorry for missing so much of your early life. You were my first and favorite blue-eyed baby. And your own journey of reinvention after the age of 50 inspires me to ignore the numbers, too. To Doug, songwriter and guitarist extraordinaire, no longer with us on earth: How I wish I could've shared this creative journey with you! I know you'd be cheering every step.

Gratitude to my father, whose love for me grows stronger and more evident with every passing year. You gave me my love for words, literature, and writing. Thank you for passing the finest family genes on to me.

To Dan and Gwen: I'll never forget your rapturous response to this manuscript or the decades of deep friendship that preceded it. If anyone knew and loved the Marilyn in these pages, it was you. Gwen, your love and understanding kept me afloat during the darkest times. Words fail me.

To all my early readers, from the youngest, Louisa, to the 'most mature': Robert Toile and Anna Kriete—a span of nearly seventy years. There are too many readers to name. But thanks to all for affirming that this story has wide appeal. Your enthusiastic feedback kept me going through the long and daunting stage of querying agents and publishers till I knocked on the right door.

To the Kelowna Writers' Group, big thanks for giving me the pleasure of reading my short pieces aloud to you. Thanks for always letting me read, and for boosting my confidence.

To my dear friends in the Kelowna Word Guild, your spiritual support and prayers, as well as all your practical marketing tips, were also part of this successful journey. Thank you.

To June and Jennifer, my Kelowna besties: hugs and gratitude. June, as the first person to hear these pages read aloud, thanks for always being my Super Fan. Jennifer, knowing you read *Paradise Road* over the phone to Bob as he drove Canada's "Highway from Hell" on those long winter nights always makes me smile! Thanks for your abiding friendship.

To Henry, my longsuffering husband and partner in the gospel: Thank you for believing in (almost) everything I do. Thanks for your faith in my talent, for giving me space to write, and for welcoming every part of my past into your present. You are exactly who God wanted me to marry!

To my wonderful children: Thanks for simply being you. I hope you'll be inspired by all the *right* examples in this book about your mother's misadventures.

Most of all, my deepest gratitude to God. As I wrote this memoir, I realized how vulnerable young Marilyn was as she lived through these events. But You were always my protector. Thank you for giving me a story of redemption and new beginnings, and for letting me share it with the world.

ABOUT THE AUTHOR

Marilyn Kriete was born and raised in Edmonton, Canada, but she didn't stay long. After a colorful life spanning four continents and 16 cities, earning her keep as cook, chambermaid, waitress, fisherwoman, missionary, speaker/teacher, tutor, and academic writing editor, Marilyn now lives in the beautiful Okanagan Valley in Kelowna, British Columbia, Canada, with her charitable husband Henry and three demanding cats. Their two grown children were adopted from Mumbai, India, and Athens, Georgia. Besides her favorite activities—writing and sleeping—she enjoys hiking, cycling, blogging, reading, playing word games, watching documentaries, and cleaning other people's homes. Her poetry and nonfiction have appeared in *The Lyric, Storyteller, The Eastern Iowa Review, The English Bay Review*, and *Brevity Blog. Paradise Road* is her debut memoir.

MarilynKriete.com

CPSIA information can be obtained
at www.ICGtesting.com
Printed in the USA
JSHW011924180723
45004JS00004B/92